MW00795914

Kropotkin and the Anarchist Intellectual Tradition

Kropotkin and the Anarchist Intellectual Tradition

Jim Mac Laughlin

PlutoPress
www.plutobooks.com

First published 2016 by Pluto Press
345 Archway Road, London N6 5AA

www.plutobooks.com

Copyright © Jim Mac Laughlin 2016

The right of Jim Mac Laughlin to be identified as the author of this
work has been asserted by him in accordance with the Copyright,
Designs and Patents Act 1988.

British Library Cataloguing in Publication Data
A catalogue record for this book is available from the British Library

ISBN   978 0 7453 3513 1   Hardback
ISBN   978 0 7453 3512 4   Paperback
ISBN   978 1 7837 1737 8   PDF eBook
ISBN   978 1 7837 1739 2   Kindle eBook
ISBN   978 1 7837 1738 5   EPUB eBook

Typeset by Stanford DTP Services, Northampton, England

Simultaneously printed in the European Union and United States of America

To the memory of my parents,
Patrick Jerome Mc Laughlin (1906–86)
and
Ellen Teresa Mc Callion (1913–2006)

Contents

1

Anarchism Before Kropotkin

The historical roots of anarchism

'Anarchy' is a composite word that derives from the Greek. The prefix 'an', meaning 'the absence of', when joined with 'archos', denoting 'ruler' or 'authority', gives us 'anarchy', a term which originally signified 'contrary to authority'.[1] In classical Greece the term was also widely used to refer to those who lived 'without rule'. As such it referred to people living in acephalous communities 'without a leader', especially those not ruled by, or under the control of, military leaders. While many of these early 'anarchic' societies were in fact stateless, they were rarely completely leaderless. Their leaders, however, did not have access to coercive agencies of authority and were often forced to rely upon a combination of skill, luck and persuasion to maintain their influence and exert authority. Acephalous communities such as these were also characterized by only the most rudimentary forms of role differentiation and could sustain only a minimum amount of economic specialization.[2] In areas outside Roman influence, village communities and freely sworn brotherhoods of free individuals were largely beyond state control. Kropotkin was to claim that the 'barbarian' spirit of societies such as these lingered on among Scandinavian, Saxon, Celtic and Slavic peoples. For seven or eight centuries after the collapse of Rome, it had incited men, and women, to seek satisfaction of their needs through individual initiative, and later in the Middle Ages through free agreement between the brotherhoods of workers and craft guilds.[3] With increased usage the term 'anarchy' was applied pejoratively by supporters of state authority to primordial communities, and later in the eighteenth and nineteenth centuries to pre-colonial societies and disorderly elements within the ranks of otherwise 'orderly' state societies. All of these were deemed 'anarchic' precisely because they were beyond the reach of state authority, or were only tenuously linked to state societies governed by the rule of law. Gradually, however, the term was also used in a derogatory fashion to describe those who constituted a threat to the authority of church and state.

There was a widespread assumption in the sixteenth and seventeenth centuries that the rural inhabitants of the pre-colonial world lived anarchic lives. This was because in large tracts of Africa, Latin America, India, and much of the Islamic world until comparatively recently, cities were considered cradles of luxury and refinement. 'Disorderly' elements were either excluded from, or granted only limited or temporary access to, these centres of 'refined' living. In the early colonial city, privileged citizens and those in authority would come together to construct their own versions of civic culture. They also took pains to contain any anarchic elements in their midst. Even as late as the eighteenth century, anarchy was said to lurk beyond the boundaries of city walls. The further one moved from the city, the more barbaric, disorderly and *anarchic* did life become. Indeed, for centuries the boundary between town and country was diligently policed in order to prevent cities growing so large that their inhabitants literally became uncontrollable.[4] Rulers in these cities were generally drawn from the *demos*, as was the case in classical Greece, or from educated privileged elites, as was the case in colonial India, Latin America and Africa. As recently as the nineteenth century, 'encroachment laws' in India defined those who had the right to live in the city. Here laws were designed to control such seemingly 'anarchic' manifestations of urban life as street trading, vagrancy and the development of shantytowns, all of which were considered blighted spots on the face of an ordered civility. Similarly in the early years of Maoist China, the gates of the country's larger cities were only opened temporarily to accommodate the huge numbers of refugees, ex-soldiers and peasants who were displaced by war. They were subsequently closed in the 1950s to stem the flood of impoverished peasants who sought a new life in the urban centres of post-revolutionary China. In Maoist China, as in the military dictatorships of Latin America, peasants were kept on the land, both because they were required to work there, and because they were more easily controlled in the countryside than they would be in the cities. Thus for example in French West Africa up until the 1950s, colonial authorities regulated the movement of the rural poor to the city, and consigned refugees from the countryside to the grim peripheries of Algiers, Dakar, Brazzaville and Abidjan.[5] In all of these cases, as famously also in tsarist Russia in the nineteenth century and the Soviet Union in the twentieth, those living outside the city were regarded as second-class citizens. As 'people without history' they were also considered 'disposable people'.[6] To those in authority they were simply trapped in an endless cycle of hardship. Their lives literally lacked direction, and their history, unlike that of their social superiors, did not appear to lead anywhere. As such they were deemed to have no place in the settled and orderly landscapes of 'civilized' peoples. Thus, in the colonial world of the nineteenth century, migration to the city was often discouraged because it was believed that untrammelled urban expansion might contribute to the physical, and even *moral* destruction of urban civilization.

While anarchists associate anarchism with a whole range of doctrines that condemn the institutions of government as unnecessary and detrimental to social and economic development, their enemies have equated anarchy with social chaos and violent disorder. This disparagement of anarchism, and the categorization of anarchists as mindless fomenters of social chaos, has had a long history in Western Europe. Long before Peter Kropotkin's defence of 'scientific anarchism' in the latter half of the nineteenth century, opponents of authority were derogatorily described as 'anarchists'. In the sixteenth and seventeenth centuries, figures of authority began applying the term to opponents of ecclesiastical authority. As the focus of political dissent shifted from church to the monarchy, and later to the institutions of the modern state, anarchists were indiscriminately lumped together with all those who sought to challenge abuses of ecclesiastical and state authority. These included those who, unlike 'true anarchists', sought to reform rather than abolish the institutions through which the authority of church and state was mediated. Whenever anarchists sought to distinguish themselves from other critics of authoritarian regimes they were required to take an intellectual stand quite distinct from their radical confrères. In doing so they set about rewriting history in order to challenge some of the most cherished beliefs of the social order from which they sought to liberate society. They challenged the 'founding principles' of political authority, and condemned the foundational belief systems of political regimes. The latter, they argued, extolled the virtues of government and social order, while mischievously associating statelessness with violent social turmoil and political chaos. While anarchist praxis can best be described as a principled opposition to government that rejects all forms of authority, anarchist theory has always implied a sustained intellectual challenge to the authority and the very territorial organization of the state. Thus anarchists sought to undermine state authority, attacked the foundational principles of authoritarian rule, and criticized the political and intellectual establishment for covering their state-centred objectives beneath the mantle of objective rationality. Their greatest achievement has been their intellectual defence of the state of statelessness. Throughout their long history of anti-authoritarian struggles, anarchists have always managed to articulate a 'vocabulary of desire'.[7] This has sustained the possibility of a stateless society throughout centuries of state formation, nation-building and imperial expansion. From the seventeenth century onwards, anarchists were to argue that cooperation and individual initiative, rather than competitive struggle and the suppression of individualism, should be the guiding principles of social progress. They also insisted that self-governing autonomous communities were the only rational alternatives to the bureaucratization of the state and the centralization of authority in both capitalist and pre-capitalist societies. Far from being a utopian dream, they insisted that the anarchist society of the future was grounded in the present and sustained by already-existing practices of mutual support and decentralized decision-making. Thus 'practical' anarchists counteracted the utopianism of philosophical anarchism, just as they criticized the egotism of individualist anarchism.[8] They also challenged the utter pessimism of bourgeois pragmatists who have tended to reduce anarchism to wishful thinking and caricature anarchists as mindless individuals with no other objective than the wilful destruction of orderly society. As a vehicle for antithetical thought, practical anarchism has also been ideologically distinct from the 'individualist' anarchism of those whose rejection of authority was motivated by the quest for artistic freedom. For practical or 'social anarchists' anarchism was always to remain a means to an end, which in principle had to be as uncharted as it was undefined. The dilemma confronting all anarchists was how to visualize a federalized alternative to the capitalist state without becoming ensnared in prescriptive constructs that risked of placing new restrictions on social and economic progress.[9] As political realists, anarchists have certainly been aware of the many historical instances that showed just how easily ideals could be compromised or 'canonized' in a rigid set of dogmatic beliefs about the relationship between the individual and the state. Experience has often taught them to be alert to the dangers of utopian thinking and the ossification of political protest in 'repressive dystopias'. Keeping the anarchist project to the fore when proposing changes to existing societies, they constantly reminded their followers that the anarchist alternative to the capitalist state was well within the realms of possibility. The stateless society of the future, they argued, was literally inherent in the present order of society.

Not the least of the paradoxes surrounding any historical analysis of anarchism is the fact that the term originated in Greece, the birthplace of democracy, where moderate-sized city-states experimented with a limited degree of 'citizen rule' some 500 years before the dawn of the Christian era. From the fifth to the third century BCE, classical democracy provided a comparatively small number of privileged citizens with a voice in decision-making. However, the more authoritarian among the Greek philosophers taught that civilization required the protection of the state. These men regarded democracy as an unstable form of government because it could easily descend into anarchy, in the pejorative sense of that term. Indeed Aristotle considered those who resided outside the limits of the state as lawless and dangerous beasts. Like Plato, he believed that law-abiding and hierarchical state societies required protection from social chaos and the threat of barbarism, which he argued was constantly lurking outside state borders.

Not all Greek philosophers defended the state or adopted an authoritarian attitude to social order. Indeed ancient Athenian democracy was predicated on the very concept of *autarkia*, which fostered individual self-sufficiency and a sense of civic duty and sought to uphold the values of social responsibility. Similarly the Stoics favoured cooperation and self-sufficiency as alternatives to the authoritarian state, which caused Kropotkin to label the philosopher Zeno of Citium (336–264 BCE), the 'best exponent of Anarchist philosophy in ancient Greece'.[10] Nevertheless, in the compact city-states of ancient Greece, the *demos*, namely those eligible to vote, could gather together as a social collective, rather than as individuals, to impose order and determine the political character of their city-states. Their mass meetings of citizens closely approximated what we today would consider direct democracy. However this classical age of Greek democracy lasted only around 200 years and famously excluded women and slaves from the democratic process. Nevertheless these early expressions of Greek democracy are of interest to contemporary students of democracy and anarchists alike. While disagreeing on the scope of enfranchisement, the entitlements and responsibilities of citizenship and the functions of the state, anarchists and democrats alike agree that collective decision-making works best when the body politic is small and relatively homogeneous. Thus Kropotkin was to suggest that the 'fatal error' of most cities, not just those of classical Greece but also those of Europe in the sixteenth and seventeenth centuries, 'was to base their wealth upon commerce and industry to the neglect of agriculture'. This 'estrangement of cities from the land', he argued, not only 'drew them into a policy hostile to the land', it also caused port cities in particular to engage in 'distant enterprises' that contributed to colonial warfare and unrestrained urban expansion on the maritime fringes of Europe.[11] This, he argued, hastened the disintegration of the communal systems of self-reliance, undermined local autonomy, and concentrated wealth in the hands of state elites. This in turn aggravated social divisions between town and country, and separated the urban rich from the growing numbers of the urban poor in the expanding cities of early modern Europe.

Thus classical discourses on democracy and anarchism were concerned with the scale and geographical distribution of power, and the degree to which citizens could participate in decision-making processes. Some political commentators have suggested 'direct democracy' can run into grave difficulties in groups larger than 10,000, and that it is literally impossible in towns and cities with more than 50,000 inhabitants.[12] While anarchists have been branded utopians for demanding their 'impossible community', it could be argued that the classical Greek model of democracy is no less a utopian dream in today's globalized world of centralized authorities. Quite apart from the huge numbers of people living under authoritarian regimes, including teeming populations of displaced persons and the inhabitants of 'failed states', an increasing proportion of the global population today live in mega-cities that are exponentially larger than the city-states of ancient Greece. In defending these early manifestations of democracy, Kropotkin showed that 'men lived in societies without states for thousands of years before having known the State'.[13] He also regarded the state as an historical development and recognized that 'state' and 'government' were fundamentally different concepts. State power, he argued, was always a 'top-down' affair; just as states themselves represented the territorial concentration of social and political functions of society in the hands of the few. Like Weber, he believed that the modern state was characterized by a territorial jurisdiction of variable dimensions, a bureaucratic administration of power and authority, and a monopolization of legitimate force by state authorities. States, moreover, also presumed territorial jurisdictions of certain dimensions, which meant that classical city-states were not states in the modern sense of the term.[14]

Plebeian anarchism and radical Protestantism

The spread of Protestantism in Europe in the sixteenth and seventeenth centuries paved the way for religious radicals who had their own interpretations of what the English religious dissenter, Gerrard Winstanley, called 'righteousness' (i.e. moral probity or 'uprightness'). Martin Luther called the leaders of these dissenting sects 'mad saints'. Their followers included Anabaptist opponents of conventional baptism who insisted that the sacrament marking a child's reception into the church should be a voluntary act undertaken only by consenting adults. Only then, it was argued, could it have spiritual significance.[15] However, Anabaptists and their radical associates in the plebeian world of protest were never simply religious dissenters. They were also to the forefront of political protest against religious authorities throughout the sixteenth century. As early as 1502, the followers of Münster-born Anabaptist and insurrectionist Henry Nichlaes believed that heaven and hell could be experienced in this world. In refusing to separate the politics of the church from those of the state, his followers rejected the Christian injunction to 'render unto Caesar the things that are Caesar's, and unto God the things that are God's'.[16] Their plebeian scepticism, together with their opposition to ecclesiastical authority in general, subsequently developed into a sustained critique of all forms of authority. They opposed the payment of tithes, condemned the payment of taxes, opposed conscription and military service, and regarded compulsory service on magistracies as repugnant to all followers of true religion. Many of them were also proud egalitarians who condemned social inequality and the private ownership of property. Crucially, in refusing to recognize childhood baptism, Anabaptists also undermined the territorial structure of the national church. In its place they proposed congregations of the elect who would function as self-governing 'praying republics'. Had they succeeded, they would have shattered forever the territorial integrity of the Christian world and the reach of its state-centred institutions.

Because Anabaptists were often to the forefront of religious dissent, more conservative Protestants were opposed to the 'mad saints' who led their anti-authoritarian followers. Indeed the religious fissures in sixteenth-century dissenting Europe appeared to follow fairly clear-cut social and geographical lines. Radical dissent and anti-clericalism had attracted large numbers of the urban and rural poor in England, Germany, the Low Countries and Scandinavia. Spain, Italy, Austria, Poland and Lithuania on the other hand remained predominantly Catholic, but still tolerated the presence of small Calvinist minorities in their midst. While widespread emotional support for religious reform in the former countries had to be taken seriously by state authorities, conservative reformers and large numbers of the clergy readily dissociated themselves from the 'mad saints' and radical dissenters of this Reformation Europe. Critical of the 'habit-ridden indifference' of the Catholic Church to ecclesiastical reform, these 'respectable reformers' were nevertheless willing to cooperate with the state, particularly if it furthered their social and political objectives.[17] Preaching respect for the authority of the reformed church and Parliament, they transformed heresy into a respectable religion and policed the politics and the moral conduct of their 'flocks'. If not contained, it was argued, plebeian anti-authoritarianism could threaten the comfortable civility of more respectable Lutherans, Calvinists and other authoritarian Protestants. It was for these reasons that the latter condemned as anarchism the anti-authoritarianism of the more radical plebeian Protestants.

Historically, therefore, opposition to ecclesiastical authority was inseparable from plebeian resistance to monarchical authority and the social, economic and political privilege of landed wealth. Both strands of anti-authoritarianism originated within the ranks of radical Protestantism. By the mid seventeenth century, 'anarchism' was already used as a term of abuse to describe the heretical beliefs of those who threatened to lead the urban and rural poor of northern Europe not only from the church altar but also along the path to social revolution. During the English Revolution, for example, radical Levellers were branded 'Switzerising anarchists'. Doubly condemned as 'foreigners' and opponents of religious authority, they were thrown, like most plebeian opponents of church and state, onto the dust heaps of history. Because they appeared to be 'demanding the impossible', these early anarchists had no friends on the reformist left or the political right. Their radical disavowal of social and political authority cast them in the role of friendless revolutionaries.[18]

Gerrard Winstanley and the anti-authoritarian tradition

The seventeenth and eighteenth centuries witnessed massive changes in the social and economic landscapes of the United Kingdom of Great Britain and Ireland. The collapse of feudal privileges fostered the development of a market-centred economy, facilitated an early form of nation-building under the auspices of substantial landholders, promoted state centralization, and gave Parliament new powers to regulate social and economic activity on an unprecedented scale. The power blocs of this new Puritan Britain sought to literally refashion the country in their own image. This in turn led to the privatization of property and the increased commercialization of agriculture, particularly in the country's rural heartlands in the south of England. Here large-scale enclosures nurtured the seeds of an emerging Puritan hegemony, which in turn threatened the traditional moral economy of the rural poor, while simultaneously contributing to the proletarianization of many smallholders and tenant farmers. Massive developments in agriculture and transportation also threatened to further reduce the regional and cultural diversity, and the parochialism, of late feudal Britain. This transformed even Britain and Ireland's remotest districts into functioning communities that were linked to the national state structure and indeed the global economy.[19]

This was the environment in which Gerrard Winstanley produced an astonishing output of religious and political writings that laid the foundations of modern anarchism. In 1648 he began to publish the religious tracts that brought him to the attention of the London poor, and of the civil and military authorities. Accused of fomenting anarchy by churchmen and the English gentry, Winstanley conspired to 'level men's estate' by making a number of critical interventions in English revolutionary politics between 1648 and 1652. Baptized in Wigan on 10 October 1609, he was the son of a textile dealer of modest means who had Puritan sympathies.[20] The young Winstanley grew up in a parish strongly associated with rural radicalism that was dominated by powerful landlords and aggressive landowning clerics. This may have prompted his later criticisms of landlordism and authoritarian religion. The fact that he possessed some knowledge of Latin suggests that he may have attended the local grammar school. However, in an England where poor schoolmasters tutored pupils in their own homes, it is not improbable that his knowledge of the language could have been acquired in a less authoritarian atmosphere outside of school. In 1630, Winstanley left for London where he was apprenticed to the widow Sarah Gater, who carried on her deceased husband's trade as a merchant tailor in the impoverished parish of St Michael, in Cornhill. We know that he shared the house of his female employer until 1638, and that she was a devout and comparatively learned woman who had her own small library of medical books and religious tracts. However, there is no evidence to suggest that the widow Gater was the source of Winstanley's religious radicalism. Quite the contrary indeed, as it would appear that she was of a conservative disposition and one of the overseers of her last will and testament was no other than her staunchly royalist cousin, Izaak Walton, the author of *The Compleat Angler*, published in 1653. In London, Winstanley ran a small shop in the parish of St Olave where he probably took in items of clothing for resale. Four years later the business was in jeopardy and he was forced to divide up his stock to pay off creditors. He moved to Cobham in 1643 where he lived near his wife's family.[21]

Winstanley could not have been unaware of the social and intellectual ferment in London in the early 1640s. Neither was he immune to the impact of the civil war on the daily lives of the London poor. He certainly appears to have been acutely aware of the revolutionary potential of the 'giddy multitude' of London and the 'glorious flux and intellectual excitement' that engulfed the city in these years. Convinced that 'the old world [was] running up like parchment in the fire',[22] he welcomed its demise and set about preparing citizens for the new anti-authoritarian society which he believed was about to emerge from the political chaos and millenarian hopes of these brief years. As Christopher Hill has suggested, anything seemed possible in revolutionary England between 1648 and the restoration of the landed gentry under the Protectorate of Oliver Cromwell. In these years the urban and rural poor not only challenged the authority of church and state – they questioned the very foundational values of early modern capitalism, not least its work ethic and its moral code of respectability. In his account of this 'world turned upside down', Hill has shown that mid seventeenth-century England was the site of at least two major social revolutions. The one which succeeded went on to defend the rights of property, abolished feudal tenures, put an end to arbitrary taxation, granted political authority to property holders and Parliament, and removed all impediments to the triumph of the Protestant ethic, the ideology of all men of substantial property. The other revolution, with which Winstanley and his Digger followers identified, never succeeded. It was waged by men and women of no property who were fundamentally opposed to the authority of Parliament and the political rights that property conferred on its owners. Had these masterless men and women succeeded in abolishing the authority of church and state in society, they would have established communal property, rejected the Protestant work ethic, democratized political and legal institutions, disestablished the church and initiated a process of radical reform that could well have resulted in the decentralization of decision-making and the withering away of the state.[23]

As major critics of ecclesiastical authority, Winstanley and his confrères among the more radical Levellers argued that church ministers should be elected by their congregations and paid through the voluntary contributions of their members. Like the more radical of his peers, he also denied the need for a separate clergy, preferring instead to have 'a gifted layman preach on Sunday whilst labouring with his hands the other six days of the week'. As he put in his *Watch-word to the City of London*, published in 1649:

All men have stood for freedom, ... and those of the richer sort of you that see it are ashamed and afraid to own it, because it comes clothed in a clownish garment ... Freedom is the man who will turn the world upside down, therefore no wonder that he hath enemies ... True freedom lies in the community in spirit and community in the earthly treasure, and this is Christ the true manchild spread abroad in the creation, restoring all things unto himself.[24]

An early critic of the church's control of education and a staunch advocate of free education, Winstanley also suggested that religious sermons in chapels throughout the land should be replaced by lectures on the natural sciences and human rights. In a period of intense religious and ethnic conflict, he visualized a society where churches would be 'torn to pieces' so that national divisions could be swallowed up in 'the brotherly unity of all peoples'. Adam's sin, he argued, was not responsible for shutting the doors on Paradise by condemning men and women to live by the sweat of their brows. Instead it was private property and human greed that contributed to the Fall. It was when 'self-love began to rise in the earth' that 'man began to fall'. Man's fall began, he argued, 'when mankind began to quarrel about the earth, and some would have all and shut out others, forcing them to be servants'. Writing in 1649 he suggested that the 'poor must be picked out' and prepared for the new democracy and that the common people should become 'part of the nation' and have equal rights with the gentry and the clergy.[25] For Winstanley, the righteousness of the gospels could only be realized through communism, which in turn was predicated on the elimination of privilege and the subversion of existing order. In a statement that would have met with approval from such twentieth-century revolutionary thinkers as Franz Fanon and Paulo Freire, he wrote: 'If you would find true majesty … go among the poor despised ones of the earth … These great ones are too stately for Christ to dwell in; he takes up his abode in a manger, in and amongst the poor in spirit and despised ones of the earth.'[26]

A pioneer in the practice of seventeenth-century anti-authoritarianism, Winstanley called on the poor to defend their rights by demanding an end to the 'ancient custom bred in the strength of kingly prerogative' that deprived them of their entitlement to work common land. Like French syndicalists and British trade unionists some two centuries later, he urged the poor to withdraw their labour and farm labourers in particular to cease working on landed estates. Like the followers of Winstanley in mid seventeenth-century England, they believed that the social contract binding landless labourers and powerful landowners together in an unequal bond of servitude was as unjust as it was one-sided. They certainly would have agreed with Winstanley's followers among the revolutionary Diggers who argued that: 'Rich men receive all they have from the labourer's hand, and when they give, they give away other men's labourers, not their own. Therefore they are not righteous actors on the earth.'[27] In attacking the deferential attitudes of some workers, and criticizing the humiliation of the poor by the rich, these seventeenth-century proto-anarchists refused to 'go with cap in hand and bended knee to farmers, begging and entreating to work with them for 8d or 10d a day'. Deference, they insisted, literally belittled the workers and enabled the gentry and rich farmers 'to tyrannise over the poor'.[28]

Building on the popular radicalism and political alertness of 'the giddy crowd', Winstanley argued that God sanctioned righteousness. As such it could be used to challenge the authority of those who excluded the poor from the body politic, condemning them to an impoverished life without rights or security. Thus he asked the landlords, 'What would you do if you had not such labouring men to work for you?'[29] He preached a seventeenth-century variant of modern liberation theology and asserted that private property was incompatible with social justice; that power corrupted those who wielded it; that property and the abuse of power were the true cases of crime; that men and women could only be happy in a society without rulers, where work and its products were shared equally; and that people should act, not in accordance with laws imposed by their political and religious superiors, but in accordance with their own enlightened consciences. Like Kropotkin, he also insisted that freedom was not an abstract political principle. It was something that was literally within reach of those who sought to abolish private property and social and political privilege. Arguing that the political authority of the monarchy and the moral authority of the church were an affront to God and man alike, he stated:

> Let all men say what they will, so long as such are rulers as call the land theirs, upholding this particular property of mine and thine, the common people shall never have their liberty, nor the land be freed from troubles, oppressions and complainings; by reason thereof the Creator of all things is continually provoked.[30]

Like Kropotkin, Winstanley also believed that 'past laws' could fetter progress in the future. In the latter half of the nineteenth century, Kropotkin would argue that social chaos could also be transmitted from one period to another as a result of colonial conquest. He showed how the tyranny of the Persian Empire and the oppressive laws of the 'Eastern autocracies' were transmitted to Greece. He further suggested that the authoritarian character of the Roman Empire was passed on to the 'young barbaric States' of Europe following the fall of Rome. By such means, Kropotkin argued, 'foreign' laws and 'laws of the past' were able to 'fetter the future'. Kropotkin also argued that the Roman Empire had all the characteristics of a state, just as Roman concepts of law and sovereignty subsequently influenced the bureaucratic evolution of the medieval state. While recognizing that Greek city-states were as prone as any political regime to the 'arrogance of power', he admired their civic culture because it was based primarily on rhetoric and persuasion rather than force, and on the collective action of equals rather than the 'enforced laws of slaves'.[31] Similarly Winstanley argued that judicial decisions based on 'ancient custom bred in the strength of kingly prerogative' deprived people of their rights to common land.[32] Thus he argued that the overthrow of the monarchy in 1648 should have been accompanied by the repeal of unjust laws which granted lords of the manor property rights in the commons, thereby closing them off to those most in need, namely the urban and rural poor. By 1650, his Digger followers were demanding that all lands belonging to church, crown and the royalists should be given to the poor. By then Winstanley was also calling for the repudiation of land sales authorized by Parliament and believed that lands confiscated by the crown at the dissolution of the monasteries should go towards a Commonwealth land fund. Like Kropotkin, he argued that food shortages were caused by social and economic rather than natural forces, and that food production would grow astronomically once the wastelands of Britain were cultivated by the deserving poor. He estimated that one half to two thirds of England alone was improperly farmed, chiefly because large landlords would not permit the poor to cultivate the land. He also suggested that communal cultivation was not a barrier to economic progress, and that it would encourage capital investment and agricultural improvement without damaging the interests of the commoners. He further believed that Britain possessed enough farmland to feed its population several times over. In a statement that would be echoed by Kropotkin's writings on agricultural improvement in such classic anarchist texts as *The Conquest of Bread* and *Fields, Factories and Workshops*, Winstanley stated: 'If the wasteland of England were manured by her children, it would in a few years become the richest, the strongest and [most] flourishing land in the world.'[33]

Digging for anarchism

Like a number of other seventeenth-century anarchists, Winstanley's anti-authoritarianism had a strong rural bias. Thus he envisaged a world where reason and righteousness would prevail over unjust authority, where the moral authority of the poor would replace that of hierarchical authorities, and where upright rural communities would create such an abundance of the necessities of life that they would be able to supply the needs of all who worked for the common good. He urged his followers to 'work together [and] eat bread together', adding that 'he that works for another, either for wages or to pay him rent, works unrighteously; … but they that are resolved to work and eat together, making the earth a common treasury, doth join hands with Christ to lift up the creation from bondage, and restores all things from the curse'. Having come to London to set himself up in the clothing trade, he was ruined by the onset of a recession shortly after his arrival. In London, he wrote, 'I was beaten out both of estate and trade, and forced to accept the goodwill of friends crediting to me, to lead a country life.'[34] Thereafter he favoured a simple rural life over the 'diseasednesse, injustices and uncertainties of urban commerce'. He attributed his own disillusionment with city life to 'the cheating sons in the thieving arts of buying and selling' who beat him 'out of both estate and trade' in London. Having been forced to rely on the goodwill of both friends and creditors, he decided to 'live a country life' sometime around 1648–49.

Like Kropotkin, personal inspiration rather than books informed Winstanley's conception of 'the good life'. However his thoughts on land reform and smallholding society were never as completely original as they appeared. They had close parallels with the new radicalism of dissenting Christians whose reading of the Bible challenged the authority of the landed gentry and the hierarchical church. Writing in a pre-scientific age of reason and experiment, Winstanley believed that the study of the prophetical works of the Bible would put 'the science of prophecy' on a more rational footing. Properly interpreted, he argued, the Bible was capable of liberating man from superstitious beliefs and predestination. If its teachings were subordinated to human needs, instead of being used to legitimize the authority of church and state, then duties, customs and tradition would no longer be capable of restraining the lives of the poor with their strictures. Thus he asserted that once freed from superstition and clerical authority, man 'needs not that any man should teach him'.[35] This radically new plebeian interpretation of the Bible differentiated between the authority of the 'Bible without' and the 'Bible within', insisting that the latter contained truths that coincided with private conscience. As such it was superior to the 'Bible without', which derived its authority from the teachings of an authoritarian church. Thus John Everard, the 'perpetual heretic' whose writings were familiar to Winstanley, claimed that 'letter learning' was no substitute for the religious experience of those who 'know Jesus Christ and the Scriptures experimentally rather than grammatically, literally or academically'. Yet for Winstanley the Bible was the ultimate basis of all truth, and like Hobbes he made selective use of its texts to illustrate conclusions arrived at by rational means. The scriptures, he believed, were a better blueprint for the just society than 'book learning' and 'university knowledge'. Like Kropotkin, he showed that 'university learning', which was the monopoly of wealthy men, prostituted reason in its defence of social hierarchy and the authority of the state.[36] Unlike Kropotkin, Winstanley based his social philosophy on folk custom and the plebeian radicalism of the leaders of 'the meaner sort of men' of England in the 1650s. Individual thinkers who may have inspired him included the printer Giles Calvert, the radical Leveller William Walwyn, and William Everard, the 'scoffer at ordnances' whose influence on the early Diggers rivalled that of Winstanley.

Winstanley's Diggers were men and women who set out to perform something close to a sacred act of magic on themselves, and on the land they struggled to cultivate.[37] When Winstanley led a group of Diggers onto common land outside London in 1649, the site that he chose, St George's Hill, and the date, April Fool's Day, were steeped in moral and political significance that would not have been lost on his followers. St George symbolized the triumph of holiness over evil, while April Fools' Day was a 'Robin Hood day', the day when the poor, in an act of ritual reversal, literally took from the rich to give to their poorer brethren. As a dissenting radical Christian, Winstanley sought to make every day a 'Robin Hood day'. As 'true Levellers', his Diggers were accused of conspiring to 'level men's estates' and overthrow the social order of landed society. Winstanley called for the digging up of common land and the establishment of self-sufficient communes under the organizational control of the 'righteous' poor. The Diggers' opposition to enclosure, especially when that resistance involved the cultivation of common land by the common people, was considered a religious act of great practical, political and spiritual significance. For Winstanley, true social revolution taught men and women how to live 'in community with the globe and … the spirit of the globe'.[38] As such it had profound environmental as well as social implications. Like the nineteenth-century French anarchist, Élisée Reclus, Winstanley wished to open men's eyes to the beauty of the world and exhorted men and women to live in accordance with the laws of nature and sound environmental practice. This meant that the

Diggers were radically different from squatters and traditional cottagers. They were never, however, like latter-day hippies, whose lifestyles could generate scandal and become a burden on others. Thus Winstanley condemned sexual promiscuity as well as overindulgence in 'meat, drink, pleasure and women'. He warned against 'excessive community of women' on the grounds that sexual promiscuity could contribute to venereal disease and threaten the harmony of the family. While critical of the work ethic of authoritarian Protestantism, he nevertheless condemned idleness on the grounds that it 'inflamed' the hearts of men and women and led to 'quarrelling, killing, burning houses or corn'. Thus his views on work and leisure wavered between Quaker asceticism and the 'excessive community of women' for which the 'scandalizing Ranters' were famous. Because so many of his followers moved freely between the Ranters and the Diggers, Winstanley was careful to distinguish between the promiscuity of the former and the respectability of the latter, especially when it came to the question of marriage and the family. By no means an ascetic, Winstanley was a confirmed monogamist in an age where there was no effective method of birth control, but considered sexual freedom an illusion because it applied only to men and kept women in a permanent state of 'embondage'.[39]

Winstanley's earliest writings describe his tortuous quest for right-eousness and spiritual enlightenment in an age of social and economic dislocation due to failing harvests, falling trade, heavy taxes, disease and the intense military manoeuvres around the south-east of England before and after the Puritan revolution. The armed forces were literally pushing the London poor beyond the margins of the city, where they were often forced to subsist on wasteland. It was at this stage that Winstanley's spiritual awakening infused his political thinking and transformed him into the revolutionary leader of the Diggers. His appeal to plebeian common sense was pitted against the elitist arguments of church and gentry based on legal precedent and biblical authority. His religious and political pamphlets were also crucial to the development of popular English prose. Like some of the leading anarchists of the nineteenth century, not least Kropotkin, he wrote in a style that was at once decorative and polemical. However his writing could also be reasoned, argumentative, rhetorical and poetic. Indeed this was the reason why he could appeal to such large numbers of readers, and listeners, in the revolutionary turmoil of the 1640s. Like the great radical polemicists of the nineteenth and twentieth centuries, he was less concerned with the literary worth of his writings than with their social and political impact. In an assessment of his literary output, the editors of a two-volume collection of his complete works recently stated:

> Winstanley compares with the finest writers of that glorious age of English non-fictional prose that extended from the contrasting accomplishments of John Donne and Francis Bacon, through the pyrotechnic power of John Milton, to the fierce, sardonic wit of Andrew Marvell and the resonant simplicities of John Bunyan, before the Williamite Revolution ushered in a calmer and less ambitious aesthetic in prose communication … His arresting and original biblical mythmaking … is crucial to his literary achievement. [His] first tracts demonstrate an astonishing and mature capacity to stitch from a mass of biblical allusion and a declarative and eloquent exposition that is unmistakably his own … Even in the early theological treatises he develops a style of plain exposition that smoothly becomes the measure for a measured and potently reductive reasoning.[40]

Winstanley, like Kropotkin in a later era, appreciated that 'state' and 'government' were fundamentally different concepts. Laws and rules were essential to the smooth running of the 'impossible community' that he struggled to construct. The idle, the ignorant and the unruly were for him 'ended spirits' whose anti-social behaviour should be condemned, even punished. His Digger followers believed that their occupation and cultivation of the land had divine approval. Both activities were directed towards spiritual as well as political ends. Instead of practising traditional methods of farming, they planted carrots, parsnips, beans and turnips. These were the very crops that transformed English agriculture in the seventeenth century, making it possible to feed large numbers of people and keep cattle and sheep alive throughout the harsh winter months. Agricultural surpluses, they argued, were 'to be a stock for ourselves and our poor brethren though the land of England … to provide us bread to eat till the fruit of our labours in the earth bring forth increase'.[41] Insisting that the woods of England belonged to the poor rather than the rich because they were essential to the survival of rural communities, Winstanley's Diggers called on the lords of the manor to cease felling trees and clearing woodland. Trees were to be used for building and heating homes for the poor, rather than going towards mining, shipbuilding and the construction of swathes of new urban housing. The collective 'manuring' of the commons was also deemed a religious act because it imposed a sacred order on the landscape and literally sanctified the land that the poor subsequently worked. As one radical parson put it, 'a hedge in the field is as necessary as government in the church or commonwealth'. While Winstanley's Diggers may have rejected armed force and taken comfort from the Bible in their war against enclosure, they hoped that their seizure of wasteland would inspire the urban and rural poor to engage in a mass invasion of marginal and common lands throughout the country. As radical Christians they branded all 'sacred ordinances of magistracy and ministry' profoundly offensive to 'the levelling multitude'. By digging land without orders from superiors, the Diggers were severing the servile links that bound the landless poor to their 'non-righteous' superiors. The righteous poor could only come into their earthly inheritance by taking hold of land and other property that had been taken from them by those who usurped the word of God. In the political turmoil of the 1640s this strategy was bound to appeal to the anti-authoritarian poor because digging without the consent of their lords would make the poor masters of their own fate and contribute to their social and economic independence.

Winstanley and the 'natural history' of anarchism

To the political and religious establishment of seventeenth-century Britain, entire sections of the national population were nothing short of 'natural anarchists'. To the ecclesiastical establishment they were 'unreformed' and incorrigible sinners. From the fifteenth to well into the nineteenth century, maritime communities and the urban underclass in particular, together with the inhabitants of mountainous fastnesses and remote rural districts, were as often as not beyond the reach of state authorities. Whether in town or country, the inhabitants of such places were notorious for their irreligion, 'strong talk', heavy drinking, ribald behaviour and loose sexual morality.[42] To their anti-authoritarian supporters however, they were noted for their neighbourliness, strong sense of comradeship and community, and cooperative 'associationism'. Even as late as the nineteenth century, places like these retained folk customs and social practices that were clearly at odds with the political and moral orthodoxy of their state-centred superiors. It was then that their ranks were thinned by famine and emigration, and the administrative apparatuses of the state, including police stations, army barracks, workhouses and religious institutions, penetrated practically every corner of metropolitan Europe. Not until then, however, could the capitalist nation-state mobilize the full panoply of state controls to purge rural and working-class culture of seasonal excess and 'anarchic disorder'.

Thus it is important to note that the social calendar of Britain and Europe in Winstanley's time was punctuated with civic days of festive relief and riotous public displays of social inversion. At such times the prosperous and the powerful were expected to offer the fruits of harvest bounty to their poorer dependents. These events were often occasions of low-intensity class warfare that could easily descend into social chaos as the rich and powerful lost control over their anti-authoritarian and anarchic subordinates. Among the most notable of these public holidays were the seasons of Christmas and April Fools' Day. Christmas in particular, which in many European countries began in the first week of November and stretched to 'Plough Monday' around 6 January, was the season when those at the bottom of the social hierarchy could mock their superiors in anarchic displays of plebeian disobedience.[43] However, May Day, Halloween, New Year's Eve, Shrove Tuesday and All Fools Day were also occasions for seasonal excess. At such times social hierarchies and the accepted norms of decent behaviour were literally turned upside down as the raucous conviviality of the poor threatened the established social order, not least the authority of the church, landowners and the merchant classes. These plebeian outbursts of anarchic 'misrule' could often act as safety valves that allowed the poor to express their resentment at the established order in a fashion that was jovial and apolitical, and therefore acceptable to the powerful. What was new about the mid 1640s, when Winstanley was writing his politically charged religious tracts, was the idea that the world of established authorities might be permanently overturned in an anarchic upsurge of popular radicalism. When it was the poor, not the gentry, who in their festive seasons temporarily severed the servile bonds that linked the former to the latter, then the ritual reversal and social inversion that characterized such festivities could easily blossom into full-blown dramas of political anarchy. When the rich and powerful lost their grip on these public rituals of plebeian boisterousness, they often assumed a strong oppositional form. This, more than anything else, frightened the landed gentry, challenged social hierarchy and threatened the very foundations of religious authority. Newspapers wrote of the very real fear that the country would 'be embroiled in anarchy and subjected to strangers and foreigners'. Their fears seemed justified, particularly during the periodic depressions of the mid seventeenth century. They could also be justified in slack times throughout the year when poor harvests and downturns in trade brought huge numbers of the 'giddy poor' onto city streets in search of food and strong drink. When public holidays coincided with periods of want and unemployment, they ceased being harmless displays of political theatre directed by the poor at their wealthy audience. To members of the gentry they were close to revolutionary displays of political anger that allowed the anarchic poor to claim the streets and threaten the authority of the powerful. Thus plebeian carnivals of seasonal disorder and excess transformed from street theatre into anarchic outbursts of class rage.[44]

It is easy to imagine groups like the Diggers emerging from these bands of disorderly opponents of political and religious authority. Distinguishing themselves from Levellers who favoured limitations on democracy and accepted the sanctity of property, the Diggers regarded themselves as True Levellers and had considerable support among the armed forces and the London poor. Unlike their more moderate and constitutional confrères, they were less concerned with the constitutionality of their actions than with the bread and butter issues that were central to the survival of the poor in periods of revolutionary ferment.

One of the problems in placing Winstanley within the anarchist tradition is the fact that his writings, like his political career, never represented a seamless narrative.[45] That said, only those who privilege political consistency over political expediency will condemn him as an opportunist. The fact that the 'unitary' Winstanley never existed does not mean that his life's work should be devalued. Always the revolutionary pragmatist and never the dogmatist, his literary interventions during the tumultuous years of the English Revolution reveal a writer and political activist who always rolled with the flow of revolutionary events. His political thinking oscillates between impassioned pleas for the survival of the disappearing world of small traders, craft workers and farmers, to visionary blueprints for an anarchist society of the future. More concerned with making history than securing a place in literary history, he believed that 'Words and writings were all nothing, and must die, for action is the life of all, and if thou dost not act, thou dost nothing.'[46] Like George Orwell in the 1930s, and the Irish-born author Frank McCourt, he wrote about poverty and social displacement from the depths of his own experiences.[47] Like his near contemporaries Milton and Defoe in the seventeenth century, and many young Muslim writers today, he struggled to come to grips with the problem of how to keep faith with his God in a materialist age. He tried to resolve this issue by casting his lot with those who were literally being pushed to the margins of society, while simultaneously constructing a Paradise in his imagination where the answers to moral dilemmas became clear and where social conflicts were resolved. In his proto-anarchist writings Winstanley managed to unite the plebeian radicalism of Civil War England with the peasant rebellions, millenarian yearnings and antinomian doctrines of the heretical religious sects of Europe in the late Middle Ages. Like Kropotkin two centuries later, Winstanley wrote of the closed worlds of the marginalized poor just as they were being turned upside down due to the collapse of feudalism and the coming of global capitalism. As one of the more prominent historical personalities to be forged on the anvil of the English Civil War, he articulated an anti-politics of religious heresy that appealed to those on the margins of English society because it was infused with a popular revolutionary desire to dispense with all forms of religious and political authority and create a world from which the poor would no longer be banished. Although he published a huge volume of work in four short years from 1648 to 1652, his writings on political issues, social philosophy, religion and history have nevertheless earned him a place among the finest writers in the English language in the sixteenth and seventeenth centuries.

An antinomian rejection of the power politics, moral authority and religious practices of the hierarchical church, Winstanley's denunciation of authority was by no means confined to the realms of religion. Formulated in the cauldron of English Civil War politics, his anti-authoritarianism also extended to an anarchist variant of civil society. The civil wars that raged in England, Scotland and Ireland in the mid seventeenth century were not unlike the wars in countries as far apart as Yugoslavia and Rwanda in the 1990s. Driven by religious hatred and misunderstanding, ethnic hostilities and political violence, they were responsible for religious massacres, ethnic cleansing and mass murders and other political atrocities. This was the background against which Winstanley and his followers sought to articulate their vision of a decentralized society free from religious and political coercion, a society informed by a radically new approach to living and working in town and country alike. His anti-authoritarian sermons and political pamphlets sought to dispense with political authority, abolish private property, encourage voluntarism, cultivate liberty, promote equity and foster the development of social and economic arrangements free from the political coercion of government. The visionary quality of Winstanley's anti-authoritarianism is especially evident in such radical pamphlets as *The Law of Freedom in a Platform* and *The New Law of Righteousness*. Like Franz Fanon's anti-colonial masterpiece *The Wretched of the Earth* some 300 years later, this was addressed to 'the despised ones of the world' and purported to provide a 'Glimpse of the new Heaven, and New Earth, wherein dwells Righteousness'. His religious tracts were at once reasoned attacks on the ecclesiastical establishment, and the basis for a new ethics of the marketplace and a new geography of social welfare. In *Truth Lifting up his Head Above Scandals*, he denied that parishes were simply religious administrative units and suggested instead that they were 'made for civil good sake'.[48] In a blanket condemnation of the mystifications of religion and the iniquities of monarchical authority, he insisted that a 'universal law of equity' was about to usher in a new egalitarian social order in Civil War England. When this happened, he prophesied:

> none shall lay claim to any creature and say, This is mine, and that is yours. This is my work and that is yours. But everyone shall put their hands to till the earth and bring up cattle, and the blessing of the earth shall be common to all; … There shall be none lords over others, but everyone shall be a lord over himself, subject to the law of righteousness, reason and equity, which shall dwell and rule in him, which is the Lord.[49]

In a statement that would be echoed by Mao's contention that 'political power grows out of the barrel of gun', Winstanley, the bête noire of the landed aristocracy, insisted that 'the power of property was brought into creation by the sword'. In *The Law of Freedom in a Platform*, published in 1652, he outlined his vision of a new social and economic order devoid of private property and unbound by any cash nexus. It was a vision for the future that harkened back to a past when, this argument suggested, basic needs like food, shelter, security and water had historically been provided within the confines and moral structures of peasant society. These were now endangered by the enclosure system and the emergence of powerful landowners and the new merchant class whose obsession with private property could only result, Winstanley argued, in social discontent and greater inequality. Like those who sought to transform Britain into a country fit for heroes in the aftermath of the Second World War, he repeatedly insisted that social transformation was the necessary recompense for the thousands of ordinary men and women who had helped to overthrow monarchy, including those who had fought in Parliament's armies.

William Godwin: the anarchist lover of order

William Godwin was born in Wisbech, in north Cambridgeshire, on 3 March 1756. The seventh of 13 children, he belonged to a family of Dissenting ministers, and his grandfather and one of his uncles had been prominent preachers. His father, a strict pastor, presided over a series of Independent congregations in Norfolk, a region that had seen strong opposition to land enclosures in the mid sixteenth century, and had also been the backbone of a movement for more political independence during the English Revolution. The young Godwin was steeped in this culture of dissent. The English Dissenters in Godwin's day constituted a separate cultural group who were prohibited from registering the births of their children and were barred from public office. From an early age, the deeply religious and intellectually precocious Godwin displayed a tendency to follow in the family footsteps. His favourite childhood pastime was said to be preaching sermons to his fellow students, which suggests that his belief in the powers of persuasion was formed at an early age.[50] According to his friend and contemporary, William Hazlitt (1778–1830), 'He blazed as a sun in the firmament of reputation; no one was more talked of, more looked up to, more sought after, and wherever liberty, truth, and justice was the theme, his name was not far off.'[51]

Godwin, like Hazlitt, attended Hoxton Academy, one of a number of independent colleges established by Dissenters during the eighteenth century to compensate for the fact that they were debarred from England's universities. From 1778 to 1783, he served as minister over a succession of small non-conformist chapels in East Anglia and the Home Counties, following which he set off for London to live as a writer. Although he wore clerical garb to the end of his long life, he abandoned any kind of Christian belief in 1790, just three years before the publication of his *Enquiry Concerning Political Justice, and its Influence on General Virtue and Happiness*. This work was followed in 1794 by *The Adventures of Caleb Williams*, a psychological thriller and 'anarchist parable', which, some two centuries before Foucault, showed that 'the spirit and character of government intrudes itself into every rank of society'.[52]

Godwin was not a revolutionary by temperament, and his influence was limited chiefly to English early socialist thinkers and the Romantic poets. That said, *Political Justice* did reach working-class readers in the larger towns of the midlands and north of England, and along with Paine's *Age of Reason* did much to promote the spread of free thought and atheism among craft workers in England's industrial cities. Nevertheless, as Joll has suggested, it is as a constructor of theories rather than a practical revolutionary that Godwin remains a subject of interest for anarchists today.[53] He was practically forgotten until the late nineteenth century, when his anti-authoritarianism appealed to anarchists looking for rational doctrines to justify the construction of a stateless society. His writings are a reminder of what anarchism owes to the Enlightenment. *Political Justice* in particular made a powerful philosophical case against government, the law, property and the institutions of the state in the late eighteenth century and early nineteenth. Like Tolstoy, he was a major literary figure as well as an educationalist and anarchist philosopher. While he stood outside any anarchist movement and avoided the term 'anarchy' because of the negative connotations it acquired during the French Revolution, he anticipated the anti-authoritarianism of many nineteenth-century anarchists. As a product of the Enlightenment, he regarded education as the key to liberation, without which, he argued, men's 'ungoverned passions would incite them to grasp for power'.[54] Yet he preferred extreme disorder to a life spent subordinate to the will and authority of others. Next to Kropotkin, he is anarchism's greatest intellectual. His influential friends and acquaintances included Percy Bysshe Shelley, Samuel Taylor Coleridge, Robert Owen, Francis Place, Charles Lamb, William Wordsworth, Edward Bulwer-Lytton and Robert Southey. He was famously, and briefly, married to Mary Wollstonecraft, author of *A Vindication of the Rights of Woman* (1792), who died in

London in 1797 just 11 days after giving birth to daughter Mary, who would grow up to be Mary Shelley, author of *Frankenstein* (1818).

Godwin's philosophic anarchism

Kropotkin credited Godwin with laying down the principles of anarchism in his 'truly remarkable' *Political Justice*, where he 'boldly' attacked the law, proved the uselessness of the state, and argued that 'only with the abolition of courts could true *justice* become possible'. This work, Kropotkin suggested, made Godwin 'the first theoriser of Socialism without government – that is to say, of Anarchism'. Godwin, he added,

> was also aware of what went on in England under the cover of parliament: the pillage of communal lands, the sale of advantageous posts, the hunting of children of the poor and their removal from workhouses, by agents who travelled all over England for the purpose, to the factories of Lancashire, where masses of them soon perished.[55]

Although he was a lover of order, Godwin nevertheless welcomed the disorder of anarchy because it 'awakens minds, diffuses energy and enterprise through the community ... though it does not effect this in the best manner'. He regarded anarchy as transitory and despised despotism because it 'tended towards permanence' and 'trampled the mind into an equality of the most odious sort'. His greatest achievement was to separate happiness from a selfish individualism, which rendered pleasure and the pursuit of happiness 'the principle and necessary object of all existence'. Saint-Just once described happiness as 'a new idea' in eighteenth-century revolutionary Europe. Happiness, Godwin insisted, could not be obtained individually, for 'all must partake of it or the few will never enjoy it'.[56] If justice was to have any meaning, he argued, it should contribute to the happiness and well being of the entire community, not just the privileged few.

When he wrote his *Enquiry Concerning Political Justice*, Godwin was influenced by the French *philosophes* and had already become an atheist. Nevertheless, unlike Proudhon, Bakunin and Kropotkin, his moral and political outlook had largely been shaped by his Calvinist upbringing. As Marshall has perceptively observed, he took Aquinas' notion 'of the stewardship of the good things of the earth' and turned it into a foundational principle of anarcho-communism.[57] Similarly, his anti-authoritarianism resulted in the transfer of the Dissenters' right of private judgement from the purely religious realms of church politics to the secular world of power politics. As a boy, Godwin had been deeply influenced by Samuel Newton, pastor of an Independent congregation in the city of Norwich. Newton was a disciple of Robert Sandeman, leader of a small fundamentalist sect that had been expelled by the Presbyterians for their opposition to all forms of church government. Sandeman's followers remained Calvinists, espoused a harsh conception of 'the elect', and insisted that the Bible contained all that was necessary for the salvation of man. In denying the validity of all government, not just church government, Godwin rejected the limited anti-authoritarianism of the Sandemanians. While the latter believed that 'religious man' had no business with the state, Godwin insisted that those of a true moral disposition should likewise shun the state. Justice, he argued was the 'general appellation for all moral duty'. While the Sandemanians created an organization of independent congregations with no ordained ministers, Godwin envisaged a network of independent parishes without rulers as the ideal structure for his libertarian society.[58] While the Sandemanians believed in the 'community of property' and taught that savings were sinful and should be distributed to the poor, Godwin envisaged a community of goods to be shared according to need. Like Sandeman, he laid specific stress on the moral evils of 'accumulated property'. However, he maintained that the poor did not have the *right* to be supported by the rich, and argued instead that the rich had a *positive duty* to support the poor. Thus Godwin differed from many of his fellow radicals in rejecting the concept of natural rights. As a lover of order he also denied workers the right to resist oppression, but nevertheless was unsparing in his condemnation of the social, political, legal and ecclesiastical institutions of late eighteenth-century Britain.[59] Thus at the dawn of a new age of factory production, when factory towns and urban expansion were changing the face of Britain, and new ways of using and abusing the land were transforming rural life, Godwin and his followers sought a rational alternative to this harsh new capitalist order that was ultimately based on 'accumulated property'. As Joll has suggested, it was

the disruptive example of the French Revolution and the growing challenge of the new emerging industrial society that were to produce the circumstance in which both heretics and rationalists could join in a movement that provided a fundamental criticism of the old society and a programme of violent action to remedy its defects.[60]

Godwin's *Political Justice* has rightly been praised for the astonishing completeness with which it anticipated the many aspects of libertarian thinking in the nineteenth and twentieth centuries. It still remains one of the most thorough expositions of anarchist thought. Godwin was one of the earliest social theorists to consciously confront in his own work the extreme implications of a post-Reformation, Kafkaesque world wherein, for the first time, the Absolute State faced the Absolute Individual.[61] This was a theme that he developed in his novel, *The Adventures of Caleb Williams* (1794), which was a call to end the abuse of power by a tyrannical government. Intended as a popularization of ideas presented in his *Political Justice*, Godwin used the novel to show how legal and other institutions can and do destroy even the most just individuals. He insisted that freedom was not something that could be decreed or protected by laws and states – instead it was 'something you shape for yourself and share with other men. States and laws are its enemies ... the state is evil and brings not order but conflict. Authority thwarts the natural impulses and makes men strangers to each other.'[62] Nurtured by the tradition of English Dissent and two decades of careful reading in the Greek classics and English and French literature, *Political Justice* was conceived independently of events in France and at a time when the French Revolution had already descended into violence and dictatorship. However this did not cause Godwin to abandon his basic beliefs in anti-authoritarianism. It led him to insist that political change was futile unless accompanied by changes in moral attitudes. Criticizing all forms of 'governmental organization', he insisted that the stateless society could only be constructed consequent upon the complete reconstruction of personal conduct and the reform of social behaviour. Five years before the French Revolution he could write:

> The state of society is incontestably artificial; the power of one man over another must always be derived from convention or from conquest; by nature we are equal. The necessary consequence is, that government must always depend upon the opinion of the governed. Let the most oppressed people under heaven once change their mode of thinking,

and they are free … Government is very limited in its power of making men either virtuous or happy; it is only in the infancy of society that it can do anything considerable; in its maturity it can only direct a few of our outward actions. But our moral dispositions and character depend very much, perhaps entirely, upon education.[63]

The idea of necessity, or determinism, pervades Godwin's work. Thus he argued that impersonal and immutable forces, expressed through natural laws, determine human actions. This genre of 'necessitarianism' is analogous to the scientific determinism we encounter in Kropotkin's *Modern Science and Anarchism* (1912). Far from being fatalistic or a justification for inertia, however, it optimistically maintained that people were the makers of their own destiny, and that human effort could hasten the arrival of a new millennium. Thus like all anarchists, Godwin not only rejected the authority of church and state, but insisted that, left to itself, the human mind would detect error and make its own way towards that which was true. He regarded government as abhorrent because it 'lays its hand upon the spring that is in society and puts a stop to its motion'. In so doing, he added, it also gives substance and permanence to human errors and blind ambition. Thus government:

[r]everses the genuine propensities of mind, and instead of suffering us to look forward, teaches us to look backwards for perfection. It prompts us to seek the public welfare not in innovation and improvement, but in a timid reverence for the decisions of our ancestors, as if it were the nature of mind always to degenerate and never to advance.[64]

Godwin's stateless society

Like other anarchists, Godwin refused to outline a blueprint of his stateless society on the grounds that to do so would contradict many of his most important teachings on progress and social justice. Nevertheless, he believed that human perfectibility was possible because man, he argued, was born without any innate ideas, and his mind and character were capable of being influenced to an infinite degree by external 'suggestions'. Thus he added, 'Whips, axes, gibbets, dungeons, chains and racks are the most approved and established methods of persuading men to obedience and impressing upon their minds the lessons of reason.

Hundreds of victims are annually sacrificed at the shrine of positive law and political institutions.'[65] However, he insisted that the dissolution of the authoritarian institutions of government should be preceded by a period of education and enlightenment. Otherwise, he argued, all would descend into mob violence. As early as 1784 when he planned to set up a private school, he published *An Account of the Seminary that Will be Opened on Monday the Fourth Day of August at Epsom*. Described as 'the most incisive and eloquent account of libertarian and progressive and free education,'[66] it reads like a preliminary essay on the evils of authoritarianism that he later developed in his better-known work *Political Justice*. He proclaimed that children are born innocent and benevolent, and that teachers should foster their individual talents without the use of restraint. Marshall has credited Godwin with presenting the 'most remarkable and advanced ideas on education ever written.'[67] Education in the stateless society, Godwin argued, should be beyond the reach of church and state alike. It should foster happiness, develop critical minds, and allow children to learn at their own pace. Thus he believed that 'national education ought uniformly to be discouraged on account of its obvious alliance with national government'. Given the crucial role of state-centred education in inculcating respect for authority, and for figures of authority, in eighteenth-century Europe, this was a revolutionary ideal that was also opposed to propaganda and the authoritarian indoctrination of students. While he rejected the authority of church and state, the Puritanism and asceticism of Calvinism pervade much of Godwin's teachings on education and social reform.

Joll has suggested that Godwin, like Proudhon and Kropotkin, was an anarchist who could accept some degree of association for minimal administrative purposes. However, Godwin also insisted that such associations should be as inclusive and decentralized as possible. The parish was the unit on which the new society would be based, and no central assembly was necessary for the functioning of the stateless society.[68] Men's needs, he argued, were few, and 'little would be required in a society where the motives of vanity and ambition, the desire to outshine one's neighbour, has been eradicated by the inculcation of a true scale of values.'[69] Yet, as Marshall has shown, Godwin was by no means opposed to the industrial process. He looked to 'technology (what he described as "various sorts of mills, of weaving engines, steam engines") and even one day to an automatic plough, to reduce and alleviate unpleasant toil'.[70]

ANARCHISM BEFORE KROPOTKIN

Godwin's ideal was a society where wisdom could be transmitted without the intervention of institutions, a society that was devoid of authority and command and governed only by persuasion. Small social groups were preferable to large political assemblies. In such a society:

> opinion would be all-sufficient; the inspection of every man over the conduct of his neighbours, when unstained by caprice, would constitute a censorship of the most irresistible nature. But the force of this censorship would depend on its freedom, not following the positive dictates of law, but the spontaneous decisions of understanding.[71]

In arguing thus, he clearly ignored the dangers of exhortation becoming as oppressive as compulsion. If public opinion were to become the sole arbiter of behaviour, then intolerance of difference could easily lead to an Orwellian world of social conformity and blind obedience of the opinion of the majority. Thus anarchists like Godwin failed to give due weight to the dangers of moral tyranny replacing the legal and moral tyranny of the authoritarian state. Instead Godwin trusted that the enlightened localism of small anarchist communes would not lead to narrow parochialism. Rather, he hoped that it would transform the world into a single great republic wherein people could move freely without the impediment of national barriers. As an advocate of 'small is beautiful' and the decentralization of decision-making, Godwin condemned complex centralized states as harmful and unnecessary for social progress. Their dissolution, he argued, would lead to localized forms of administration that would impose limits upon, and reduce the scope for, grasping ambition. 'Sobriety and equity', he maintained, were 'the obvious characteristics of a limited circle'.[72] In these new local units of society legislation would rarely be needed; the whole community would participate in administration and officials would be concerned with providing information and concerns of a practical nature. Only in exceptional circumstances might it be necessary to go beyond the parishes and form regional assemblies.

Like most nineteenth-century anarchists, Godwin envisaged a drastic simplification of life. He felt that work was necessary for human happiness, that luxury was a corrupting influence, and that the rich deserved pity as much as the poor. Unlike Tolstoy, however, he did not see dignity in unnecessary manual labour. Thus he maintained that appropriate technology 'would not only lessen the enforced cooperation imposed by the present division of labour, but increase the incomparable wealth of leisure in which people might cultivate their minds'.[73] Like Kropotkin, he believed that technological developments were not incompatible with anarchism, and that science 'might one day make mind omnipotent over matter, prolong life, and ... even discover the secret of immortality!' Thus his decentralized society was one wherein forward-looking, organic communities were engaged in industrial as well as agricultural work. Again like Kropotkin he also believed that new technologies would facilitate the decentralization of production. The break-up of giant monopolies would in turn result in the decline of mega-cities, thereby contributing to the growth of smaller urban centres organically linked to their own hinterlands.

His ideal was 'independence of mind, which makes us feel that our satisfactions are not at the mercy either of men or fortune, and activity of mind, the cheerfulness that arises from industry properly employed about objects of which our judgment acknowledges the intrinsic value'.[74] He envisaged the enlightened person 'making individual calculations of pleasure and pain and carefully weighing up the consequences of his or her action'. In stressing the importance of individual autonomy to social and moral progress, he called for 'a mental space for creative thought' and could see no value in sacrificing one's identity to that of the community or wider society. Thus he argued: 'Every man ought to rest upon his own center, and consult his own understanding. Every man ought to feel his independence, that he can assert the principles of justice and truth without being obliged treacherously to adapt them to the peculiarities of his situation and the error of others'.[75]

While emphasizing the value of individual autonomy to social progress and personal development, Godwin repeatedly reminded his readers that, as social beings, they were required to live in society. Only in society, he argued, would their best qualities reach their optimum development. Like Kropotkin, he argued that society 'originated in men's consciousness of the need for mutual assistance'. Its 'moving principle' was justice, which he defines as 'a rule of conduct originating in the connection of one percipient being to another'. Like other nineteenth century anarchists he believed that we should avoid 'setting up the general good ... as something above or outside individuals'.[76] He preferred democracy to monarchy and aristocracy, regarding it as a system of government in which 'every member is considered as a man and nothing else'. Democracy, he believed, 'restores to man a consciousness of his value, teaches him by the removal of authority and oppression to listen only to the dictates of reason, gives him confidence to treat other men as his fellow beings, and induces him to regard them no longer as enemies against whom he must be upon guard, but as brethren whom it becomes him to assist'.[77] Yet he condemned electioneering as 'a trade so despicably degrading, so eternally incompatible with moral and mental dignity that I can scarcely believe a truly great mind capable of the dirty drudgery of such vice'.[78] As an uncompromising critique of the iniquity of government he wrote:

> Above all we should not forget that government is an evil, an usurpation upon the private judgment and individual conscience of mankind, and that, however we may be obliged to admit it as a necessary evil for the present, it behoves us, as friends of reason and the human species, to admit of it as little as possible and carefully to observe whether, in consequence of the gradual illumination of the human mind, that little may not hereafter be diminished.[79]

Meanwhile at the other end of Europe, Peter Kropotkin was to become an even harsher critic of democracy and the rising power of the centralized nation-state. Unlike Winstanley, Godwin and Proudhon, he looked to the sciences, including the newly emerging social sciences, in order to provide anarchism with a rational foundation. In so doing he presented 'scientific anarchism' as an alternative to the political violence to which his opponents pointed when they wished to castigate anarchists as an incorrigible underclass whose efforts to construct the 'impossible community' were, they argued, utopian at best or insane at worst. The product of European and Russian cultural traditions, Kropotkin fused the best principles of the Enlightenment with the 'new knowledge' of the natural and social sciences. This allowed him to extend his critique of Russian autocracy to attack all forms of authority, including that of state-centred sciences and the academic establishment of nineteenth-century Europe.

Pierre-Joseph Proudhon and the French roots of anarchism

Many anarchists have objected to the identification of anarchism with its best-known theorists – Godwin, Proudhon, Bakunin, Malatesta and

Kropotkin – preferring instead to trace the roots of modern anarchism to the slave revolts of ancient Rome, the peasant rebellions of medieval Europe, the anti-authoritarian Diggers of seventeenth-century England, and the plebeian radicalism of the French Revolution. Indeed Colin Ward has suggested that Kropotkin himself was so concerned with unearthing the folk roots of anarchism in the French Revolution that he failed to discuss in any great detail the ideas of anarchist groups like *Les Enragés* who were closely associated with the impoverished *sans culottes* of Paris and Lyons in the late eighteenth century.[80] *Les Enragés* first appeared on the historical stage in 1793. Like the Diggers, they emerged during a period of economic recession when the urban poor of those two cities were reacting against the encroaching power of the ascendant middle class. Because they lacked organization and had no common policy, *Les Enragés* were never a party in the modern sense of the term. Nevertheless they fit within the anarchist tradition as a group of like-minded revolutionaries who rejected Jacobin views on the authority of the state. Their most articulate spokesmen were Jacques Roux and Jean Varlet. The latter was a full-time activist of independent means who, like Proudhon, believed that the self-interest and political aspirations of Les Girondins were selling the French Revolution short and betraying groups like the *sans culottes* (i.e. the 'trouserless' ones). Roux's teachings on radical egalitarianism derived from his experience of serving a sprawling inner-city parish in the revolutionary district of Saint-Nicolas-des-Champs in the centre of Paris.[81] From the start, however, Roux and Varlet attracted the attention of radical clubs, but they also had a following among revolutionary journalists like Jean-Paul Marat, who defended food riots as a legitimate response to the over-pricing and hoarding of food by shopkeepers and petty merchants. Roux, the most celebrated of *Les Enragés*, was a country clergyman and a strict Christian ascetic who, prior to his arrival in Paris, had been accused of inciting the poor to rebel against landowners who attempted to enforce their seigniorial rights to tribute payments from their tenants. Some 30 years before Proudhon, he claimed that the land of France belonged to all. He also identified closely with the workers of Paris' Gravilliers quarter and railed against profiteering shopkeepers, who, he argued, were bleeding the poor dry with high prices for basic foodstuffs. He frequented the Club of the Cordelier (the Society of Friends of the Rights of Man and of the Citizen) and eventually became a member of the General Council of the Paris Commune. The failure of the Revolution to fulfil its promises to the poor made him a rebel against 'senatorial despotism', which, he argued, 'chains the people without their knowing it, and brutalizes and subjugates them by laws they themselves are supposed to have made'.[82]

A confirmed internationalist who despised political boundaries, Pierre-Joseph Proudhon, the son of tavern-keeper, was born in Besançon, in Franche-Comté, on 15 January 1809. A proud son of the French soil, he was also an ardent regionalist who once boasted that he had been 'moulded with the pure limestone of the Jura'.[83] Pre-nationalist regionalism, based on the territorial unit of the traditional French *pays*, was at the heart of his writings on anarchism and federalism. Growing up on a peasant holding, he experienced the distress that land enclosure and the privatization of property bought to this remote corner of France in the aftermath of the Napoleonic wars. This partially accounted for the puritanical and patriarchal values that characterized his writings on anarchist society and anarchist economics. The rural environment of his birth not only fostered an attachment to rural values – it also encouraged in the young Proudhon an ecological sensibility that caused him to lament the loss of that 'deep feeling of nature' which had always been at the heart of French rural life, and which was rapidly disappearing in the first half of the nineteenth century. Writing in 1840, he felt that 'Men no longer love the soil. Landowners sell it, lease it, divide it into shares, prostitute it, bargain with it and treat it as an object of speculation. Farmers torture it, violate it, exhaust it and sacrifice it to their impatient desire for gain. They never become one with it.'[84]

His fellow Frenchman and composer, Élie Halévy (1799–1862), considered Proudhon 'the real inspirer of French socialism'.[85] Unlike Marx and Engels, however, he rejected the political path to socialism, believing that this would inhibit the freedom of the individual and end in political oppression. Fifty years after the French Revolution, and despite his deeply misogynistic attitudes, Proudhon's prose, like the best of Zola, invigorated popular French literature and whetted the appetite of post-revolutionary France for radical social change. His writings on social justice were admired by no less than Baudelaire (1821–67), Flaubert (1821–80) and Hugo (1802–85). Like Winstanley, he was renowned for the vivid phrase. His biographer, Arthur Desjardins, aptly described him as a 'plebeian sculptor of words' and ranked him alongside the great French classicists. 'No less than Molière', he argued, Proudhon should have been nominated to the Académie Française.[86] His provocative prose and revolutionary ideas extended beyond the world of his birth, and even beyond the much wider world of French anarchism and socialism. His political and economic writings influenced the Russian Narodniks in Kropotkin's time, and Spanish federalists in the 1930s. His thoughts on war and history attracted the attention of Tolstoy, who borrowed the title of his own masterpiece, *War and Peace*, from Proudhon's *La Guerre et la Paix*.[87]

From the age of 12, Proudhon worked as a cellar-boy in his father's tavern but nevertheless still managed to win a scholarship to the College de Besançon, the town's most prestigious school. Here he rubbed shoulders with the sons of local merchants and substantial landowners. His education was cut short after his father was declared bankrupt in 1827, and the young Proudhon then became a printer's apprentice. In so doing he entered a world that allowed him to continue his education, while also nurturing that deep sense of comradeship that characterized rural and village life in early nineteenth-century France. As a printer's apprentice he inevitably came in contact with local socialists. He may even have supervised the printing of Charles Fourier's classic work on rural reconstruction and cooperative living, *Le Nouveau Monde industriel et societaire*, which was published in 1829. Fourier, also from Besançon, sought to adapt the rural economy to human needs and his ideas on the wastefulness of competitive capitalism foreshadowed those of Marx. A strong believer in the merits of sustainability, his teachings have been central to the development of the cooperative movement and modern ecology. In his early years in particular, Proudhon was profoundly influenced by the 'bizarre genius' of Fourier.[88] He was particularly attracted to his teachings on 'immanent justice' and the inevitability of revolution. However, his peasant upbringing may have prevented him from accepting Fourier's rural utopianism, just as his puritanical background may have prevented Proudhon becoming an advocate of free love and sexual liberation.

While employed as a printer (of mainly religious publications for the local clergy), Proudhon also published an obscure essay on philology. This earned him the Suard pension, offered once every three years by Besançon Academy to a young scholar of exceptional academic ability, which enabled the recipient to study in Paris. In his submission to the city's academicians, the young Proudhon made a forthright declaration of the class values that he would uphold for the remainder of his life. As an enthusiastic working-class organic intellectual, he vowed to protect the interests and values of the rural and proto-industrial working-class communities that had nurtured him:

> Born and brought up in the working class, still belonging to it, today and forever, by heart, by nature, by habit, and above all by the community of interest and wishes, the greatest joy of the candidate, if he gains your votes, will be to have attracted in his person your just solicitude for that interesting portion of society, to have been judged worthy of being its first representative before you, and to be able to work henceforward without relaxation, through philosophy and science, and with all the energy of his will and the powers of his mind, for the complete liberation of his brothers and companions.[89]

George Woodcock has described Proudhon as 'a connoisseur of paradox' and 'an aficionado of antinomial thinking'.[90] Kropotkin credited him with laying the foundations of modern anarchism, while Bakunin considered him the first real anarchist socialist. His doctrine of spontaneous action, together with his views on free associations, fostered an anarchist theory of society that was devoid of governmental regulation and state protection. In a recent reappraisal of anarchist theory, Richard J. Day described Proudhon as 'a rationalist perfectionist'. Nevertheless Proudhon was convinced that not even anarchists could construct a world completely free of relations of power. His passionate diatribes against the capitalist state and modernity were, Day suggests, 'driven by a pragmatic desire to make the best of existing institutions rather than replacing them with alternative modes of organization'.[91] Today he is principally respected in anarchist circles for his views on federalism and his complex critique of private property. He was also the first classical anarchist to apply the term 'anarchy' to what Kropotkin described as the 'no-government system of socialism'. Nevertheless, this great advocate of 'mutuellisme', the founder of an anti-politics of anarchism, was a profound misogynist. As an arch individualist he stressed the importance of individual freedom and distrusted the very word 'association'. This placed him in a paradoxical position in relation to other anarchists for whom mutualism and associationism were to become stepping-stones to revolution and the hallmarks of an anarchist society. In Proudhon's anarchist society, laws would be replaced with mutually agreed contracts, and each citizen, each town and each industrial union would 'make its own laws'.[92]

A quintessentially French anarchist, the influence of his peasant upbringing remained with Proudhon throughout his life. Similarly, the ideal of a self-sustaining peasant society was a shaping influence on his moral philosophy and political thinking. His comparative neglect by British and American anarchists may have been attributable to 'the peculiarly Gallic nature of his genius'.[93] His writings have proven difficult to translate, while those that have been translated from the French do not match the literary quality and stylistic flourishes of the original texts. It could be argued that Proudhon's anti-clericalism, coupled with his emphasis on rural rather than urban society, limited his appeal outside of rural Europe for much of the nineteenth century. A spokesman for the propertyless who was nevertheless cautiously in favour of private property, Proudhon was opposed to the absolute rights of ownership that permitted the wealthy to exploit the labour and poverty of others. Absolute ownership, he argued, transformed resources into capital, allowed the wealthy to charge interest on credit, and enabled landowners to accumulate wealth through the imposition of rent. In *What Is Property?*, in terms reminiscent of Kropotkin's treatment of the evolution of the state, he described the origins of property and political authority:

Man, in order to procure as speedily as possible the most thorough satisfaction of his wants, seeks *rule*. In the beginning this rule is to him living, visible, and tangible. It is his father, his master, his king. The more ignorant man is, the more obedient he is, the more obedient he is, and the more absolute is his confidence in his guide. ... In proportion as society becomes enlightened, royal authority diminishes ... Thus, in any given society, the authority of man over man is inversely proportional to the stage of intellectual development which that society has reached; and the probable duration of that authority can be calculated from the more or less general desire for a true government – that is, for a scientific government. And just as the right of force and the right of artifice retreat before the steady advance of justice ... so the sovereignty of the will yields to the sovereignty of the reason, and must at last be lost in scientific socialism ... As man seeks justice in equality, so society seeks order in anarchy. Anarchy, the absence of master, of a sovereign, – such is the form of government to which we are every day approximating, and which our accustomed habit of taking man for our rule, and his will for law, leads us to regard as the height of disorder and the expression of chaos.[94]

'Property is theft'

Proudhon's famous assertion that 'property is theft' needs to be seen in its historical and indeed regional context. Private ownership of land had only emerged in France in the 1760s. There was nothing to suggest that, if left unchallenged, privatization of land could develop along English lines and contribute to the rise of a powerful landed aristocracy. However, eighteenth-century France, like seventeenth-century England, seethed with rural unrest. The landless poor opposed enclosure and fought hard to retain their traditional rights of access to common lands. Nevertheless, wealthy merchants, buoyed up by a sustained period of rising prices for cereals, continued to buy up feudal estates. This contributed to the privatization of large tracts of land throughout the east and south of the country in particular. *Geometres*, or land surveyors, measured the precise extent of private properties which they then mapped onto estate maps that were subsequently used in legal disputes to defend the rights of landowners. From the 1780s onwards, this new French-speaking elite used the Legislative Assembly to abolish communal grazing of peasant livestock on arable land. By then, the opponents of privatization were vociferous in their claims that the land should belong to the nation, and that 'natural property' did not 'extend beyond the body of each individual'.[95] Rousseau's *Social Contract*, published in 1762, had argued that it was 'manifestly against the Law of Nature that a handful of men wallow in luxury, while the famished multitudes lack the necessities of life'.[96] Reflecting his Calvinist background, Rousseau, like Proudhon, ascribed selfishness to grasping landlords and suggested that the state should only protect such property as was required for an individual's safety and subsistence. Viewed thus, the right of each individual to own landed property was always to remain subordinate to the rights of the community.

In his definitive 1905 article on the evolution of modern anarchism in the *Encyclopaedia Britannica*, Kropotkin applauded Proudhon's subtle distinction between the absolute right to property which allowed owners to 'use and abuse' it, and the limited rights of those whose possession of property was confined to the lesser privileges of usufruct.[97] For Proudhon, as for Kropotkin, possession of property without the absolute rights that Roman law conferred on its owners was a vital protection against collectivization and other forms of state encroachment that characterized the rural economy of post-revolutionary Russia. Thus Kropotkin praised Proudhon for his repudiation of state-aided socialism, which, he argued, could only drive mankind into 'communistic monasteries or barracks'. His first 'memoir' on property, published in the 1840s, suggests that Proudhon was cautiously in favour of private property, and, unlike Marx and Engels, he was opposed to the violent dispossession of property owners. Instead he sought to encourage social equality through mutual aid and a banking system that would cater to the needs of all those engaged in the process of production. This, he argued, would prevent landowners from earning interest from their properties. It would also prevent the rural poor falling victim to the authority of property owners. Raised among poor peasants and smallholders, Proudhon believed that those who sought the collectivization of property risked subordinating the rights of the individual to those of the collective. He insisted that the workers' right to the produce of their work did not entitle them to outright ownership of the means of production. Instead, a communal system of 'mutuellisme', that would certainly have been familiar to Kropotkin, would allow all those engaged in the process of production to exchange their produce at cost-value. Labour cheques, based on the number of hours required to produce any given commodity, would ensure that all such exchanges would be strictly equivalent. From this Proudhon was able to argue that private property was incompatible with social justice because it excluded the majority of workers from their right to the products of collaborative work.

Quite clearly Proudhon's views on private property were underpinned by a social philosophy that privileged the productive potential of workers over 'cowardly proprietors' who lived off the wealth of others. His defence of the rural poor was also in stark contrast to Marx's denigration of the peasant way of life and his infamous portrayal of peasants as subhuman creatures who lacked the organizational capacities of the urban proletariat.[98] It was also much more in line with Kropotkin's ardent advocacy of the rights of the rural poor in Russia following the abolition of serfdom. In his trenchantly anarchistic *Avertissement aux proprietaires*, Proudhon celebrated all workers, not just the urban proletariat, as champions of social reconstruction who would liberate all of humanity and not just its most oppressed sectors:

Workers, labourers, men of the people, whoever you may be, the initiative of reform is yours. It is you who accomplish that synthesis of social composition which will be the masterpiece of creation, and you alone can accomplish it ... You, men of power, angry magistrates, cowardly proprietors ... Do not provoke the outbreaks of our despair, for even if your soldiers and policemen succeed in suppressing us, you will not be able to stand up before our last resource. It is neither regicide, nor assassination, nor poisoning, nor arson, nor refusal to work, nor emigration, nor insurrection, nor suicide; it is something that is seen but cannot be spoken of.[99]

Workers, he argued, were to be the agents of their own liberation and should not place their trust in political leaders. Thus he suggested that the 'social revolution' would be seriously compromised if it were predicated on the prior success of the 'political revolution'. Nothing short of a 'war of the workshops' was necessary to bring about the birth of socialism. Like Winstanley, he rejected political violence and relied on the power of reason and good example to achieve his social revolution. This caused Marx to categorize Proudhon's theory of spontaneous revolution as a *pot pourri* of optimistic conjecture that placed a brake on the intellectual development of scientific socialism. Utopian socialists, Marx argued, imposed 'new hallucinations and illusions' on the people. Rather than confining their attention to the 'social movement' of oppressed groups in concrete regional and historical settings, they sought the liberation of all humanity, or at least those sections that inhabited Western Europe and its colonial outliers. In so doing they failed to produce a 'single, objectively verifiable socialist narrative'.[100]

In a statement that had clear implications for the future of syndicalism, Proudhon also called for a 'social republic' and a 'new edifice of industrial institutions' based on contractual 'associationism' and inter-regional cooperation. This would create a new historical disjuncture that would bring to a close 'governmental, feudal, and military rule, imitated from that of former kings'.[101] Criticizing trade unionists for limiting the revolutionary potential of the working class, he called for the formation of new associations of workers to undermine 'the rule of capitalists, usurers, and governments, which the first revolution [i.e. the French Revolution] left unconquered'. Thus Proudhon's workers' associations were to replace capitalist relations of production. Unlike conventional trade unions, they could never become ends in themselves. As agents of radical reform, they were to be stepping-stones to a truly socialist republic and would counterpoise the idea of a social contract to that of authoritarian government. This concept of an egalitarian social contract was also intended to foster new forms of citizenship and promote mutual respect. Thus he added: 'Between contracting parties there is necessarily a real personal interest for each [because] a man bargains with the aim of securing his liberty and his revenue at the same time. Between government and governed … there is necessarily an *alienation* of part of the liberty and means of the citizen.'[102]

Proudhon on federalism and revolution

Proudhon, again like Kropotkin, regarded anarchism as a means for asserting the indefinite perfectibility of the individual and of the race. He claimed that 'the principle of federation' was the 'one correct system' that represented 'the greatest triumph of human reason'. Federalism, he claimed, would eliminate the random hostilities based upon conflicts of opinion and partisan divisions that bedevilled the revolutionary left even before the French Revolution. The new federalism was not to be an authoritarian imposition from above which allowed the state to exert control throughout the national territory. Instead it was to be constructed from the ground up and was to function as a strategy for reducing 'the sway of government'. For Kropotkin also, self-reliance and federalism were political principles that underpinned the body politic of urban Europe in the twelfth century. Federalism, Proudhon argued, 'arose when mighty states made their appearance', and as such was a strategy used by independent cities to 'resist strongly-organized centres of authority which had their own armies of serfs at their disposal'. For Proudhon federalism was not simply about the revival of the ancient rights of cities. It was a balkanizing force, which protected regional diversity and counteracted the over-centralization of power in modern nation-states. As a fundamental feature of anarchism, it was a system that greatly enhanced political autonomy in the present, which also preserved the traditional rights of rural communities. As Proudhon saw it:

The federal system is applicable to all nations and all ages, for humanity is progressive in each of its generations and people; the policy of federation ... consists in ruling every people, at any given moment, by decreasing the sway of authority and central power to the point permitted by the level of consciousness and morality.[103]

Thus Proudhon regarded federalism as 'the salvation of the people' because it marked the 'end of rule by the public square', and 'saved the people [from] the tyranny of their leaders and from their own folly'. Each new federal arrangement was designed to protect the citizens of the federative states from capitalist and financial exploitation, both within them and from the outside. In this new federalized anarchist society, political functions were to be reduced to industrial functions, while social order would be maintained through social contracts and contractual exchanges of goods and services. Only then, Proudhon argued, could 'each man ... say he is the absolute ruler of himself'. History, he believed, was 'leading Humanity inevitably' to this new system, just as 'the fecundity of the unexpected' (i.e. social spontaneity) was welcomed because it prevented humanity from settling for a predetermined course of social and economic development.[104]

For Proudhon, again as would be the case for Kropotkin, revolution was not just a historical event – it was a historical process. This did not mean, however, that it would achieve the perfect anarchist society, or that it would once and for all sound the death knell of power relations in any post-revolutionary society. Thus although he was convinced that even anarchists could not construct a world completely free of relations of power, he believed that revolution was also an historical inevitability, an ancient and unavoidable force that had clear parallels in the world of nature. For Proudhon, a revolution was:

a force against which no power, divine or human, can prevail, and whose nature it is to grow by the very resistance it encounters ... The more you repress it, the more you increase its rebound and render its actions irresistible ... Like the Nemesis of the ancients, whom neither prayers nor threats could move, the revolution advances, with sombre and predestined tread, over the flowers strewn by its friends, though the blood of its defenders, over the bodies of its enemies.[105]

Similarly both Proudhon and Kropotkin claimed that the Great French Revolution had left intact those social forces that had continually hampered human development. Limiting their aims to the arena of 'governmental metaphysics' the revolutionaries failed to initiate the structural changes demanded by the demise of the *ancien régime*. 'The Republic', he argued, 'should have established Society; it thought only of Government. ... Therefore while the problem propounded in '89 seemed to be officially solved, fundamentally there was a change only in governmental metaphysics.' In a letter to Marx in 1846 he also warned against the dangers of political and economic dogmatisms. He regarded it as his duty,

> and the duty of all socialists, to maintain for some time yet the critical or dubitive form; in short, I make profession in public of an almost absolute economic anti-dogmatism ... I believe we have no need of it in order to succeed; and that consequently we should not put forward *revolutionary action* as a means of revolutionary reform, because that pretended means would simply be an appeal to force, to arbitrariness, in brief, a contradiction. I myself put the problem in this way: *to bring about the return to society, by an economic combination, of the wealth which was withdrawn from society by another economic combination.*[106]

Always alert to the contradictions inherent in conventional wisdom, Proudhon cautioned against the misleading nature of bourgeois discourse. 'If God exists', he wrote,

> he is entirely different from our accepted image of him ... I affirm that God, if there is a God, bears no resemblance to the effigies which the philosophers and the priests have made of him; that he neither thinks nor acts according to the law of analysis, foresight and progress, which is the distinctive characteristic of man; that on the contrary, he seems to follow an inverse and retrogressive path; that intelligence, liberty, personality, are constituted otherwise in God than in us; and that this originality of nature ... makes of God a being who is essentially anti-civilized, anti-liberal, anti-human.[107]

Transforming this scepticism into a philosophic principle, he privileged social and historical experience over mere appearances. Like Kropotkin, he habitually questioned the authenticity of the foundational 'truths' of political systems and submitted them to the rigours of reasoned criticism. As he wrote in *The System of Economic Contradictions*:

> The essential contradiction of our ideas, being realized in work and expressed in society with a gigantic power, makes all things happen in the reverse way to that in which they should, and gives society the aspect of a tapestry seen the wrong way round, or a hide turned inside out. ... The non-producer should obey, and by a bitter irony it is the non-producer who commands. *Credit, according to the etymology of its name and its theoretical definition, should be the provider of work; in practice it oppresses and kills it.* Property, in the spirit of its finest prerogative, is the making available of the earth, and in the exercise of the same prerogative it becomes the denial of the earth.[108]

2

Kropotkin:
The Education of an Anarchist

Historical context

Peter Kropotkin lived through one of the most turbulent periods of Russian and European history. He was born into a Russia that was 'a few steps behind the civilized world', where the military despotism of Tsar Nicholas I had hardened into a tyrannical regime that was to last until 1855.[1] This was two years before his authoritarian father sent the young Kropotkin off to military school in St Petersburg. The basic structure of Russian society in Kropotkin's youth still retained many of the hallmarks of the feudalism that had been imposed upon it by Ivan the Terrible (1547–84) and Peter the Great (1672–1725). In large tracts of Moscovy where serfdom had originated, including the western provinces more recently acquired in successive partitions of Poland, approximately four-fifths of the entire population were proprietary serfs. In these rich heartlands each layer of society was hermetically sealed off from the one above and below it by strong cultural traditions and well-defined status differentials. At its apex were the powerful oligarchs, the landed aristocracy and hereditary noblemen. These groups still retained social and political privileges that had long since disappeared, or been seriously eroded, in much of Western Europe.

Among the 'living relics' of feudalism that survived in Russia well into the post-Napoleonic era were the church and the landed aristocracy. The aristocracy in particular still cherished their feudal rights, administered justice according to their principles, and extracted heavy dues and taxes from their serfs and other vassals. Right up to the 1860s, the armed forces, the nobility, the church and the administrative apparatus of an increasingly centralized state provided the political power that allowed the Romanovs to extend their rule from St Petersburg almost as far eastward as Siberia.

For much of the nineteenth century, the Russian economy continued to rest, as it had done since the Middle Ages, 'on the labours of peasants in the fields who worked the land using methods and tools that were little different from those used by their medieval ancestors'.[2]

The history of Russia was still primarily concerned with the activities of the tsar, the nobility, the military establishment and the Russian Orthodox Church. Russia's peasants and serfs were to all intents and purposes effectively written out of history. They existed outside the framework of official time, and were confined instead to that which was changeless and timeless. At best, they regarded the tsarist court as a meaningless institution that had no bearing on their lives of drudgery. At worst, the court was to be feared because it forced them to pay tribute to harsh overlords, or took their sons away to fight foreign wars when they were most needed to tend their own tiny plots at home. Like the peasants in Carlo Levi's classic account of peasant life in southern Italy in the 1930s, the only wars that touched their hearts were those that they fought to 'defend themselves against civilization, against history and government'.[3] These wars they waged under their own pennants, without military leadership or training. The underground world of the serfs and the peasants had neither training nor discipline. In the half-century after the great rebellion of Pugachev and his Cossack followers in the 1770s, their wars were sporadic outbursts of revolt, which were always doomed to repression. Still their world survived well into the nineteenth century, yielding up the fruits of the earth to their aristocratic masters, all the while imposing upon them their own measurements of time and space, their earthly divinities and superstitions, and their ethnic languages and rural dialects.

High-ranking army officers and state bureaucrats, the social strata to which Kropotkin's family belonged, were ranked below that of the oligarchy and powerful nobility. Throughout much of the eighteenth and well into the nineteenth century, they continued to look to France for their cultural values. Under Nicholas I, Emperor of Russia from 1825 to 1855, they adopted the strict disciplinarian Prussian methods of social organization that were later despised by the young Kropotkin and his liberal peers. Below the powerful aristocracy came poorly paid clerks and army officials, many of whom supplemented their incomes through bribery, extortion and other nefarious means. At the bottom of Russia's social pyramid were state peasants and private serfs. The latter were literally owned by the landed nobility. Although tied to the land, state peasants were not considered serfs as they neither paid rent nor worked on behalf of landlords. For that reason also they were not considered the private property of the nobility. Although they did not hold title to the lands that they tilled, state peasants lived in rural communes and could dispose of their plots as if they in fact owned them. However state peasants were not permitted to leave their villages, and were obliged to pay a higher 'soul tax' than proprietary serfs. All serfs were obliged to provide the state with conscripts and supply the army with vital provisions in times of war. Prior to their emancipation in 1861, the greatest concentrations of 'pure' serfs were to be found in the central and western provinces of Russia. Serfdom was far less significant in the distant peripheries of the Russian Empire. It was practically unknown in Siberia when Kropotkin served there as an army officer in the early 1860s.[4]

Like many advocates of social change in nineteenth century Russia, Kropotkin appears to have acquired his populist convictions and concern for the poor from a childhood spent among his family's serfs. In *My Past and Thoughts*, Alexander Herzen (1812–70), the father of Russian socialism, recalled the affectionate bonds that existed between members of the feudal nobility and their household serfs. Serf 'nannies' and 'uncles' were also widely revered in the memoirs of other members of the liberal nobility.[5] Herzen, Kropotkin, Tolstoy and Gorky were the most famous Russian authors whose writings transformed a childhood spent among caring family serfs into a veritable literary cult. In so doing they literally 'reinvented childhood', transforming it into an enchanted realm in an otherwise brutalized feudal society. As sons of the Russian nobility, Herzen, Kropotkin and Tolstoy were all raised in the stifling atmosphere of what Marx chose to define as 'oriental despotism'. Indeed Kropotkin remembered that the Russian autocracy in his day had been 'terrifyingly strengthened by Prussian militarism, and overlaid with a veneer of French culture'.[6] While recognizing the inevitability of revolution, each of these writers was to advocate very different solutions to their country's social and political problems. However, despite very obvious differences in political philosophy, their commitment to social justice transformed men like Tolstoy and Kropotkin into larger-than-life figures. Certainly Kropotkin's life as a Russian prince, an army officer, a court aide, a revolutionary activist, an anarchist theorist, a scientist, an explorer and a respected geographer seemed to encompass the lives of not one but of many men.

The gentle sage

Paradoxical as it may seem, Kropotkin's privileged background, together with his experiences of army life in eastern Siberia in the early 1860s, go a long way in explaining his coming of age as Europe's foremost anarchist intellectual in the last quarter of the nineteenth century. His biographers have overwhelmingly affirmed the benign nature of his character and the essential unity of his life. In commenting on his benevolence, several of his contemporaries sanctified and practically deified the man. To many of those who knew him, and to several of those who subsequently wrote about him, Kropotkin was at once a prince among anarchists and an anarchist prince. Adopting terms that are today reserved for such iconic figures as Mahatma Ghandi, Martin Luther King, Nelson Mandela, Eva Perón and Aung San Suu Kyi, some biographers have portrayed him as a God-like prince who walked among mortals. Although she considered him too 'bookish' and never shared his 'reverence for the people', Emma Goldman (1869–1940) was enthralled by Kropotkin's benign disposition and thought that this gave him the character of a saint.[7] To Paul Avrich, Kropotkin's most sympathetic biographer, he was quite simply 'a saint without God'.[8] George Bernard Shaw once famously described him as 'amiable to the point of saintliness … with his full red beard and lovable expression [he] might have been a shepherd from the Delectable Mountains'. Kropotkin's public image was that of 'a gentle sage or liberal saint'.[9] His fellow anarchist, Errico Malatesta, who often clashed with him on points of political strategy, described him as:

a really good person, of that goodness which is almost unconscious and needs to relieve suffering and be surrounded by smiles and happiness. One would have said that he was good without knowing it … and his goodness was the first of his qualities. He would rather boast of his energy and courage – perhaps because these latter qualities had been developed in, and for, the struggle, whereas goodness was the spontaneous expression of his intimate nature.[10]

Discussing Kropotkin in 1899, the Danish critic Georg Brandes wrote: 'Seldom has there been a revolutionist so humane and mild ... He has never been an avenger but always a martyr. He does not impose sacrifices upon others; he makes them himself.'[11] His benign character and aristocratic background may have helped to 'soften' the public image of anarchism and enhance its intellectual qualities. Certainly compared to Bakunin and others who believed in the efficacy of anarchist-inspired acts of political violence, Kropotkin represented the reasonable face of European anarchism. Writing some 60 years after Brandes, George Woodcock suggested that:

Kropotkin's benign presence as a platform speaker, the sweet reasonableness which in his writings replaced the fulminations of Bakunin and the wilful paradoxolatry of Proudhon, and the talent for amiability that made him as easily at home in the country houses of aristocrats as in the terrace cottages of Durham miners, all contributed to the transformation of the image of anarchism.[12]

Roger Baldwin, founder of the American Civil Liberties Union, regarded Kropotkin and Emma Goldman as the two major influences on his life. In 1970 he could still claim that Kropotkin was:

remembered chiefly as he became in his later years, a kindly, beaming philosopher-scientist, whose light blue-grey eyes looked out through spectacles with serenity and penetration. Bald, with a wide forehead and bushy white beard, he at once impressed all he met as a man of great intellectual force, but without the slightest self-consciousness or sense of superiority. Though his kindliness and courtly manner marked him in all relations, they were not of the patronizing aristocrat, but of a genuine lover of his fellowmen who made no distinction between them. Whether lecturing to a scientific association or an anarchist group, dining with the aristocrat or working people, he was simple, warm, earnest – overflowing with feeling for the cause he had at heart, no sense of leadership or position.[13]

Other contemporaries who provided similarly glowing images of this 'anarchist prince' who moved among mere men and women included Ford Madox Brown, Oscar Wilde and Herbert Read. By the 1880s, when

Kropotkin was Europe's most respectable anarchist, he was mixing with the foremost radical intellectuals of his day, including William Morris, Kier Hardie and Edward Carpenter. His *Memoirs of a Revolutionist* (1902), along with Alexander Herzen's intellectual autobiography, *My Past and Thoughts* (1861–67), Tolstoy's fictionalized trilogy, *Childhood, Boyhood*, and *Youth* (1852–57), and Maxim Gorky's *Childhood* (1913), *In the World* (1915) and *My Universities* (1923), have been widely acclaimed as autobiographical classics. Indeed popular perceptions of Russian society in the century before the Bolshevik Revolution have been strongly influenced by 'the marvellously rich stream of personal memoirs, particularly of childhood and youth' of these authors in particular.[14] Their writings reveal a deep attachment to the Russian rural landscapes of their childhood. Despite the horrors of serfdom, Kropotkin's *Memoirs* capture the underlying beauty of rural life prior to the 'uglification' of Russia's landscapes and the brutalization of its people in the Stalinist era. Taken together the autobiographical works of all of these authors tend to evoke 'a world of birch trees, governesses, samovars, sailor suits and sleigh rides', a world where 'the taste of tea and jam was sharpened and sweetened by the sense of the vast empty steppes beyond the garden and the imminent end of it all'.[15]

It has been suggested that Kropotkin was more like an argumentative *philosophe* of the eighteenth-century Enlightenment than a nineteenth-century anarchist. In his introduction to Kropotkin's *Memoirs*, Colin Ward has described him as 'methodical, hard working, intensively serious, immensely well-read, self-confident and absolutely certain that his opinions were correct'. As a late Victorian moralist with a 'fondness for plain living and high thinking', he always had one foot in the turbulent world of revolutionary politics, and another in the refined world of the European scientific establishment.[16] Martin Miller, undoubtedly Kropotkin's most meticulous biographer, has suggested that 'it is a curious irony of history that Peter Kropotkin, one of the fiercest opponents of all government and national states, was a direct descendent of the original princes who governed his country'.[17] To understand how he became the leading anarchist theorist of his day, writers have looked to his early years for the roots of his anti-authoritarianism. They may have been encouraged to do this by those who suggest that all 'true' rebels, especially anarchists, are born rather than made. One such 'born rebel', Kropotkin's sister anarchist, Emma Goldman, once claimed:

'Environment can only bring out what is inherent in human beings. It can never put anything in sterile ground. If I had not been born with the love of freedom and the intense hatred of injustice, I do not believe I would have become what I am.'[18]

Kropotkin seemed to hold with the motto that the child is father of the man. In his memoirs, written in the 1890s, he suggested that 'human character is usually settled in a definite way at an earlier age than is generally supposed'. He also felt that on leaving home at 15 to enrol at St Petersburg's strict military school, his 'taste and inclinations were already determined'. He insisted that his fundamental concerns as a mature anarchist theorist – the abuses of authority, the degradation of the peasantry, social and political reform, and the protection of pre-capitalist communities from the ravages of capitalist modernization – were already evident at a tender age. Yet to assert that anarchists are born rather than made is a gross misrepresentation which caricatures them as 'wild-eyed free spirits' and 'slightly cracked' eccentrics, pathologically incapable of submitting to the norms of 'normal' society. It also implies that anarchism, unlike other 'isms', is a behavioural trait that is acquired at birth and has its roots in the realms of the irrational rather than reason. In challenging this view, this study will show that, unlike many of his anarchist individualist associates, Kropotkin's scientific and philosophical anarchism never allowed 'passion to bow to wisdom'. His anarchism was the product of prolonged, multi-disciplinary, theoretical investigations into the historical origins of the state, the functions of political authority, the contribution of mutualism to the survival of individual species and entire societies, and the long-term prospects for the inter-communal and international association of free individuals in a stateless world. He envisaged an anarchist society wherein the mutual relations of individual members would be regulated not by laws or even elected authorities, but by social customs and mutual agreements between free individuals. Thus his anarchism was rooted in an antithetical tradition that challenged the very nature of the state. As we shall presently see, he was also critical of state-centred science and opposed to political parties that claimed that radical social change did not require the prior abolition of the state. His concerns over abuses of authority, social injustice, urban and rural poverty, and the destruction of communalism may well have been evident from an early age. Yet they would not become defining features of his anarchist philosophy until the 1860s and 1870s. Only then did he replace

Bakunin as Europe's foremost anarchist intellectual. Thus Kropotkin did not become an anarchist until his thirties, and did not publish his seminal texts on anarchism until he was into his fifties. Far from being a 'natural anarchist', everything about his privileged upbringing and educational background suggested that he would become a staunch defender of political authority. For the first 20 years of his life he, like his brother Alexander, was groomed for a military career in the service of an autocratic state. Looking back on his privileged upbringing in the 1840s and 1850s, he recalled:

'Everything seemed to prepare us for the military career: the predilection of our father (the only toys that I remember his having bought us were a rifle and a real sentry-box); the war tales of M. Poulain [their tutor]; nay, even the library which we had at our disposal.'[19] The library in his father's house had once belonged to General Repninsky, his mother's grandfather, and 'consisted exclusively of books on military warfare, adorned with rich plates and beautifully bound in leather'. In his memoirs he recalled that their 'chief recreation, on wet days, [was] to look over the plates of these books, representing the weapons of warfare since the times of the Hebrews, and giving plans of all battles that had been fought since Alexander of Macedonia'. These boyhood fascinations with battles and military history, however, were soon to fade, and he was 'not many years old' when he grew to hate the 'absurdity' of military life. In later life Kropotkin famously described his father as a man 'enamoured of the military uniform and utterly despised all other sorts of attire; whose soldiers were trained to perform almost superhuman tricks with their legs and rifles ... [and who] ... could show on parade a row of soldiers as perfectly aligned and as motionless as a row of toy soldiers'.[20]

Subscribing to the Proustian contention that an essential unity binds the personal life of an individual from the act of creation to the fact of death, several of Kropotkin's biographers, most notably Miller, have delved deep into his family history to locate the green shoots of his proto-anarchist rebellion against his militaristic, patriarchal and privileged upbringing. Some have even hinted that his anti-authoritarianism was rooted in the Oedipal rebellion of an obedient son against a militaristic father. This has also been traced to a narcissistic obsession, inspired by his mother, to serve the downtrodden victims of poverty and oppression with whom he spent his childhood years. In tracing some semblance of a pattern in his personal history, in seeking as it were to find the embryo of the man in the life of the boy, his biographers have turned to his childhood in order to understand his early development as an anarchist. We know that the young Kropotkin decided to drop his princely title in his twelfth year, and adopted the signature 'P. Kropotkin' when signing documents. As he subsequently admitted, this was influenced by 'the general Republican tone of Russian literature'. Yet this was a decision from which, despite the 'remonstrances of his chiefs', he never departed in military school or in the armed forces. Thus it could be argued that those seeking to understand Kropotkin's anarchist 'personality' have adopted an overly psychoanalytical approach and have ignored the far more important social and cultural influences that contributed to his intellectual development as an anarchist. Whatever the merits of this approach to the artistic development of novelists, poets and musicians, it is arguably far less useful in tracing the complex intellectual development of an anarchist theorist of Kropotkin's stature. Born into an aristocratic world where Ivan Turgenev (1818–83), Mikhail Bakunin (1814–76) and Alexander Herzen (1812–70) were already radicalizing Russia's intellectual elite, Kropotkin played no small part in shattering the isolation of aristocratic and autocratic Russia. Far from being a 'born anarchist' it was not until his encounter with the radical literature of working-class activists in the late 1860s that the lessons of his privileged upbringing were 'wiped out'.

Home and family life

Born in the Old Equerries' Quarter of Moscow on 9 December 1842, Peter Kropotkin was the youngest of three sons of Prince Aleksey Petrovich and Princess Catherine Kropotkin. With the keen eye of the social geographer he later described the Moscow where he spent the first 15 years of his life as 'a city of slow historical growth' whose 'different parts, at least up until the 1890s, had wonderfully retained the features which have been stamped upon them in the slow course of history'. Historically, this corner of Moscow was home to the city's old noble families who, by the 1850s, were already dying out. Although the heads of these families were 'frequently mentioned in the pages of Russian history before the time of Peter I' they had largely disappeared to make room for 'men of all ranks' when Kropotkin was a boy. Because they felt that they had become increasingly 'supplanted' at court, lesser nobles like Kropotkin's father and uncles had already retired 'to their picturesque estates in the countryside around the capital'.[21] His father was deeply contemptuous of 'the motley crowd' of families which 'came from no one knew where to take possession of the highest functions of government in the new capital on the banks of the Neva'. The young Kropotkin recalled that when he was a boy the lesser nobility 'had tried their fortunes in the service of the state, chiefly in the army; but for one reason or another they had soon abandoned it, without having risen to high rank'. The more successful, including his father, often obtained minor honorary positions in the city. Yet no matter how widely they ranged 'over the wide surface of Russia ... they always somehow managed to spend their old age in a house of their own in the Old Equerries' Quarter, under the shadow of the church where they had been baptized, and where the last prayers had been pronounced at the burial of their parents'.[22]

Like most middle-ranking officers from the period of Nicholas I, Kropotkin's father was also a wealthy landowner who, in addition to a mansion in the city, owned 1,200 male serfs and large tracts of land in the province of Kaluga to the southeast of Moscow. Kropotkin's own recollections of country life and the rural landscapes around Moscow at this stage evoke a tranquil world of privilege that was effectively wiped out after the Bolshevik Revolution. His descriptions of the lost world of his privileged youth are all the more important due to the significance he subsequently attached to rural development and urban and rural relations in his anarchist writings of later years. Calling to mind the rural milieu around Nikolskoye where he spent such a large part of his own childhood, he wrote:

For the quiet life of the landlords of these times Nikolskoye was admirably suited. There was nothing in it of luxury which is seen in richer estates; but an artistic hand was visible in the planning of the building and the gardens, and in the general arrangement of things. Besides the main house ... there were, round a spacious and well-kept yard, several smaller houses, which gave a greater degree of independence to their inhabitants without destroying the close intercourse of family life. An immense 'upper garden' was devoted to fruit trees, and through it the church was reached. The southern slope of the land, which led to the river, was entirely given up to a pleasure garden, where flower-beds were intermingled with alleys of lime-trees, lilacs and acacias. ... The woods; the walks along the river, the climbing over the hills to the old fortress ... there was no end of new and delightful impressions. Large parties were organized in which all the family took part, sometimes picking mushrooms in the woods, and afterwards having tea in the midst of the forest, where a man a hundred years old lived alone with his little grandson, taking care of the bees. At other times we went to one of my father's villages where a big pond had been dug, in which golden carp were caught by the thousand – part of them being taken by the landlord and the remainder being distributed among all the peasants. My former nurse, Vasilisa, lived in that village. Her family was one of the poorest; besides her husband, she had only a small boy to help her and a girl, my foster sister, who later became a [Nonconformist] preacher. ... There was no bound to her joy when I came to see her. Cream eggs, apples and honey were all she could offer; but the way in which she offered them, in bright wooden plates, after having covered the table with a fine snow-white linen tablecloth of her own making, and the fond words with which she addressed me as her own son, left the warmest feelings in my heart.[23]

Aside from the insights they provide into the family life of the privileged, recollections like these are of interest to students of Russian anarchism for a number of reasons. Firstly, they display little of the guilt that caused the revolutionary sons of the Russian nobility to disown their past and denigrate the privileged lives of their ancestors. Secondly, they emphasize the self-sufficiency of the landed estates and portray country living as infinitely superior to 'modern life' and the filth and squalor of overcrowded working-class districts in Russia's industrializing cities. From an early age, indeed, the young Kropotkin had an aristocratic dislike of the untrammelled forces of urbanization and industrialization that were already transforming the face of Russia in his day. Thus he envisaged a new Russia where federated networks of autonomous agrarian communities and rural townships would have control over their own affairs. The roots of this vision of a new rurality can be traced to a childhood spent in the countryside around Moscow. Thirdly, far from idealizing the past, Kropotkin considered the historic landscapes of mid nineteenth-century Russia as carefully maintained man-made environments that were part of the country's national heritage. He suggested that these places were aesthetically beautiful and worth preserving, not as the private domains of privileged individuals, but as sites where self-sustaining, healthy, egalitarian communities could make a living for themselves. Like his fellow anarchist and geographer, Élisée Reclus, Kropotkin wrote affectionately about the rural landscapes around his family's ancestral estates. He perfectly understood the attractions that estate life had for his immediate ancestors and rural neighbours. He once lovingly suggested that the 'fertile prairies' of one such estate at Ryazan near Moscow 'might tempt anyone by the beauty of its shadowy forests, winding rivers, and endless meadows'.[24] His lyrical descriptions of the countryside also point to the significance of Kropotkin's rural upbringing for his early development as an anarchist. Thus he fondly remarked that it was in the forests of his youth that his love of nature and the first 'dim perception of its eternal life were born'.

Yet there is in Kropotkin's writings, especially his memoirs, no sentimental yearning for a return to a past suffused with the deference and subservience of an oppressed peasantry that one finds in the writings of some of his contemporaries. This was a Tolstoyan world of passionate love affairs, excessive gambling, reckless horse racing, colourful hunts and extravagant balls. Its pleasures were of a different scale, and kind, to those that appealed to the young Kropotkin. It was a world of misty forests and wooded valleys, inhabited by aristocratic lords and courtly ladies, and described with such panoramic verve in the novels of Czesław Miłosz and Miklós Bánffy.[25] In the hands of these authors, it reeked of nostalgia for a lost paradise of aristocratic privilege that the young Kropotkin rejected. Turgenev coined the term 'superfluous men' to describe an entire generation of young noblemen who lived privileged lives on their fathers' estates and 'vented their frustrated energies in desperate gambling, carousing, duelling, and cruelty, or else sank into inertia'.[26] Many of Russia's landed estates, including the Kropotkin's estate near Moscow, had become cosy 'gentry nests' by the mid nineteenth century. In stories such as 'Peasants' and 'My Life', and in plays such as *The Three Sisters* and *Uncle Vanya*, Anton Chekhov described these country seats with their urban mansions as 'stifling cages' for young men and women of ability whose political and intellectual ambitions ran counter to the hierarchical social order that these structures represented. While repeatedly commenting on the kindnesses he experienced from serfs in his own childhood, Kropotkin was highly critical of the oppression and deprivation that prevailed on Russia's landed estates. Ivan Tolmachev, who managed the Kropotkin estate at Kaluga, referred to the family's serfs as 'peasant cattle'. Kropotkin's own father wondered if serfs were 'really people'. Right up to the eve of their emancipation in 1861, his estate manager was already devising ways for strengthening his master's control over the family's proprietary serfs.

The Kropotkins famously claimed descent from the legendary Varangian Prince Rurik, founder of the ninth-century Russian dynasty of Rurikids. These Scandinavian adventurers had established a loose principality of Eastern Slavs that extended from Novgorod to the northwest of Moscow, right around to Kiev in central Ukraine. Credited with compiling the first legal code in pre-Romanov Russia, the Rurikids fostered the spread of Christianity in the country. They also organized the territories of the Eastern Slavs into a cohesive confederation that was presided over by warrior princes living in cities, along the strategic trade routes that linked the rural interior of Russia with the Black Sea. Kropotkin once described his father as a 'coarse and stubborn' man who was 'very proud of the origin of his family … [but] not much versed in Russian history'.[27] His own ancestors included the Grand Princes of Smolensk who ruled extensive territories at the epicentre of this extensive trade route. However, like many of the seventeenth-century nobility, they were 'driven into the background when … the Romanovs, enthroned at Moscow, began the work of consolidating the Russian state'. None of Kropotkin's immediate ancestors had any special liking for state functions. His great-grandfather and grandfather, Peter recalled, had 'retired from the military service when quite young men, and hastened to return to their family estates'. Kropotkin was particularly fond of his paternal grandmother, Princess Gagarin. Her brother, a well-known and passionate lover of the stage, scandalized all his relations by marrying the genial actress Semyonova, 'one of the creators of dramatic art in Russia, and undoubtedly one of its most sympathetic figures'. He was also proud of another ancestor who had published a book of poetry, which was something that his father 'always avoided' mentioning. With such an illustrious ancestry, it is not surprising that fellow revolutionaries would taunt Kropotkin with the suggestion that he had more right to the throne of Russia than Emperor Alexander II, who after all was 'only a German'. The young Kropotkin literally had the Russian state on his doorstep and an illustrious family history in his blood. This renders his subsequent rejection of a titled position in the tsarist state for the puritanical life of an anarchist activist all the more remarkable.

Several of his biographers have alluded to the fact that neither of the young Kropotkin brothers inherited any of the personality traits of their patriarchal and militaristic father. They belonged to a generation of young aristocratic Russians who were historically, and intellectually, a world apart from their conservative, serf-owning fathers. Thus whereas Kropotkin's father was made 'of coarser clay', his son Peter was considerate, sensitive and generous, and would later be described as 'a man of immense benevolence'. His biographers have particularly noted that Peter had a much stronger attachment to his mother than to his father. The daughter of a military officer, his mother died in 1846 from 'an inflammation of the lungs that brought her to an early grave'. Peter, who was then only three and a half years old, recalled that 'all who knew her loved her'.[28] The family's servants 'worshipped her memory' and it was 'in her name that Madame Burman took care of us, and in her name the Russian nurse bestowed upon us her love. … We were her children, we bore likeness to her'. Forty years after her death, Kropotkin still described his mother as 'tall, slim, adorned with a mass of chestnut hair … a remarkable woman for the times she lived in'. Always 'vivacious and often careless', she was 'fond of dancing'. Peasant women told tales of how 'she would admire from a balcony their ring-dances – slow and full of grace –and how finally she would herself join in them'. Kropotkin described his mother as having 'the nature of an artist'. He recalled how in his late fifties he found:

> in a corner of a storeroom of our country house, a mass of papers with her firm but pretty handwriting: diaries in which she wrote with delight of the scenery of Germany, and spoke of her sorrows and her thirst for happiness; books which she had filled with Russian verses prohibited by censorship – among them the beautiful ballads of Ryleyev, the young poet whom Nicholas I hanged in 1826; other books containing music, French dramas, verses of de Lamartine, and Byron's poems that she had copied; and a great number of water-colour paintings.[29]

Thus Kroptokin's childhood was, as he himself admitted, certainly 'irradiated' by the memory of his mother. After her death, it was mostly in the households of the family's serfs that he encountered 'that atmosphere of love which children must have around them'. Two years after her death, his father took another wife, 'one of several daughters of an admiral of the Black Sea fleet', who immediately set out 'to expunge all traces of the previous paradise' in which the young Kropotkins had spent their formative years. Describing the changes to his life after his father remarried, Kropotkin simply recorded that:

> winter came, and a new life began for us. Our house was sold and another was bought and furnished completely anew. All that could convey a reminiscence of our mother disappeared – her portraits, her paintings, and her embroideries. ... All connections with our uncles and aunts and our grandmother were broken.[30]

Thereafter it was chiefly the family's serfs who would 'conspiratorially keep alive the warm sentiments' of his mother, as 'often in some dark passage, the hand of a servant would touch Alexander or me with a caress; or a peasant woman, meeting us in the fields, would ask "Will you be as good as your mother was? She took compassion on us. You will, surely."' Peter, who throughout his childhood was regularly pressurized to become 'a warrior like Papa', bided his time, accumulated experience, and frequently struck out against 'the very principle of paternal authority'.[31] Much later in life, these childhood rebellions would be eclipsed by a lifelong struggle against all forms of authority and the abuse of power.

Education and military training

French tutors, whom Kropotkin labelled 'the debris of Napoleon's Grande Armée', were frequently responsible for the education of the sons of Moscow's nobility in the early part of the nineteenth century. As a child, he was subjected to a rigid regime of formal instruction by an autocratic father who also regulated much of his free time. Peter, who later in life was to become a strong advocate of educational reform, described the 'very simple plan of education' of his first tutor, Monsieur Poulain:

> After having woke us up, he attended to his coffee, which he used to take in his room. While we were preparing the morning lessons he made his toilet with minute care: he shampooed his grey hair so as to conceal his growing baldness, put on his tail-coat, sprinkled and washed himself with eau-de-cologne, and then escorted us downstairs to say good morning to our parents. We used to find our father and

stepmother at breakfast, and on approaching them we recited in the most ceremonious manner, 'Bonjour, mon cher papa', and 'Bonjour, ma chère maman', and kissed their hands ... Then our work began. M. Poulain changed his tail-coat for a dressing gown, covered his head with a leather cap, and dropping into an easy chair said 'Recite the lesson'.[32]

In addition to good manners and deportment, the young Kropotkins were taught French grammar and conversation, 'universal geography' and 'world history'. By the time he left home in 1855 to enrol in the Corps of Pages in St Petersburg, Peter was also 'able to think in French' and had learned 'to write correctly in that language'. Unlike the more liberal environment that had prevailed in the early 1850s, 'opinions', he recollected, 'were not much in vogue' in the homes where he and his friends spent their young adult life. He recollected that 'All was quiet and smooth' at home when he was a boy, 'at least on the surface'. It was chiefly in the 1860s that many of these mansions witnessed 'struggles between fathers and sons ... that usually ended either in a family tragedy or in a nocturnal visit to the state police'.[33] Thus Kropotkin's early education was no different from that of his aristocratic peers. Neglected by his father and educated by a succession of tutors, he was introduced to the niceties of French culture, including French ideals of equality. The Kropotkin brothers also took instruction from 'a Russian teacher' who taught them 'the "Russian" subjects – grammar, arithmetic, and history'. N.P. Smirnov, a student at Moscow University, instilled in Peter a love of Russian history and folklore, introduced him to the stories of Gogol and Pushkin, and may even have familiarized him with the radical journalism of Nikolai Chernyshevsky. Thus it was at this stage that the young Kropotkin learned to more fully appreciate the humanity and essential goodness of the serfs whom his father branded 'peasant cattle'. His earliest publication, written when he was 12 years old, described the lives of serfs on the estates around his home. To ascertain how they would fare after emancipation, he compiled statistical tables outlining the products they could tender for sale, together with the prices they expected to obtain for them. This in itself was a quasi-revolutionary act in a country where little was known about the lives of peasants. Liberal politicians elsewhere in Europe had championed the collection of statistical data as a valuable tool of social progress. In Russia, however, the spectre of politics severely hampered the development of the new disciplines of demography and statistics. Nicholas I had been so cautious about placing Russian society under the microscope, particularly where serfs and state institutions were concerned, that he simply banned the collection of social statistics. Indeed it was not until the 1880s that poorly paid members of the intelligentsia began conducting censuses in villages on behalf of local government, and it was not until 1897 that the first national census was completed. Thus Kropotkin's early attention to statistical detail and his penchant for field studies were certainly out of line with official state policy. Statistical accuracy and regional detail were to become defining features of such seminal anarchist works as *Fields, Factories and Workshops* (1899), *The Conquest of Bread* (1906) and *Modern Science and Anarchism* (1901).

Contact with serfs was unavoidable in Kropotkin's home, which was organized like a military establishment. Fifty servants cared for the family at their Moscow mansion, 'and half as many more' were employed in their country residence. There were four coachmen to attend a dozen horses, 'three cooks for the masters and two more for the servants, a dozen men to wait upon us at dinner … and girls innumerable in the maid-servants' room'. To maintain such numbers in their Moscow mansion 'would have been ruinous if all the provisions had to be bought at Moscow; but in those times of serfdom things were managed very simply'. When winter arrived in Moscow, his father compensated for his lack of ready cash by organizing long and tortuous pilgrimages to the family estate in Kaluga to procure enough provisions to see the family through the winter. His estate manager back in Kaluga was simply ordered to 'load twenty-five peasant sledges, each drawn by two horses, [with] so many quarters of oats, wheat, rye … as also with all the poultry and geese and ducks'. More tellingly, this list also contained 'an enumeration of the penalties which would be inflicted in case the provisions should not reach the house … in due time and in good condition'. Kropotkin remembered some Christmases when as many as 'twenty-five peasant-sledges … entered our gates, and covered the surface of the wide yard'.[34]

Trips to the country accompanied by the family's servants and serfs also whetted Peter's appetite for geography and natural history at this stage. As 'an inexhaustible source of enjoyment', these trips gave the young Kropotkin new insights into country living. He described one such trip as follows:

The stages were short, and we stopped twice a day to feed the horses
… The beautifully kept high road from Moscow to Warsaw, which we
followed for some distance, was covered … with a variety of interesting
objects: files of loaded carts, groups of pilgrims, and all sorts of people.
Twice a day we stopped in large, animated villages, and after a good
deal of bargaining about the prices to be charged for hay and oats,
as well as for samovars, we dismounted at the gates of an inn. Cook
Andrei bought a chicken and made the soup, while we ran in the
meantime to the wood, or examined the farmyard, the gardens, the
inner life of the inn.[35]

These trips between town houses and country mansions on family
estates were regularly undertaken by many of Peter's social peers in the
landed aristocracy. To the indolent and unambitious, the pampered life
of these young aristocrats appeared perfectly acceptable. It allowed the
sons of the nobility to live 'half-lives' by feasting, gambling, hunting and
socializing, while entire swathes of peasant society laboured under the
most appalling conditions. However, for talented and ambitious young
men like the Kropotkin brothers, it was stultifying in the extreme. In these
years Kropotkin also witnessed floggings of serfs that were carried out
as 'a regular part of the duties of the police and the fire brigade'. Military
service, an ever-present feature of serf life on his father's estate, brought
its own horrors. Nobles and merchants were exempt from military
service, and 'when a new levy of recruits was ordered, the landowners
had simply to supply a certain number of men from their serfs'. While
those defined as 'field serfs' kept a list of those eligible for conscription
within their communities, 'house servants were entirely at the mercy of
their lord, and if he was dissatisfied with one of them, he sent him to
the recruiting board'. Kropotkin later recalled how landowners earned
a 'considerable sum' each time this happened. Military service usually
lasted 25 years, during which time common soldiers were subjected to
barbaric punishments for the slightest infringement of military discipline.
Although he was to discover that students at the military academy he
attended were not immune from the harshest of punishment, the lot of
the peasants and serf soldiers was, he wrote, 'far worse':

If they were unfortunate enough to face court martial they could be
whipped by a thousand men … placed in two ranks facing each other,

every soldier armed with a stick the thickness of the little finger, and the condemned man [was] dragged three, four, five, and even seven times between these two rows, each soldier administering a blow. Sergeants followed to see that full force had been given. After one or two thousand blows had been given, the victim, spitting blood, was taken to the hospital and attended to, in order that the punishment might be finished as soon as he had more or less recovered from the effects of the first part of it.[36]

Students at the young Kropotkin's Corps of Pages could also receive 'a thousand blows with birch rods' for infringements as petty as smoking. However, it was his peers, rather than his superiors, who were his main problem at this military academy. Here senior students wielded 'enormous power', compelled everyone 'to do their bidding', and meted out harsh punishments for the 'slightest resistance' to their authority. Kropotkin portrayed General Giradot, the French director of the academy, as 'a despot by nature, capable of hating – immensely hating – a boy who did not submit to his influence'. Not surprisingly, it was from these youthful experiences that the young Kropotkin developed a deep revulsion against military discipline and abuses of authority.

Kropotkin's experience of military authority was greatly intensified when, at the age of 13, he was taken to St Petersburg and enrolled in the Corps of Pages. Only the sons and grandsons of top ranking military and state officials could automatically qualify for this prestigious military academy. On completion of their training, the brightest boys often served as aides in the courts and palaces of the tsar, or else entered one of Russia's celebrated Guards regiments. In Kropotkin's time at least, the top four Guards regiments were the Preobrazhenskii, the Chevalier Guards, the Horse Guards and the Hussar Life Guards. As the 'privileged nucleus of the army', these regiments 'supplied tsarist Russia with theoreticians, thinkers and drunken profligates'. Throughout much of their history, they functioned as 'something between a band of brigands and a cultural avant-garde'. At crucial junctures in Russian history, their members were 'in the thick of things, either because of their proximity to the tsar or through the old-boy network of former Guardsmen'. Like the Guards, the Corps of Pages was unashamedly elitist in ethos, and its students usually set the standards of snobbery for the entire country. Kropotkin entered the academy just as its inner life was undergoing significant changes.

Gone was the censorship and 'the terrible nightmare' that prevailed throughout the reign of the 'iron despot', Nicholas I. Had these still been in place when he entered, Kropotkin admitted that his will 'would have been totally broken, or [he] should have been excluded from the school with no one knows what consequences'. Although at the time of his enrolment, the Corps of Pages was still 'run with all the discipline of a military unit', the educational life of the academy had become far more relaxed. A number of university lecturers consented to offer courses in the academy. The most outstanding of these, Vladimir Klassovsky, a graduate of Moscow University, was an authority on Greek and Roman history, and Russian and Latin languages. Kropotkin recalled how he had 'an immense influence [on all his students], which only grew with the years'. Klassovsky had a holistic approach to historical studies and he encouraged students 'to seek out that generalized conception of the development of the human mind which lies beyond the scope of each subject when taught separately'.[37] Kropotkin would subsequently adopt this approach to great effect in his own research on medieval history, geography, criminology and historical sociology. His preference for a holistic approach to the study of social and environmental process was only partially motivated by a desire to 'see things in the whole'. Ever the critic of narrow specializations that were already becoming a feature of academic life in Russia as elsewhere in Europe, he was also no defender of academic boundaries. Instead he would call on academics to circumvent what he considered the needless fragmentation of social and scientific knowledge. More than that, he also criticized state-centred disciplines for aiding and abetting the centralization of intellectual capital and widening the gap between educated elites and the uneducated masses. Thus the practical exercises that he learned at the military academy had an important influence on his later development as an anarchist. Much of the time spent training to be an officer was devoted to routine building projects and field research. Here also he learned the value of balancing intellectual with manual work that was to become such a feature of his later writing on anarchist economics and educational philosophy.

By the time the young Kropotkin entered the Corps of Pages the pro-fessionalization of the armed forces was already fostering powerful career structures in the Russia's military establishment. As elsewhere in Europe and in Latin America, the militarist values underpinning state ideology attached immense importance to macho values of honour, social order and obedience to authority. The 1850s and 1860s also witnessed the tentative modernization of Russian society, which resulted in a growing concentration of power and decision-making in St Petersburg. Modernization was also accompanied by the aggravation of class conflict in Russia's larger cities, a widening of the social distance between rich and poor in town and country alike, and the forceful assimilation of many of Russia's scattered ethnic minorities into an increasingly powerful national network of state control and military surveillance. Change was particularly evident in the shift of power from the countryside to the city. However, socio-economic disparities were equally evident in the spatial concentration of production in fewer hands in the countryside, and in Russia's larger cities. All of this was accompanied by huge strides in the modernization of the armed forces and the surveillance capacity of the tsarist state. The military establishment now had the power to monitor the modernization of the economy and control many aspects of Russia's social and political life.

By the mid nineteenth century the military establishment was also acutely aware of the importance of cartography and a sound geographical education for the exercise of power and the extension of state influence to Russia's expanding territories. When Kropotkin began his military training in 1857, 'a new spirit' that was at once 'studious and serious' already prevailed in the Corps of Pages. The grading system that ensured students would automatically become officers in a prestigious regiment was reformed. The moral tone of the academy was also improved as the old manners associated with the feudal order were now looked upon with disgust. Thus the decades after the Crimean War were a period of intense scientific experimentation in Russia's military academies and state colleges. Feverish activity in chemistry, physics, astronomy and mathematics led to the establishment of new laboratories and academic journals to report the most recent experiments and findings. Professors were appointed to university chairs in the natural sciences, geography, geology and zoology, and government directives were issued to provide more support for academic research. For many young student cadets at this stage the sciences offered personal fulfilment and were a recipe for healing the wounds of national disillusionment after the shameful debacle of the Crimean War. However, to the more radical students in the universities, and to a minority in Russia's elitist military academies, science was both the key to the future and a call to revolt. It gave meaning to life and provided students with new roles in the future development of Russia. Addressing students in 1855, two years before Kropotkin was enrolled at the Corps of Pages, A.S. Norov, the country's progressive minister of education, declared: 'Science, gentlemen, has always been for us one of the most important necessities, but now it is the first. If our enemies possess a superiority over us, it is solely on the strength of knowledge.'[38] From the start, therefore, the promotion of the applied sciences was to be a state-centred project motivated by powerful, state-building objectives. As nation-builders and nationalists, young graduates were expected to literally build the new Russia from the ground up. In an autocratic state like Russia, the control of scientific education widened the gap between the powerful and powerless, contributed to the uneven economic development of the country, enhanced the position of privileged sectors in Russian society, and sustained the authoritarian structures of the tsarist regime.

As a defining event in the history of nineteenth-century Russia, the Crimean War also had an indirect impact on Kropotkin's education and family life. He learned of its physical horrors from his stepmother's sisters who had been forced to leave their home in Sebastopol as a result of the war. He was also acutely aware of the sense of foreboding that war brought to the families of peasants and serfs in his own neighbourhood:

> In the country the war caused much gloominess. The lines of recruits followed one another rapidly, and we continually heard the peasant women singing their funeral songs. The Russian people look upon war as a calamity which is sent upon them by Providence, and they accepted this war with a solemnity that contrasted strangely with the levity that I saw elsewhere under similar circumstances.[39]

We know from the memoirs of other army officers that in the first half of the nineteenth century experiences of war were already 'softening' relations between a minority of officers and the peasant soldiers under their command. In Tolstoy's *War and Peace*, for example, the social distance between officers and their serf soldiers was gradually eroded on the battlefield. As the sons of the nobility began to appreciate the bravery, humanity and patriotic character of their serf soldiers, they learned to treat them as human beings in their own right. While war with the West had undermined the traditional faith of the Old Russian elites in the merits of French-style westernization, it also caused many young officers to appreciate the plebeian patriotism of peasant soldiers and to re-evaluate their relationships with rural Russia. For the vast majority of peasant soldiers, however, military service was a wrenching experience that dragged young men away from their families and communities, and exposed them to the harshest of discipline at the hands of officers who continued to regard common soldiers as 'peasant cattle'.

Nevertheless, war and military experience had thrown the sons of the nobility into the world of the peasantry, and this led to the development of new expressions of humanitarianism at the edges of aristocratic society. It famously also caused Russia's leading poets, dramatists and novelists to transform serfs and peasants into subjects of art in their own right. Young officers and intellectuals now began to 'rediscover' the Russian peasant, and Kropotkin clearly identified with this new generation that treated serfs as virtuous human beings with almost unlimited capacities to endure hardship on the land, and on the battlefield. More than anything else, it was their capacity simply to endure that attracted the young Kropotkin to the rural poor. In years to come, this would force him to seek an anarchist alternative to the state-centred revolutionary visions of Russia's much less significant industrial working class. The Decembrist leader, Sergei Volkonsky (1788–1865), also known as the 'peasant prince', epitomized this section of the liberal nobility to which Kropotkin was attracted even from an early age. Volkonsky's wartime experiences and travels in Europe convinced him of the personal dignity of all human beings, especially Russia's serfs.[40] In dedicating themselves to the cause of peasant reform, men like Volkonsky were engaged in a democratic mission to learn about the common people in order to unite their country on genuinely Russian principles. They encouraged landlords to become enlightened guardians of serfs, and reminded them that their duties to their serfs were as important as their duties to the state. As the foundations of the old aristocratic culture of their fathers slowly collapsed under the corrosive effects of European militarism, many young Russians, including Kropotkin, were to commit themselves to a life of service working in the interests of those at the social, political and indeed geographical margins of Russian society. Revolutionary populism led many of them to monumen-talize the daily toil of the peasantry and thereby expose the extravagance and frivolity of aristocratic culture. This in turn aggravated inter-genera-tional tensions and caused many of the sons and daughters of the nobility to question the service ethos of Russia's patriarchal and status-conscious state elites. This new intelligentsia challenged the hierarchical structures of Russian society, planted the seeds of civil society in the country's political landscape, and dedicated themselves to the demilitarization of Russian politics and popular culture. From the mid nineteenth century onwards, their ethnographic accounts of rural life formed the basis of a cultural renaissance in Russia. They peopled the Russian landscape with 'saintly princes' and 'beatified' it.[41] Others eulogized the rural poor, and used the material elements of Russia's symbolic landscape – vernacular architecture, ancient monuments and sites of historic significance – to provide Russians with 'points of physical and ideological orientation' that would help to guide them in an increasingly turbulent world.[42] Many of those who returned from Crimea sought a more authentic existence by devoting themselves to the cause of the poor, and demanded constitutional reform and the abolition of serfdom.

The explosive expansion of the administrative and surveillance powers of the military establishment and the Russian state in the 1850s was accompanied by cameralist efforts to increase industrial and agricultural production. The state now sought to develop the country's regional economies and unite them within a national matrix of state control. State officials, especially young officers who had been trained in the more advanced military academies of St Petersburg and Moscow, were now charged with compiling statistical data for every corner of the empire, promoting social and economic reform, facilitating the military governance of rural areas, and consolidating governmental control over Russia's growing population and expansive territories. To rule this huge landmass of an empire, the government trained surveyors in the principles of scientific geography and cartography, established printing houses for the production of maps for military as well as civil use, launched geodesic surveys of Russian territories, and amassed a huge amount of cartographic data on the general condition of the state's territorial possessions.[43] All of this contributed to the militarization of Russia's political landscape and created new territorial divisions of the Russian countryside that were increasingly now under the control of the military establishment rather than civilians.

It was in this way that the *esprit géométrique* of the administrative geography taught to students at institutions like the Corps of Pages contributed to the aggrandisement of the tsarist state. Military academies and universities now dispatched thousands of army officers, government officials, land surveyors, scientists, geologists, geographers, mining experts and agronomists to the distant borderlands of the Russian Empire. All of this facilitated the growth of Russia's territorialized state, a state that was increasingly presided over by 'a highly space-conscious elite'. The latter's ambitions for shaping and governing the national territory of Mother Russia were distinctly different from the political agendas of Russia's rulers in the eighteenth and early nineteenth century. Ruling elites now perceived Russia as 'a European country with an Asian extension', a geographical formation that needed to be unified under the control of the tsarist state. It consisted of an historical rich heartland centred on Moscovy and the eastern provinces, and a non-Russian periphery that stretched far away to the outer limits of Siberia and Manchuria in the east. Atlases produced while Kropotkin was a student in St Petersburg continued to emphasize the territorial extent and immense grandeur of this nation that had ambitions to become an empire. In highlighting each province as 'a distinct space cut out from the state', Russia's imperial modernizers stressed the underlying importance of the empire's provinces.[44] People and land in this greater Russia were to constitute an organic and symbiotic whole. Just as mother Russia was portrayed as the nurturer of her people, the national territory was to become the legitimate homeland of the Russian people. By the mid nineteenth century, therefore, Russian rulers were predisposed to appropriate and administer state territory as the fundamental objectives of government policy.

Those responsible for Kropotkin's education at the Corps of Pages shared these views on the role of government in the new Russia. Students were taught a range of skills that would allow the state to deepen its physical and conceptual grip on the country. While this was not a new development, it certainly acquired a renewed momentum in the 1860s as authorities in St Petersburg sought to reinvigorate the state by introducing a series of major changes in the country's social and political order. As far back as the eighteenth century, state schools had been preparing candidates for state and military service, while primary schools and individual estate owners and owners of serfs were left with the task of teaching practical skills, religious knowledge and morality to those under their care. While the quality of recruits entering military academies and other third level institutions improved markedly throughout this period, the gulf separating educated elites from the mass of society continued to grow substantially in the first half of the nineteenth century. The further down the educational ladder one went, the poorer the standard of education. Thus while other European countries were experimenting with primary education, the bulk of the Russian countryside was still served by a meagre network of small, poorly run, parish schools.[45] The state's continued need for qualified professionals led to the construction of a 'ladder' to ensure that promising students could, in theory at least, move from one level of society to another. In reality, however, the social distance separating the educated from the uneducated meant that education was not merely beyond the reach of the vast majority of Russian youth. It was used by the autocratic state like a quasi-colonial foreign force to keep the majority of Russian people in their place. That said, the old established universities in Moscow and St Petersburg were to play a crucial role in the modernization of Russia from the 1820s through to the 1860s.

Certainly in the 1860s, universities and military academies were to the forefront in teaching the skills of statecraft. This raised the civic-mindedness of students and equipped them with the skills required for civil and military service. Despite the autocratic nature of the state, universities, and to a lesser extent Russia's military academies, also served as 'staging points' for revolutionary change. They became places where students could gather together 'to discuss the injustices of the social order, the shortcomings of the government's reform programme and the possibilities of communal life'.[46] However the autocratic nature of tsarism militated against the development of academic freedoms and the prevailing view suggested that a cameralist or vocational education was more than adequate for candidates entering either civil or military service. In the 1860s, the state still regarded a combination of European philosophy, a good knowledge of the classics, religious-moral instruction, and conservative Russian nationalism as the only sound foundation of official state ideology.

As in many other European countries, education was a crucial variable in determining rank and status in Russia when Kropotkin was a student in St Petersburg. Russia's earliest academies had been established by the state in the eighteenth century and had a strong state-centred and utilitarian ethos. These state schools and specialized academies taught navigation, medicine, engineering, mining and foreign languages, particularly French and German. While the old nobility looked with disdain upon these 'cipher schools', attitudes changed when state-run military academies guaranteed graduates automatic entry to positions of privilege in the military and state establishment. The Corps of Pages, the Imperial Law School and the School of Guards' Sub-Ensigns were among the most elitist academies in Russia in Kropotkin's day. In addition to training officers for military service, these schools also taught good manners and inculcated codes of etiquette and social grace that were considered appropriate to state officials who had to mix with their European counterparts. Thus students at institutions like the Corps of Pages sought to distinguish themselves in cultural as well as admin-istrative and military pursuits. In addition to reading classical French drama, promising students like Kropotkin also read Voltaire, Kant, Hegel, Montesquieu, Racine, de Lamartine, Marcus Aurelius and the Greek and Roman Classics. Their education was elitist in a dual sense. On the one hand, the educated were obliged to 'to mark off their social standing against competitors from below' by protecting their privileges and literally keeping their distance from the poor and uneducated. On the other hand, they had to adopt the educational mores and standards of European polite society, especially that of France. While this wholesale borrowing from Western Europe may have helped to narrow the cultural divide between the Russian nobility and their European counterparts, it simultaneously widened the gap between educated elites and the bulk of Russian society. This placed the educated nobility in an incongruous position in relation to the rest of society.[47]

When Kropotkin entered the Corps of Pages in the mid 1850s, the sciences, including scientific methodologies of inquiry, were already contributing to a radical re-examination of the entrenched social, religious and political assumptions underpinning the authority of Russia's tsarist state. All across Russia, enlightened citizens were talking of education. As Kropotkin remarked:

The ignorance of the masses of the people, the obstacles that had hitherto been put in the way of those who wanted to learn, the absence of schools in the country, the obsolete methods of teaching, and the remedies for these evils became favourite themes of discussion in educated circles, in the press, and even in the drawing rooms of the aristocracy ... As if by magic a number of men and women came to the front who ... not only devoted their lives to education but ... proved to be remarkable practical pedagogists.[48]

As a student in the Corps of Pages, Kropotkin had already developed a strong interest in popular education. Like many young liberals he had taken part in a scheme to provide free education for liberated serfs in schools that were to be staffed by voluntary teachers. This scheme had to be abandoned when tsarist authorities interpreted any effort to ameliorate the position of the poor as revolutionary in intent. He continued to raise issues associated with social reform and community service at the Corps of Pages. In a pamphlet lamenting the intellectual stagnation he encountered at the academy, he wrote: 'My main purpose was to arouse the Corps to the false tendencies which dominated us; i.e. in vain [students] think that autocracy is the best government, that military service is the best kind of activity, and that one may be a respectable fellow only in the Preobrazhenskii and guard regiments.'[49] It was at this stage that he began to criticize and expose the conspicuous consumption of court life.

Like many young Russians from privileged backgrounds, Kropotkin's civic-mindedness expressed itself in an altruistic desire to perform useful services for the poor and uneducated. As a young and talented member of the nobility, he felt increasingly alienated from the regime he was being trained to serve. Reminding fellow students of their social and ethical responsibilities, he wrote:

> Everyone must be a useful member of society. Of course, no one demands that he should sacrifice himself in such a way as to go barefoot. But he must by the measure of his strength try to satisfy the needs of society … What is demanded … is no more than an honest fulfilment of his responsibilities, i.e., to conform with the needs of the majority and not with one's personal conviction.[50]

In 1873, when still in his early thirties, he produced a detailed manifesto entitled 'Must We Always Occupy Ourselves with an Examination of the Ideal of a Future Society?' This was to be his first major political statement and in it he outlined many of the features of the future anarchist society. Here, for example, he considered it necessary to reiterate that it was 'absolutely necessary' to acknowledge 'the superfluity of that class which enjoys a privileged type of occupation; in other words, the acknowledgment of the necessity of manual, muscular labour for all members of society, along with the acknowledgement of complete freedom for each individual in choosing these occupations – if he can prove his capability in the selected type of occupation'. This type of society, he added, had no need of heroes to keep the people in a state of enthralment. In periods of political turmoil and social change, such men and women would 'appear of themselves, from among the most ordinary people'. He also believed that 'the grouping of men' in the future 'must not merely be national ... it must extend across all artificial frontiers and boundary lines'. In outlining the qualities needed in those who wished to serve the people effectively, rather than lead them, he stated:

> We need people who, once having come to a certain conviction, are for its sake ready to withstand all possible deprivations day in and day out. But activity among the peasants and workers demands precisely this rejection of every comfort of life, a lowering of one's prosperity to a level attainable by the worker, and – work, without fail, work. ... If any sort of deprivation was to be assumed expiatory penance or exclusively a means of education, then we, of course, would not consider it: we are not a monastic order.[51]

Kropotkin's concept of service was completely different from the state-centred and militaristic ethos of his father's generation. In a letter to his brother Alexander describing how his father's view equated service to the state with military service, Peter lamented the fact that 'outside of military service' his father was unable to imagine himself 'as anything respectable'. Now retired from the army and living on a state pension, his father considered his entire life as meaningless simply because he failed to achieve the desired rank of General. This, for Kropotkin, was far too restrictive a definition of service, and he lamented the fact that his father had wasted his entire life currying favour with his superiors in pursuit of a goal that he never achieved. At 17, Kropotkin was already familiar with the radical literature that circulated more freely in Moscow and St Petersburg after the death of Nicholas I. We know that he was familiar with socialist ideas picked up through reading Alexander Herzen's journal, *The Pole Star*. Published in London, it was secretly circulated in Moscow and St Petersburg in the 1850s. Kropotkin was especially struck by the beauty of Herzen's style, and by 'the breadth of his ideas and his love of Russia'. He also expressed an affinity with the five Decembrists who were hanged by Nicholas I in 1825, and whose images adorned the title page of *The Pole Star*. Advocating 'nothing more radical than a constitution for Russia', contributors to this journal brought the young Kropotkin into contact with mid nineteenth-century Russia's vibrant intellectual tradition. When he left the Corps of Pages in 1862, Kropotkin had read widely in European literature and philosophy. His natural agnosticism developed from a close reading of the works of Voltaire and Kant. Although he found Kant's *Critique of Pure Reason* difficult going, he was enthralled with Voltaire's *Dictionnaire Philosophique*. He was particularly impressed by the manner in which Voltaire structured and presented his arguments in an accessible style that both amused and informed his readers. This was precisely the style that he himself would choose when he wished to disseminate his anarchist teachings among the working class and rural poor of Europe. He also developed a strong interest in mathematics and physics at this stage, and even began writing a textbook on physics. It was at the Corps of Pages that 'the never-ceasing life of the universe, which [he] conceived as life and evolution, gradually became an inexhaustible source of higher poetic thought'. 'Gradually', he added, 'the sense of man's oneness with nature, both animate and inanimate – the poetry of nature – became the philosophy of my life.'[52]

Thus Kropotkin's privileged upbringing influenced his conception of anarchism in a variety of ways. Firstly, the Corps of Pages taught him the benefit of balancing manual with intellectual labour that was to become such a feature of his foundational anarchist texts, *Fields, Factories and Workshops* and *The Conquest of Bread*. Secondly, the military-inspired principles of self-sufficiency and survival that he acquired as a young officer were adapted, albeit in far more elaborate forms, in his writings on economic planning and regional development. Thirdly, Kropotkin's anarchism displayed a landed aristocrat's preference for the countryside over the industrialized city. Like many of his aristocratic peers, he also expressed a preference for federated networks of townships and cities that were organically linked to their rural hinterlands. These were considered eminently more desirable than the industrialized agglomerations that were absorbing thousands of peasants who were forced to leave the land for a life of drudgery in the city. Fourthly, Kropotkin's 'urge to serve' and 'wish to be useful' were by no means unrelated to the paternalism that was such a marked feature of the liberal nobility and enlightened elites of nineteenth-century Europe. The fact that he adapted these goals to the cause of revolution is only one of the many paradoxes linking the life of this anarchist Russian prince with the poor and the powerless of Europe.

Finally, and in contrast with Bakunin's fascination with political violence and the 'anarchism of the deed', Kropotkin's lifelong commitment to the constructive possibilities of anarchism was partially inspired by an aristocratic distaste for the violent actions of 'wild-eyed' anarchists at this crucial juncture in the development of modern anarchism.

The Siberian years

The period between 1862, when he graduated from military school, and 1871, when he rejected an offer of a position in the prestigious Imperial Geographic Society of Russia, has been described as Kropotkin's 'decade of wandering'.[53] However, far from being aimless, his life remained deeply purposeful throughout these years. Indeed they could more accurately be described as Kropotkin's most transformative period. He began the decade as a young officer serving the interests of the tsarist state in Eastern Siberia and ended it by renouncing both a military and an academic career and dedicating himself to the revolutionary cause of a stateless society. He transformed his own life and was now on the verge of transforming European anarchism.

We have already seen that most students from the prestigious Corps of Pages military academy automatically entered state service on graduation. The majority of these chose to serve the emperor in a variety of military and civic capacities in one of Russia's Guards regiments. As a member of an established military family, Kropotkin was certainly expected to forge a career in the service of the tsarist state. His choice of regiment, and the fact that he chose to serve in a region 'as little known as an African desert', showed just how far he was prepared to go in order to follow his desire to do 'useful' work. To the surprise of his military colleagues, and to the horror of his father, he accepted a commission in the ranks of Cossacks and chose to serve in the remote Amur River basin of Eastern Siberia. When Alexander II heard of his decision, he personally mandated him 'to go' to Siberia, adding that 'one can be useful anywhere'.[54]

In Siberia Kropotkin encountered a world of contradictions. Here he came face to face with the harsher realities of both urban and rural life in one of imperial Russia's most backward regions. In this semi-periphery of a modernizing Russia he met with the political prisoner and the inde-pendent-minded peasant, the exploited miner and the state administrator, the settled farming family and hunting and gathering communities. Here also he parted ways with the military establishment and the tsarist state and gradually converted to anarchism after the violent suppression of the Polish rebellion in 1863. By then he had reached the formative age of 21. After years of private tuition and an education in one of Russia's most prestigious academies, Kropotkin felt that the five years he spent in Siberia represented 'a genuine education in life and human character'. Here he matured into a Renaissance man of science, conducting research, much of it ground-breaking, in zoology, physical geography, sociology, ethnography and criminology. He was later to write that his experience of life 'among the natives of Siberia opened up an awareness of the complex forms of social organization which they have elaborated far away from the influence of any civilization'. This in turn allowed him 'to store up floods of light which illuminated my subsequent reading'.[55] He also insisted that all of nature could be understood by anyone who was prepared to open his eyes. This optimistic faith in human nature and society had been summed up five centuries earlier by Leon Battista Alberti when he wrote, 'Man can make whatever he will of himself.'[56] Criticizing those who insisted that the lives of men and women must always and everywhere be constrained and limited by laws and conventions, Kropotkin insisted that even the most oppressed could learn to walk on earth with dignity. Thus in Siberia he refused to acquiesce before the mysteries of nature and the majesty of the state. Instead he set out on a humanistic quest for understanding and sought out order outside the parameters of the state. He combined a faith in the sciences with a devastating onslaught on despondency and cynicism, and a robust contempt for conventional authority and all forms of superstition.

Yet there was something deeply ironic about Kropotkin's choice of Siberia as a place to lead a 'useful' life. It was here that he encountered some of Russia's most independent-minded peasants living and working alongside political prisoners and social outcasts who were under the constant supervision of state authorities. The fact that it was here that Kropotkin also formulated some of the foundational beliefs of 'scientific anarchism' rendered his decision to serve his emperor in the wastelands of Siberia all the more ironic. To appreciate the irony, it is worth recalling that in classical Greece, 'anarchy' originally meant 'without a leader', specifically a military leader, and subsequently encompassed all those living 'without rule' in demilitarized zones beyond the city-states of the ancient world. However, far from being a 'demilitarized' or 'unregulated' zone, mid nineteenth-century Siberia was governed, more often than not harshly, by military authorities. Yet the ambivalent geography of this peripheral region rendered it an in-between place somewhere between the 'civilized' world of European Russia and the 'semi-barbarism' of the Asiatic world. As such it was closely monitored and carefully administered by authorities in the capital, and by its representatives in outlying provincial cities like Irkutsk and Chita. Those officers living beyond the pale of urban civilization in Eastern Siberia lived among a people who lacked the paraphernalia of 'civilization' and led unregulated, or 'anarchic', lives beyond the reach of man-made Russian laws and good order. Yet the Siberia that Kropotkin encountered was by no means a demilitarized zone. Neither was it an 'anarchic' world inhabited by 'natural anarchists' and 'primitive rebels'. By the 1860s, it was already an integral part of the political domain of Moscow and St Petersburg and had become progressively linked into a vast, increasingly coordinated network of several hundred governmental districts that coexisted alongside a smaller number of lesser administrative units, military outposts and remote wilderness areas that were only then coming under the authority of the state.[57] All of these areas were governed from the Russian capital and its administrative outliers all across Transbaikalia. By the mid nineteenth century, while the military establishment were amassing huge volumes of scientific data on the geography of empire, the nobility continued to reside in lavish palaces, particularly in the spacious new model capital of St Petersburg. Here they assembled extravagant art collections that were often far grander than their Western counterparts, and lived lifestyles to match. On leaving St Petersburg and the urban world of the nobility, Kropotkin entered into what was becoming one of Russia's most strictly supervised and closely administered regions. Here he learned 'how little a man really needs as soon as he comes out of the enchanted circle of conventional civilization'.[58] His love of the simple uncorrupted life of rural Siberia certainly contributed to an anarchist cult of the primitive. It may also have influenced the anti-consumerist element in much of his later writings on anarchist economics and self-sufficiency.

Longing for 'a place without people', in 1863 he received permission to travel down the Amur River with a string of barges to supply food to outlying settlements. The following year he went on an expedition to Manchuria organized by the Imperial Geographic Society and effectively commenced serious geographical work. In 1866 he explored a route between the gold mines situated along the Lena River and the administrative town of Chita. At this stage Kropotkin attacked the negative image of Siberia as a land of exiles and a place lacking in natural resources and 'nature's warmth'. In dispelling the myth that it was a frozen wilderness and in helping to put Siberia on the map of a modernizing Russia, he demonstrated both his powers of description and his geographical knowledge of this vast region. Thus he wrote:

> Siberia is not the frozen land buried in snow and peopled with exiles only that it is imagined to be, even by Russians. In its southern parts it is as rich in natural productions as are the southern parts of Canada, which it resembles in its physical aspects; and beside half a million natives, it has a population of more than four million Russians. The southern parts of Western Siberia are as thoroughly Russian as the provinces north of Moscow.[59]

The Cossacks with whom Kropotkin chose to serve were among imperial Russia's least fashionable, most independent and fiercest regiments. These free-roving horsemen and stock-raisers had an historical legacy of brigandage and hunting. They ranged widely across Russia's 'wild country' where they 'learned to cope with the harsh and risky life of the steppe by forming themselves into military fraternities and mastering the skills which had reaped the Tatars such success in earlier centuries'. Derogatorily linked with barbarians by those in the West, their very name, Tatars, actually signified 'free men'. Thus all true Cossacks considered a settled agricultural life as beneath their dignity. In mixing respect for authority with their primitive democracy, they were utterly dependent upon each other for survival. Their conception of politics was to all intents stateless and devoid of any sense of responsibility for public welfare. Hence it was not surprising that Siberia taught Kropotkin his first lessons in mutual aid and self-sufficiency. Geoffrey Hosking has labelled the Cossacks 'an alternative Russian ethnos'.[60] To the radical thinker Alexander Herzen they represented the embryo of an independent and socialist Russia. Historically the Tatars were the 'shock troops' of imperial expansion, Russia's primitive 'conquistadores', who pushed the boundaries of empire to the outer extremities of Siberia. As far back as the sixteenth century, they had formed self-governing communities around Lake Baikal, the Amur basin and the Terek River.

With little to distinguish them from the indigenous Tatar tribesmen who commanded this extensive region, and from whom they may well have been descended, their semi-Asiatic lifestyle could not have been more different from the privileged lifestyle that Kropotkin experienced on his father's estate and at the court of the tsar.

Herzen was among the first to reject racist depictions of Russia's eastern peoples as the epitome of stagnation, tyranny and barbarism. Following his country's defeat in the Crimean War, in which Cossacks and serf soldiers fought so bravely, he suggested that their youth and vigour could invigorate Russia. He, like Kropotkin, was proud to proclaim himself a barbarian, at least by conviction, if not by birth. For Gogol, the Tatars were 'a people in whom the two opposite parts of the world come together, European prudence and Asiatic abandon, a strong sense of activity and a love of laziness, a drive towards self development and perfection and at the same time a desire to appear scornful of any perfection'.[61] As people who did not hold land that had to be worked by serfs, they were 'en dehors de la nation officielle ou legale', i.e. outside the pale of official Russia. As a frontier people, their spirit of adventure, and especially their struggle to sustain deeply independent and comparatively comfortable lifestyles far from the cities and rural heartlands of imperial Russia, compensated for their lack of civic refinements, at least as far as Kropotkin was concerned. The frontier zone literally made Tatars and Cossacks what they were, Russia's most independent-minded peoples who struggled to fashion the nation's frontier in their own image, not that of the landed nobility. Thus was it said that one Cossack was worth a hundred city-dwellers. The very lives of these settlers were living proof of their determination to survive and perform great feats of endurance in one of the remotest corners of the empire. When Anton Chekhov sailed down the Amur River some 30-odd years after Kropotkin had brought food and other essentials to isolated communities along its banks, he felt that he was 'no longer in Russia, but somewhere in Patagonia, or Texas'.[62] Like many of those who chose to serve here, Kropotkin and his fellow officers were often perceived as interlopers and complete foreigners.[63]

In a widely respected and paradigmatic essay on the significance of the frontier in American history, Frederick Jackson Turner suggested that frontier expansion and the 'rolling back of wilderness and savagery' allowed nineteenth-century America to forge liveable space from an unruly and uncooperative nature.[64] Thus westward expansion of robust pioneers and intrepid settlers not only added new territory to the American estate in the nineteenth century – it literally added new blood to the body politic of American society. Each wave of westward expansion, achieved through the conquest of nature and the annihilation of space, sent shock waves back east and fostered the growth of American democracy. Things could not have been more different in Eastern Siberia when Kropotkin was employed as aide-de-camp to General Kukel, the Governor of Transbaikalia. Here the expansion of empire was achieved through a conquest of nature, not by independent settlers, but by oppressed minorities, impoverished serfs and peasants, and political prisoners. Far from nurturing the growth of civic society and democracy, frontier expansion in nineteenth-century Russia was achieved at the expense of local communities and contributed to the consolidation of state authority. The further the state extended its reach beyond the Caucuses, the less autonomous and more underdeveloped did outlying communities become. In the event, groups like the Cossacks and the Dukhobors, and countless other ethnic minorities in Russia's southern borderlands, were expected to sacrifice their autonomy on the altar of the state in order to transform a backward Russia into a global power. The Dukhobors of the Amur region were part of an eighteenth-century religious sect that had rejected all external authority, including that of the Bible. They first attracted Kropotkin's attention in the early 1860s. These 'primitive anarchists' believed that their leader was the reincarnation of Christ. Having rejected priestly authority and the sacraments, the only ceremony they recognized was that of the *sobraniye*, or 'meeting', at which prayers were recited around a table set out with bread, salt and water. While their egalitarian beliefs, self-sufficiency, pacifism and opposition to conscription and other manifestations of state authority appealed to Kropotkin, they had also provoked sporadic persecutions throughout the eighteenth and nineteenth centuries. In 1801, Tsar Alexander I had settled approximately 4,000 Dukhobors on the Molochnaya River, near the Sea of Azov. Communities of Dukhobors were also to be found in Siberia in the latter half of the nineteenth century and Kropotkin was deeply impressed by 'the immense advantages which [they] got from their semi-communistic brotherly organization'. To witness the success of their colonization of this difficult region, especially 'amidst all the failures of state colonization', was, he wrote, 'to learn something which cannot be learned from books'.[65] In attaching success to the weak rather than the strong, Kropotkin was going against the full force of imperial geography and social anthropology. As we shall presently see, this was to become a defining feature of his writings on mutualism and social cooperation and his anti-statist critique of Social Darwinism.

Prior to the nineteenth century, the tsarist state was forced to accept the independence of indigenous minorities in the Russian 'outback'. By the mid nineteenth century, however, groups like the Tatars were considered part of a savage Russian wilderness that had to be tamed in order that progress, modernity and a thin coating of civility could be extended to the outer limits of the empire. The presence of such communities in modernizing Russia was often as not now a source of wonder to progressive thinkers and Russian state builders alike. Their mode of existence, not least their nomadic behaviour, religious beliefs, lack of respect for the established church, the state and the law, and especially their unconventional religious rites, resembled more the habits and customs of the inhabitants of the 'outbacks' of backward Asia, than those of nineteenth-century European Russia. As descendants of the Mongolian 'Tartars' who had threatened Moscovy in the thirteenth century, they were considered a barbaric, cruel, almost subhuman species of humanity whose superstitious practices had no place in tsarist Russia. Officially they lived within the borders of the Russian Empire. If fact they were perceived as social outcasts of official Russia. Like the nomadic Highlanders in Walter Scott's historical narratives, they were historical subjects from a different place and an earlier epoch in history. They were people who had literally to be consumed or otherwise 'used up' in an unfolding narrative of state expansion. The *geography of savagery* that lay behind bourgeois images of 'official Russia' implied that those furthest from the urban centres of European Russia were the most savage of all.[66] For that reason the firm hand of state administrators was needed to keep them in order.

Kropotkin considered the behaviour of many of the representatives of this 'official Russia' to be 'simply disgraceful'. One district chief, a police officer 'invested with very wide and indeterminate rights … robbed the peasants and flogged them right and left – even women, which was against the law'.[67] The local police failed to investigate allegations of crimes committed by state officials against political prisoners and the indigenous population. Native crime suspects were left to languish for months in prison, or released only on receipt of bribes. As in large tracts of contemporary India and Sub-Saharan Africa, the poor were often 'terrorized' by state authorities, especially by the local police and district officers. Yet when Kropotkin encountered racial and ethnic minorities like the Tatars, he did not become a champion of their right to self-determination. Instead he eulogized their spontaneity and emphasized their self-sufficiency. He paraded them as a people who, because they retained their independent way of life against all odds in one of Europe's harshest environments, could become true role models for a new form of stateless society.

When Kropotkin served as a Cossack officer in the largely unexplored region of Eastern Siberia between 1862 and 1867, he was also engaged in the study of animal life and conducted extensive field research on the physical geography of the mountainous Amur region. An early photograph taken in 1864, when he was engaged in his first explorations of this largely unmapped region, shows him wearing military uniform. Among other duties he was responsible for investigating conditions for prisoners held in penal colonies in the region. In this capacity he inspected 'lock-ups' where prisoners and miners slept, and was appalled not only at their plight but also by the primitive nature of capitalist development throughout much of Siberia. He compared the labour camps here to those described in Dostoyevsky's short story, 'Buried Alive'.[68] He also visited gold mines on the River Lena where men worked in icy water up to their waists, and inspected salt mines where Polish prisoners died of scurvy and tuberculosis. While all of this contributed to his hatred of autocratic rule and primitive capitalism, nevertheless in rural Siberia he enjoyed the 'hearty goodwill' of peasants and political prisoners, and 'appreciated the natural relations of equality that prevailed among them'. Forever the astute geographer, he painted powerful word pictures of the rivers, mountains and landscapes that captivated him. Thus he wrote:

Only those who have seen the Amur, or known the Mississippi or the Yang-tse-king, can imagine what an immense river the Amur becomes after it has joined the Sungari and can realise what tremendous waves roll up its bed if the weather is stormy. When the rainy season, due to monsoons, comes in July, the Sungari, the Usuri, and the Amur are swollen by unimaginable quantities of water; thousands of low islands, usually covered with thick willow thickets, are inundated and torn away, and the width of the river attains in places two, three, and even

five miles; water rushes into hundreds of branches and lakes which
spread in the lowlands along the main channel; and when fresh wind
blows from an eastern quarter, against the current, tremendous waves,
higher than those which one sees in the estuary of the St Lawrence,
roll up the main channel as well as up its branches. Still worse is it
when a typhoon blows from the Chinese Sea and spreads over the
Amur region.[69]

The whole tenor of modern Russian life was still completely alien to the
indigenous communities of Eastern Siberia when the young Kropotkin
served there. Throughout the final stages of his 4,000-kilometre trip
to Irkutch, the administrative capital of the region, the beauty of the
landscape, the fertility of the land and the comparative prosperity of the
local peasantry captivated Kropotkin. Feeling healthy and revived after
more than three weeks travelling, he wrote a letter home to his brother
describing the country as rich and the people as 'intelligent' and 'gay',
adding that 'they look you straight in the eye and don't shy away'. As he
was soon to discover, attitudes to Siberia, and to the administrative role of
the army in particular, were to undergo significant changes in the 1860s
and 1870s. Earlier in the century official Russia was largely uninterested
in 'the ocean of snow' that was Siberia. Partly because of difficulties with
transport, the tsarist regime used it simply as a dumping ground for the
empire's political prisoners, undesirables, criminals and members of
persecuted religious sects. Especially after the 1820s, they were conveyed
here in their thousands, having marched for weeks over frozen wastelands
to their confinement in convict camps. When Kropotkin arrived here in
the 1860s, he noted that some political prisoners were condemned to
work in appalling conditions in salt works and silver and gold mines.
Some of the more educated found employment in official posts in local
administration.

Despite its great distance from Moscow and St Petersburg, Siberia
continued to bolster the internal security of Russia right up to the mid
nineteenth century and its strategic importance outweighed its economic
importance to the state. However, Russian attitudes towards its frontier
lands were to become increasingly ambivalent in the latter half of the
century. Politically, Russia was as imperialist as any European state, and
'official Russia' was increasingly aware of the economic potential of its
far-flung peripheral possessions. Culturally, however, in addition to the

usual Western stance of superiority towards the 'Asiatic' and the 'Orient', there was a strong fascination and growing affinity with frontier zones like Siberia. As Figgis has suggested, this ambiguous geography of the East was a source of profound insecurity for many Russians who clearly defined themselves as Europeans but who were still considered 'Asiatics' by the West. Members of the country's urban elites in particular scarcely knew where Siberia began and European Russia ended. Alexander Herzen thought that Viatka, a provincial city a few hundred kilometres to the west of the Urals, was in Siberia. Others thought that Perm, a little further east but still far from the Urals, was in the depths of the Urals.[70]

The annexation of the Amur region by state forces just prior to Kropotkin's arrival was motivated by the twin desires of attaching this region to the national territory and providing the Russian fleet with access to the Pacific Ocean through the East China Sea and the Sea of Japan. Thus Russia had pressed down the Amur in the mid 1850s, and by 1860 Vladivostok was the gateway to Russia's eastern territories and the future terminus of her Trans-Siberian railroad. In taking possession of this remote region on the eve of the opening of Japan to Western Europe, Russia's Count Murav'ev-Amurskii had to rely upon the scanty means that the thinly populated Eastern Siberia could afford for this empire-building enterprise. In the summer of 1863, Kropotkin visited this 'immense domain along the Pacific coast', which he said had been annexed to Russia 'almost against the will the St Petersburg authorities'. In the following statement he remarked astutely on the difficulties of colonizing the region:

A nominal occupation would have been of no avail, and the idea was to have along the whole length of the great river and of its southern tributary, the Usuri – full 2,500 miles – a chain of self-supporting settlements, and thus to establish a regular communication between Siberia and the Pacific Coast. Men were wanted for these settlements, and as the scanty population of East Siberia could not supply them, Murav-ev did not recoil before any kind of means of getting men. Released convicts who, after having served their time, had become serfs to the imperial mines, were freed and organized as Transbaikalian Cossacks, part of whom were settled along the Amur and the Usuri, forming two Cossack communities. Then Murav-ev obtained the release of a thousand hard-labour convicts (mostly robbers and murderers), who had to be settled as free men on the lower Amur. He came himself to see them off, and, as they were going to leave, addressed them on the beach: 'Go, my children, be free, cultivate the land, make it Russian soil, start a new life', and so on. The Russian peasant women nearly always follow their husbands, of their own free will, if the latter happen to be sent to hard labour in Siberia, and many would-be colonists had their families with them ... The motley crowd of Transbaikalian Cossacks of ex-convicts, and 'sons' who were settled in a hurry and often in a haphazard way along the banks of the Amur, certainly did not attain prosperity, especially in the lower parts of the river and on the Usuri, where every square yard had to be won upon a virgin sub-tropical forest, and deluges of rain brought by the monsoons in July, intimidations on a gigantic scale, millions of migrating birds, and the like continually destroyed the crops, finally bringing whole populations to sheer despair and apathy.[71]

The tsarist state had expanded eastwards towards the furthest edge of Siberia and right up to the limits of space that convict supplies and pioneering communities of Tatars and Cossacks could effectively dominate. In the seventeenth and eighteenth centuries, the state, mindful of the vast distances separating it from metropolitan Russia, and of the precarious situation of its thinly scattered settler communities, adopted a highly pragmatic approach to the governance of this expansive region. Local communities were left to follow their traditional way of life so long as they could sustain themselves without state aid and contribute to the upkeep of the local administration. If southern Siberia provided Russia with an abundance of *lebensraum* and a reassuring sense of space, it also seemed more than ample to fulfil the young Kropotkin's desire to 'be useful' to the less privileged sectors of Russian society. Here, he later recollected, he hoped to find 'an immense field for the application of the great reforms which have been made and are coming: the workers must be few there, and I shall find a field of action for my tastes'.[72] It was chiefly in the 1860s that the exploitation of the mineral wealth and huge material resources of this region really began. Now Siberia became 'a prime example of the way in which the empire was run for considerations of great power status, not for economic ones'. The agricultural potential of the south and west was still practically untapped in the mid nineteenth century. Likewise, despite numerous geological expeditions, Siberia's rich gold, silver and salt deposits had scarcely been exploited. With the keen eye of an economic geographer, Kropotkin alluded to the awakening of state interest in navigation, fisheries and trade in the Russian portion of the Arctic Ocean in the 1860s. Always willing to give credit to the 'local heroes' who opened the region to external trade, he praised the efforts of a Siberian merchant and gold miners who 'made the most persevering efforts to awaken that interest [and] foresaw that with a little aid in the shape of navy schools ... the Russian fisheries and Russian navigation could be largely developed'. Unfortunately, he added, 'little had to be done entirely through St Petersburg, and the ruling portion of that courtly, bureaucratic, red-tapist, literary, artistic, and cosmopolitan city could not be moved to take an interest in anything "provincial"'.[73]

As early as 1863, therefore, Kropotkin was already losing faith in the state's ability to respond to local initiatives and effectively manage its imperial possessions. Implicit in his criticism of the state was a trenchant critique of imperialism and imperial expansion. In Eastern Siberia he was especially critical of local administrators and government-employed scientists who behaved like imperial overlords. While criticizing the scientific community for not appreciating the economic potential of the region, he praised the ingenuity of local communities who opened up trade routes and carved out an existence at the frontier of imperial Russia. Referring to recent developments in Siberia's coastal fisheries, he noted that 'a general interest in Arctic exploration' had been awakened by the discoveries of a handful of local seal hunters. This led to a new era of 'Arctic enthusiasm', which culminated in 'Nordenskjold's circumnavigation of Asia, in the permanent establishment of the north-eastern passage to Siberia, in Perry's discovery of North Greenland, and in Nansen's Fram expedition'.[74] Disillusioned with his role as a state-employee and regional administrator, Kropotkin increasingly turned to geography as an outlet for his intellectual abilities. Throughout his final years in Siberia he conducted detailed scientific research on the physical geography of Siberia. In 1866, under the auspices of the Imperial Geographical Society of Russia, he explored the Olekminsk-Vitim region in order to collect data on this remote region's geology, physical geography and glacial history.

To describe the years between Kropotkin's graduation from the Corps of Pages in 1862 and the death of his fellow anarchist, Mikhail Bakunin, in 1876 as momentous, exhilarating and turbulent would be an under-statement indeed. Merely to list the main events in his life in these years is to confirm that he was a larger-than-life historical figure whose life was radically transformed in these years. From 1862 to 1867 he had explored the mountain ranges of Eastern Siberia, travelled over 50,000 miles 'in carts, on board steamers, in boats, but chiefly on horseback', across huge tracts of sparsely inhabited territory, and navigated uncharted rivers, often in full flood, to bring the necessities of life to isolated communities along the River Amur, Russia's 'Mississippi of the East'. In the company of Ivan Poliakov, a promising young naturalist, he explored an extensive stretch of the River Lena to the north of Irkutsk and spent three months travelling in the almost totally uninhabited mountain deserts and marshy plateaux in Transbaikalia. After leaving military service in 1867, he spent the next five years in St Petersburg where his life was almost entirely devoted to geographical research. At this stage he was also a member of the Central Statistical Committee of the Ministry of Internal Affairs. On discovering that his duties did not absorb much of his attention, he enrolled as a first-year student at the University of St Petersburg's faculty of mathematics and physical sciences. Here, he later recalled, he 'sat on the benches among young men, almost boys, much younger than myself'.[75] In 1872, Kropotkin formally renounced his aristocratic heritage, visited Western Europe for the first time, famously met with small communities of craft workers and watchmakers in the Jura Mountains, and decided to dedicate his life to the theory and practice of anarchism.

In 1873–74 he became a leading figure in the Chaikovsky Circle, the most celebrated of Russia's Narodnik groups whose philosophy of 'going to the people' brought him into contact with workers, peasants and students, and with radical intellectuals in St Petersburg. In 1874, he was caught in a police dragnet and imprisoned for two years in St Petersburg's notorious fortress church of St Peter and St Paul. In 1876, in one of the most daring prison escapes of the nineteenth century, he escaped from the hospital wing of the prison and fled to England.[76] The following year he was back in Switzerland collaborating in editing the Bakuninist anarchist paper, *L'Avant-garde*. This was smuggled over the border to France in the hope of fostering the growth of anarchism in that country. By the time Bakunin died in 1876, Kropotkin was already revered as a prominent leftist intellectual in Europe's leading radical circles. During this period, however, the anarchist movement showed signs of division. Kropotkin, Malatesta and Élisée Reclus held congresses at which organizational matters and the issue of ownership in any future anarchist society were discussed. They also began to produce political pamphlets and philosophical statements outlining the nature of anarchism and anarcho-communist society. At the same time, however, all over Europe and North America small groups were set up, without offices or secretaries or club rooms, often consisting of only two or three people, determined to demonstrate their opposition to authority through political acts of violence. It was perhaps inevitable that prominent anarchists, including Kropotkin and Malatesta, were suspected of inspiring these apocalyptic acts of symbolic revenge against the state, many of which were in retaliation for the execution of their comrades.

Throughout the 1870s and 1880s Kropotkin began to castigate those Marxist socialists who claimed to be engaged in revolution but who doubted the revolutionary capabilities of the masses. He argued that those who subscribed to the view that peasants and petty agriculturalists represented little more than inert human masses were fated to repeat rather than make history by condemning workers and peasants to the political authority of a reformed state structure. By the late 1870s, therefore, he had shifted political gear from the agrarian populism that had been such a feature of Russian radicalism throughout the 1860s to a much broader, international anarchism that was committed to the destruction of the political authority of the modern state, not just the tsarist state, and its replacement with autonomous, decentralized communes sharing – but not owning – the resources of the earth. By then also he was addressing a far wider and much less visible readership than the small number of delegates who attended congresses of the anarchist Jura Federation, including the comparatively small readership of its Bulletin.

During the 1880s and 1890s Kropotkin acquired the status of a 'savant and sage' as he embarked on the lonely path of the international anarchist theorist. By the early 1880s he had become increasingly aware that revolutions were not made by words alone, but rather through action and political commitment to popular causes. Torn between the contemplative life of the scientist on the one hand, and that of the anarchist theorist and activist on the other, his lifelong desire to be useful to the less privileged was sufficiently strong to deflect him from a life devoted exclusively to philosophical contemplation. Instead he set about establishing small groups of like-minded anarchists who would later form the nucleus of Europe's anarchist movement. He also became deeply involved with the trade union movement and workers' struggles, and participated as the Russian delegate to the International Socialist Congress at Ghent. Following the suppression of *L'Avant-garde* in 1878, he founded *Le Révolté*.[77] With the demise of Proudhon's paper *Le Peuple* in 1850, this became Europe's leading anarchist paper. Shortly after the assassination of Tsar Alexander II, he was expelled from Switzerland and subsequently moved between England and France. In 1882, he was rounded up with 53 French anarchists and condemned, along with three other prominent anarchist propagandists, to five years imprisonment in the Old Abbey of St Bernard at Clairvaux, a remote mountain village to the north east of Lyons. In prison he suffered from scurvy and bouts of malaria. Moderate French papers, including *Le Journal des économistes*, widely condemned his sentence. A number of prominent intellectuals, writers, academics and officials at the British Museum signed a petition calling for his release. Among those who campaigned for his release were Victor Hugo, William Morris, Patrick Geddes, Alfred Russell Wallace, A.C. Swinburne and James Runciman. Following his release in 1886, he moved to England, which was to become his home for the next 30 years. The noble-born Serghei Stepniak, who was also an associate of Malatesta, described him as follows:

> His great gifts specially qualify him for activity in the vast public arena, and not in the underground regions of secret societies ... He is an ardent searcher after truth, a founder of a school and not a practical man. He endeavours to make certain ideas prevail, at all cost ... Being thoroughly versed in historical science, especially in everything relating to popular movements, he draws with marvellous effect from the vast stores of his erudition, in order to support and strengthen his assertions with examples and analogies, very original and unexpected. His words thus acquire an extraordinary power of persuasion, which is increased by the simplicity and earnestness of his explanations, due perhaps to his profound mathematical studies. ... He is an excellent journalist, ardent, spirited, eager. Even in his writings he is still the agitator.[78]

The English Marxist, H.M. Hyndman, described Kropotkin around this time as a man 'overflowing with enthusiasm and vigour'. He found it 'quite hopeless' to discuss his anarchist opinions. To Hyndman these seemed to be 'entirely out of accord with his intelligence and naturally charming disposition'. He recalled that 'you could pin him to nothing as his capacity for genial misrepresentation of social-democratic thought and principle transcended belief'.[79] Yet it was in 1870s and 1880s that Kropotkin developed into the foremost critic of those who had reconfigured Darwin's writings on evolution to produce a version of Social Darwinism that justified some of the worst practices of modern imperialism and state capitalism. As Europe's foremost anarchist intellectual, he envisaged the evolution of a radically new form of society following on from the destruction of Europe's newly emerging nation-states. His vision of an anarchist society was predicated on the emergence of federated communal organizations of workers and peasants along the lines first indicated by the Paris Commune of 1871 – which, as we shall see later, Kropotkin considered a major transformative event in the history of popular struggles. He was also convinced that reinvigorated urban and rural communes would eventually supplant the urban centres of capitalist production that had dominated Europe for centuries, and which he believed were soon to become extinct. Thus he envisaged a radically new political and economic landscape emerging in the closing decades of the nineteenth century.

Throughout this period he was equally optimistic that new methods of production, especially technological breakthroughs in energy production, transportation and communications, had the capacity to break down distinctions between town and country, and between manual and intellectual labour. This in turn, he argued, would motivate industrial and rural workers to fashion radically new living spaces, and new economic units, on their own initiative. At the same time he believed that anarchists, unlike socialists, should not form political parties, even if this were to enhance popular support for anarchist objectives. Thus there emerged a clear division in the political geography of socialism and anarchism at this stage. The more industrialized economies of northern Europe would follow a different revolutionary trajectory to that which was about to be adopted by workers and peasants in the south. Kropotkin was to play no small part in the creation of this divergent pattern of revolutionary politics at the dawn of the twentieth century. Whereas the German followers of Marx adopted a policy of 'conquering power within the existing state', Kropotkin encouraged the Belgian, French, Spanish, Italian and Swiss sections of the International to resist this reformist trend towards state-centred socialism. Like Bakunin, he insisted that the revolution should involve the negation of the state, and that it should come about through the spontaneous collective appropriation of land and other means of production by peasants and industrial workers who could resist the temptation to take over the state. In emphasizing the need for peasants and workers themselves to 'make the revolution' he reduced the role of anarchists to one of 'accentuating' the revolutionary consciousness of the masses, of stirring the 'spirit of rebellion' and raising hopes for the success of the revolution.[80] Together with James Guillaume, he reaffirmed the commitment of the Jura Federation to the principles of spontaneous action, collective anti-authoritarianism and regional autonomy. However, he was also aware that in so doing he risked losing contact with the realities of working-class life in the industrial enclaves of northern Europe, where the radical left believed that only a worker's state could advance the cause of socialism.

3

Kropotkin and the
Legitimization of Anarchism

The natural history of anarchism

It is a more or less accepted axiom of history, and of the social sciences, that political movements have generally required strong intellectual foundations for their assertions of truth. The sciences, particularly the natural and environmental sciences, were frequently mobilized to perform this role in nineteenth-century Europe and North America in order to legitimize political ideologies in state-societies. The linkages between the social and environmental sciences on the one hand, and political movements and political ideologies on the other, have been particularly evident in the relationship between Marxism and historical materialism, between Social Darwinism and political conservatism, and between Islamic law and the Islamic state. Similarly, if we move further back in history, we can discern even clearer linkages between monarchy and the religious establishment in sixteenth-century Europe, and between imperial authority and 'court philosophers' in ancient China, Greece and Rome.[1]

Kropotkin certainly believed that the truths of anarchism were scientifically verifiable. Whether he was discussing the evolution of the modern state or the social origins and ethical code of anarchism, he constantly related the discoveries of the environmental and social sciences to anarchist theories of progress and evolutionary, indeed revolutionary, social change. That said, he never used the category 'scientific anarchism' as authoritatively, or as frequently, as Marxists used the term 'scientific socialism' to loudly proclaim the legitimacy of Marxism. Nevertheless, Kropotkin regularly defended the scientific legitimacy of anarchism by demonstrating that humans are by definition social animals, and that human society and nature are bound together in a complex set of dynamic and indissoluble relationships that must never be torn asunder by man-made laws or the artificial authority of the state. If societies and individuals were ever to realize their creative potential, then the natural 'tendencies' that he claimed to have discovered through the application of deductive reasoning had to be respected by all true anarchists.

Kropotkin was by no means alone in seeking to reinforce his version of 'scientific anarchism' with truths revealed by disciplines like history, archaeology, anthropology, criminology, geography and environmental science. Beginning with the English, Scottish and French Enlighten-ments of the eighteenth century, and culminating in an efflorescence of the social and environmental sciences in the mid nineteenth century, social philosophers and scientists more or less successfully relocated the moral sentiments of human beings from the supernatural realms of the divine and the metaphysical to the secular realm of the individual and society. Nature and society, they argued, were orderly and rational phenomena, and deductive reasoning was the key to unlocking the increasingly discernible laws that seemed to govern society and the rest of organic nature. In taking this line of argument one step further by exposing the ideological kernel and scientific 'untruths' at the heart of Social Darwinism, Kropotkin set out to confirm that mutual cooperation and sociability were major factors in the evolution of all species, including humans.[2] He insisted that the historically proven *natural* tendency for humans to cooperate in order to survive also constituted the only solid basis upon which to construct a code of ethics that would foster, rather than hinder, the natural progression towards social progress. Using evidence from evolutionary theory, history and anthropology in particular, he claimed that societies 'moved in stages from the simple to the complex, from primitivism to sophistication, from conditions and situations of suffering towards the promise of mass happiness'.[3] The attainment of the maximum happiness for the greatest number of people could, he argued, only be achieved by accentuating human sociability, developing the mutual aid tendency in society, and living in a dynamic state of harmony with the organic world of nature rather than seeking to conquer it for purposes of sectional gain. If in the primordial past human survival was ultimately dependent upon people's ability to cooperate and live in harmony with nature and society, scientific discoveries and intellectual progress in the nineteenth century rendered the promise of mass happiness and social justice all the more attainable, provided of course that people were not subject to unjust laws or political or intellectual authorities.

In unearthing the roots of anarchism in evolutionary theory and grassroots traditions of sociability and mutuality, as opposed to metaphysical philosophy or political theory, Kropotkin did more than most to advance the cause of the stateless society. In so doing he sought to provide anarchism with a scientific foundation and an historical pedigree. Anarchists, he claimed, did not seek inspiration 'from on high'.[4] Instead he maintained that human sentiments of pity, sympathy and mutual aid were the natural basis of social and political morality. These same sentiments, which men and women could confirm 'through observations of their fellow creatures', were also the starting points of any effort to 'perfect little by little the experience of social life'. Thus, for Kropotkin, anarchism was not merely a political ideology. It was, he suggested:

> a conception of the Universe based on the mechanical interpreta-
> tion of … the whole of Nature, including the life of human societies
> and their economical, political and moral problems. … Its method is
> that of the natural sciences, and every conclusion it comes to must be
> verified by this method if it pretends to be scientific. Its tendency is to
> work out a synthetic philosophy which will take in all facts of Nature,
> including the life of societies … It refuses to be imposed upon by the
> metaphysics of Hegel, Schelling and Kant, by the expositions of Roman
> or Canonical law, by learned professors of State law, or by the political
> economy of metaphysicians…[5]

Insisting that its roots could be traced to 'the course taken by practical life', Kropotkin went on to suggest that anarchism was 'more than a … mere conception of a free society'. Inspired by natural law and the rationalism of the French Enlightenment in particular, his scientific anarchism was infused with a telcological conviction that a stateless society wherein citizens would live in harmony with natural and social 'laws' was the social ideal of the future. As a conception of the universe based on the 'mechanical interpretation' of nature and human society, anarchism derived its legitimacy from evolutionary theory. Unlike other political doctrines, it did not look to metaphysics to explain its growth and development, but relied on the environmental and social sciences, particularly history, for practical examples of sociability and mutual aid. Founded on the solid basis of inductive reasoning rather than the 'slippery grounds of mere analogies', the sociability and mutual aid that Kropotkin detected in human societies had clear parallels with similar 'tendencies' in organic nature.[6] Thus, for Kropotkin, the 'moral sense of man' had its origins in 'the further evolution of the mutual aid instincts evolved in animal societies long before the first man-like creatures appeared on earth'.[7]

Notwithstanding the vicissitudes of history, sociability and the 'mutual aid tendency' were so deeply intertwined with the evolution of the human race that they managed to survive right up to modern times. Whenever humans wished to adapt to a new phase of development, their constructive genius always drew inspiration from primordial tendencies of sociability, cooperation and mutual aid. In so far as they were creations of the masses and not their masters, authentic ethical systems, including new religions, often had their origins in these same 'tendencies'. Therefore, he concluded, the ethical progress of the human race, especially over the *longue durée*, represented nothing less than the gradual extension of the sociability and mutual aid tendencies of animals and the 'primitive tribe' to the large 'agglomerations' of people in modern societies.

To those who felt that Kropotkin represented humans and animals in 'too favourable an aspect', that the sociable qualities of humans and other animals were overemphasized to the neglect of their anti-social and 'self-asserting instincts', he responded by asserting that 'we already have had too much of this view of nature and man as red in tooth and claw'. It was now, he added, high time to stress the:

> overwhelming importance which sociable habits play in Nature and in the progressive evolution of both animal species and human beings; to prove that they secure to animals a better protection from their enemies, very often facilities for getting food (winter provisions, migrations, etc.), longevity, and therefore a greater facility for the development of intellectual faculties; and that they have given to men, in addition to the same advantages, the possibility of working out those institutions which have enabled mankind to survive in its harsh struggle against Nature.[8]

From the late 1860s onwards, Kropotkin relentlessly argued that cooperation rather than competitive struggle was the guiding principle of evolution. First published in pamphlet form and in academic journals, his thoughts on the relationships between evolutionary theory and modern anarchism were subsequently collated in his major 1902 treatise, *Mutual Aid: A Factor in Evolution*. This was to become a canonical text of 'scientific anarchism', and remains to this day one of the most widely consulted anarchist works. As he was at pains to point out, this work was about 'the law of Mutual Aid viewed as one of the chief factors of evolution'. It was not intended as a discussion of '*all* factors of evolution and their respective values'. To those who argued that anarchists expected too much from human nature, he replied:

> whatever the immoral acts of isolated men may be, the moral sense of mankind will perforce instinctively live in humanity so long as the human species does not enter a period of decay … in the necessary reaction of men against the anti-sociable actions of some of them, lies the force which preserves the moral sense and the moral habits of human societies, as it preserves sociability and a certain habit of self-restraint. In all social animals … this force is infinitely more powerful than the orders of any religion, or any lawmakers.[9]

Kropotkin insisted that the 'no-government' system of socialism was not a dream that could only be realized in the distant future. Neither was it a stage to be reached only after other stages had been passed through. It was, he insisted, the product of 'processes of life everywhere about us, which we may advance or hold back'.[10] He also maintained that the 'no-government' system of socialism, i.e. anarcho-communism, was the outgrowth of the two great movements of political and economic thought that characterized the second half of the nineteenth century. In common with all socialists, he believed that the private ownership of land, capital and the means of production had 'had its time', and that private property was fated to disappear. Secondly he believed that government also was fated to disappear once 'all requisites for production' became the common property of society, to be managed solely by the producers of wealth. Having claimed mutual aid and sociability as the legitimate basis for the moral growth and development of individuals as well as societies, Kropotkin then went on to argue that competition between members of the same species, whether human or animal, was not in their best interests. Competition, he declared, did not create the conditions whereby meaningful progress could occur. To counteract accusations from those who still considered anarchists utopians, he set out to demonstrate that the anarcho-communist society of the future would ultimately be the product of 'tendencies that are apparent now in society and may indicate its future evolution'.[11] Finally, in response to those who accused him of placing too much faith in evolutionary theory and too little in revolutionary action, he called on his fellow anarchists to actively 'promote their ideas directly amongst the labour organizations to induce those unions to a direct struggle against capital, without placing their faith in parliamentary legislation'.[12] This was particularly important in the latter half of the nineteenth century when hegemonic ideas about social change and political progress stressed the contribution of self-assertion, competition and struggle to the ethos of capitalism, and to the growth and assertion of imperial, and neo-imperial, authority in the global arena.

In emphasizing the historical 'depth' of associationism and anti-authoritarian mutualism, Kropotkin sought to transform anarchism into a legitimate political project. He offered his version of scientific anarchism as an alternative to the political violence and social chaos with which, rightly or wrongly, their enemies associated anarchists throughout much of its history. Contrary to the conventional caricatures of anarchists, Kropotkin insisted that they were not opposed to all manifestations of authority. They rejected only the specific forms of authority associated with hierarchy and socio-economic privilege.[13] While recognizing the many varieties of anarchism, he stressed that they all shared a common characteristic that distinguished them from other political creeds. In proclaiming the illegitimacy of 'the principle of authority in social organizations', anarchists of all hues professed a mutual 'hatred of all constraints that originate in institutions founded on this principle'.[14] This opposition to the principle of authority extended equally to anarchist activists and to philosophers of anarchism. Regardless of their status or the calibre of their political thinking, no individual anarchist or group of anarchists was permitted to formulate a libertarian 'creed' that might foster the development of canonical thinking. Neither could they devise an anarchist 'catechism' that might hamper freedom of action in the present or in the future. It was for this reason that the majority of anarchists objected to any close identification of anarchism with its best-known theorists and writers, including Bakunin, Kropotkin, Malatesta, Tolstoy and Élisée Reclus. Unlike Marxism, Marxist-Leninism and Maoism, anarchists did not canonize those who devoted their lives to the cause of the stateless society.

Basing his anarchism on the 'scientific' evidence for sociability and mutual aid in nature and human society, Kropotkin maintained that social convention and historical tradition were also foundations upon which egalitarian, self-governing societies could be constructed. Indeed, for Kropotkin, social custom and historical tradition were analogous to instinctual behaviour in the animal world. He also demonstrated that social change in human society had clear parallels with evolutionary change in organic nature. Having demonstrated that mutualism and sociability were important factors of evolution in the pre-scientific past, he went on to suggest that they would be infinitely more important in the future, particularly if underpinned by a new humanism based on anarchist principles and scientific research that served the common good rather than the sectional interests of any one class or the authoritarian state.

The historical legitimacy of mutualism

The continued survival of Russia's landed aristocracy following the abolition of serfdom in 1861 encouraged Kropotkin's initial search for a stateless alternative to the state-centred projects of Russia's emerging communist left and the authoritarian right. As he saw it, anarchism was not only a realistic political alternative to the authoritarian state – it was also a sustainable socio-economic and ecological alternative to the processes of capitalist modernization then sweeping across Europe. In emphasizing the historical and political legitimacy of anarchism, in redefining it as an anti-authoritarian expression of mutual aid and cooperation, Kropotkin rescued it from the dust heap of history and relocated it firmly within the Western intellectual tradition. In so doing he showed that, far from being a utopian dream, anarchism was a socially progressive historical force that could be harnessed by anti-authoritarian movements in the present to construct more truly democratic and sustainable communities in the future. In realigning anti-authoritarianism with traditions of mutualism and cooperation, in portraying anarchism as a progressive historical force, he emphasized the intellectual legitimacy of anarchism at a time when most anarchists were perceived as agents of social and political chaos. Thus, he suggested, the 'no-government' ideal of modern anarchists was a legitimate ideal that had the sanction of evolutionary theory. It also had the sanction of historical and anthropological research that testified to the importance of powerful traditions of sociability and mutual aid in societies past and present.

There were obvious strengths and weakness in Kropotkin's argument that anarchism derived its political legitimacy from manifestations of sociability and mutual aid in a variety of social settings, including rural communities, medieval cities, urban communes, clans, craft guilds and medieval townships. He refused to limit his search for evidence of sociability to the narrow ground of the nineteenth century, or to the very obvious achievements of modern syndicalism and the trade union movement. By emphasizing the historical longevity of mutual aid 'tendencies', both within Europe and among 'primitive' tribes in Africa, North America and South East Asia, he demonstrated the centrality of these 'tendencies' to the historic evolution of humankind.[15] In so doing he challenged the cruder aspects of historical and environmental determinism by demonstrating that mutual aid and cooperation enabled communities to confront enormous social and environmental challenges in some of the world's harshest environments.

Nevertheless Kropotkin's appeal to custom and tradition as a suitable basis for developing the stateless society of the future ignored the harmful effects of social custom and historical tradition on intellectual development and personal freedom. Even in his day, historical and anthropological evidence clearly demonstrated that the idealization of peasant society, rural traditions and archaic social customs had severely hampered individual initiative and progress. It had clearly also fostered the development of a deep-seated conservatism that was particularly detrimental to women within patriarchal societies and families. That said, as someone who was extremely familiar with village life in rural Russia, Kropotkin insisted that the 'narrowness' of the village milieu need not hinder personal development. In a letter to Nettalu in the spring of 1902 he wrote:

In the communal life in Russia, I knew people who, while remaining what the Russians called *mirskoi chelovek* (a communal man) in the fullest sense, were also individual personalities breaking with all the narrowness of their village and continuing alone, isolated on *their* way

– whether that involved an individual political revolt or a personal revolt or a moral revolt or a revolt against religion.[16]

Even a writer of the stature of his beloved Goethe, he claimed, would not have found work within a small community detrimental to his artistic development. Instead, he asserted, he 'would have been a delight to his fellow workers; he would have brought with him so much enthusiasm, gaiety, zest, and a sociable and communist spirit'. At the same time, he claimed, Goethe, with his 'great personal poetry or philosophy', would even have 'gained from the enjoyment of ordinary things in a communal *work*, while learning about a new aspect of the human genius (consider his joy in discovering mutual reliance!). His whole being and personality having developed in this new direction, another aspect would have been added to his genius'.[17] Yet Kropotkin certainly ignored the fact that historical traditions from the past were often revived – even reinvented – in the present for the precise purpose of confining women to the domestic sphere, or otherwise limiting their autonomy. Thus while he was deeply impressed with the manner in which pre-colonial communities of 'savages' governed themselves, he completely ignored the sexist bias in the decision-making processes of many of these societies. Referring to the Kabyles of North Africa, who knew 'no authority whatever besides that of the *djemmâa*, or folkmote of the village community', he described how:

All men of age take part in it, in the open air … and the decisions of the *djemmâa* are evidently taken at unanimity: that is all discussions continue until all present agree to accept, or to submit to, some decision. There being no authority in a village community to impose a decision, this system has been practiced by mankind wherever there have been village communities, and it is practiced wherever they continue to exist, i.e. by several hundred million men all over the world.[18]

For all his efforts to transform anarchism into a progressive force of history, Kropotkin also paid scant attention to the mutual aid strategies of women, even though these often sustained whole communities and contributed to the social and economic survival of entire societies. Despite the fact that 'women's work' had for centuries has been characterized by a high degree of sociability and mutual cooperation, the vast majority of his examples of mutual aid in action referred to the working worlds of men. Discussing the political gulf that opened up between young and old in Russia in the 1870s, he described how 'young liberals' were entirely alienated from their fathers and older brothers. Nevertheless, he added, this 'youthful band ... of young men had merely taken to heart, and had tried to realize in life, the intellectual inheritance of those same fathers and brothers'.[19] Kropotkin, however, was no feminist, and was regularly criticized by Emma Goldman for his sexist views on the role of women in the revolutionary process. Thus he described how young women students:

> *went about as typical Nihilists, with their short cropped hair, disdaining crinoline, and betraying their democratic spirit in all their behaviour ... The real secret of their wise and fully successful attitude was that none of the women who were the soul of that movement were mere 'feminists',* desirous to get their share of the privileged positions in society and the State. The sympathy of most of them were with the masses ... The rights they strove for – both the leaders and the great bulk of the women – were not only the individual right to higher instruction, but much more, far more, the right to be useful workers among the people, the masses. This was why they succeeded to such an extent.[20]

The authenticity of Russian anarchism

We have already seen that even as a youth Kropotkin was possessed of a powerful will to serve that was matched only by his desire to comprehend and to change the world into which he was born. From an early age also he considered the unpretentious and 'organic' civilization of rural Russia as infinitely superior to the 'inauthentic' cultural expressions of Western capitalism. Yet like Tolstoy, he was appalled by the backwardness and poverty of communities of peasant households known as the Mir that continued to survive throughout the nineteenth century. Even as late as the mid nineteenth century, these communities elected their own officials and controlled access to common land, local fisheries, forests and hunting grounds. Impressed by their historic resilience and socialist potential, Kropotkin cautiously regarded them as social foundations upon which the edifice of the stateless society of the future could be constructed. However, even throughout the seventeenth and eighteenth centuries, as peasants had become increasingly enserfed and subject to the authority of powerful landowners, it was clear that their scope for self-government had been greatly restricted. By the mid nineteenth century the Mir system of village government had been reduced to a shadow of its former self across large tracts of western Russia. Following the abolition of serfdom in 1861, the tsarist state retained an emasculated version of the Mir as a system of communal land tenure and transformed it into an administrative organ of the state. This placed thousands of previously autonomous and extremely impoverished rural communities within the 'iron cage' of the tsarist state. It also locked them into a nationwide network of authoritarian control, thereby reducing their elected officials to the status of state functionaries and tax collectors. Pan-nationalist Slavophiles and conservative landowners alike were supporters of the emasculated Russian Mir.[21] Both groups regarded peasant villages as the guardians of Old Russian values and repositories of the country's ancestral rural wisdom. To the landed nobility, the cult of the simple peasant was predicated on deeply conservative notions of the moral purity and natural humility of peasants. As paragons of Russian virtue, the uneducated poor could also be mobilized in counter-revolutionary struggles to preserve tsarist hegemony and protect Russia from 'foreign' influences emanating not only from Western Europe, but also from Russia's larger cities. Thus the leading protagonist in Pushkin's classic, *Boris Govunov*, urged the Russian poor 'to remain silent' while the tsar and the nobility maintained control over all aspects of social life in the Russian countryside.[22] However, the traditional Mir system also attracted the attention of the revolutionary Narodniks, not least small groups of Russian anarchists who regarded the reinvigorated Mir as a potential building block of a revitalized anarcho-communist society. Echoing the Romanticism of European intellectuals, writers like Kropotkin, Tolstoy, Herzen and Gorky suggested that the 'wild places' and humble inhabitants of feudal Russia could contribute to the revival of their country's spirit.[23] This, they suggested, would provide rural Russia with the *lebensraum* it needed to survive in the struggle against an alien modernity. Kropotkin's stress on the traditional rural collective as the basis of a future revolutionary order underwent significant change in the aftermath of the Paris Commune. After 1871, he also recognized the revolutionary potential of the urban collective in the social order of modern anarchism.

The more firmly Russian identity was rooted in the 'pure' landscapes of peasant Russia, the more anarchists like Kropotkin and Tolstoy regarded the rural poor as legitimate role models for their new stateless society. They both felt that the resilience of mutual aid and other rural-based expressions of sociability would enable petty agriculturalists, and a whole range of marginalized craft workers, to resist the homogenizing forces of capitalism and the centralizing forces of the modern state. From the Slavophiles of the 1830s to the Narodniks of the 1870s, many of the radical sons, and daughters, of the nobility 'worshipped at the altar of the peasantry'.[24] For Kropotkin, the villages of his childhood were not simply havens of rural simplicity – they were living proof of the importance of mutual aid and self-government to the survival and independence of rural communities. For that reason, he suggested, they were more sustainable than the urban conglomerations that were even then cropping up all across the country, including in the remote corners of his cherished Siberia. If the Mir was a potential building block of an anarcho-communist society for Kropotkin, his country's budding cities were parasitic accretions on an otherwise productive landscape. Homes to the idle and aristocratic rich, they were also dens of iniquity that reeked with the deceit and vanity of the wealthy on the one hand, and the stench of poverty on the other. These sprawling towns and cities were increasingly also overburdened with growing numbers of petty officials, government employees, administrative workers and clerical workers, all of whom leeched off the more productive countryside. Thus Kropotkin's anarchism could be regarded in part as a last-ditch attempt to halt the penetration of the state into the internal affairs of self-governing autonomous communities perched between the twin peaks of a rural past and an industrialized future. He sought to defend, and extend, the social and political autonomy of self-governing communities just as the state was initiating a whole series of agricultural reforms, which by the opening years of the twentieth century had forced millions of peasants to leave their rural communes for the city. Those left behind set about privatizing the land and other resources they had previously worked in common. Nevertheless, far from romancing the past, or favouring the asceticism of 'stone age' economics, Kropotkin sought to encourage the elected members of the Mir to extend the scope of self-government to local control over educational policy, vocational training and applied research. Rather than halt the present, or seek a simple *rapprochement* between the past and the present, he wished to inform the rural inhabitants of nineteenth-century Russia, and Europe, of the very real achievements of subaltern communities in the past. This, he argued, would not only draw them closer to the stateless society of the future – it would also enable them to reach the future through the past.

Kropotkin's youthful desire to be 'useful', like his 'urge to serve', was certainly in accord with the populist Narodnik tradition of 'going to the people' to win the hearts of the peasantry. Convinced of the moral superiority of the peasantry, unlike their Marxist counterparts, Kropotkin, Tolstoy and Bakunin were among the more prominent anarchist leaders who regarded the rural poor as a revolutionary force capable of forging autonomous egalitarian societies of the future. Together with Alexander Herzen and Nikolai Chernyshevsky – both of whom, as we have already seen, influenced his thinking while he was a young military cadet – Kropotkin believed that Russia's peasants were also imbued with the spirit of a natural socialism. In calling for the abolition of oligarchy and an end to autocracy, he believed that Russia could bypass industrial capitalism and the proletarian revolution to become a fully fledged socialist, stateless society. Unlike state-centred revolutionaries who considered the seizure of power as an indispensable prelude to the radical transformation of society, Kropotkin advocated a decentralized form of agrarian communism organized on the basis of autonomous communities and townships with collective ownership of land, factories and workshops. The most striking characteristic of the group of intellectuals with whom he identified was not their inventiveness. It was the seriousness with which they adopted the ideas of others and incorporated them into a '*mission civilatrice*' to end social and political oppression in Russia. In seeking to reunite the educated elite with the common people, they struggled to 're-knit the torn ethnic and civic fabric of Russian society … and thereby create a Russia that was both more humane and more authentically Russian'.[25]

Although often used interchangeably, the terms 'intellectual' and 'intelligentsia' should not be confused in relation to nineteenth-century Russia. Unlike intellectuals, who were educated in prestigious state colleges and military academies, the members of Russia's intelligentsia were generally drawn from the *raznochinsty*, i.e. 'the people of sundry ranks'. From the 1860s onwards, many of these '*intelligents*', including Kropotkin, were bound together in loose intellectual 'brotherhoods' dedicated to the cause of the *narod*, or 'the people'.[26] One such group, to which Herzen, belonged was described as 'a militant order of knights which had no written charter [but nevertheless] stood athwart the whole current of contemporary life'.[27] The chivalric and cabalistic qualities of the members of these brotherhoods owed much to their youth, love of intrigue, shared political convictions and radical civic mindedness. Thus, unlike the more conservative graduates of the military academies and universities, the radical '*intelligentry*' with which Kropotkin was clearly affiliated were not entirely alienated from the rest of Russian society. Like Kropotkin, they were imbued with a strong desire to serve. In disowning the inactivity and narrow sense of service of their militaristic fathers, many of the new men and women of Kropotkin's generation repudiated the authority of the tsarist state and were opposed to the inauthentic lifestyles of their social peers. For that reason they dedicated themselves to a whole variety of political causes, including socialism, anarchism, Marxism and the utilitarian doctrines of Bentham and Mill.[28] In abandoning a world where military rank and service to the state defined social status, young men like Kropotkin were also revolting against the narrower service ethos of the tsarist state. This was not a new development. Earlier in the mid nineteenth century, the more liberal landowners had established schools, set up banks to extend limited amounts of credit to the rural poor, encouraged monasteries to provide food when harvests failed, reduced levies imposed on peasants on their estates, and generally dedicated themselves to the cause of rural reform. Thus their estates became much more than economic units, mere islands of aristocratic privilege in a sea of peasant poverty. They were veritable experimental stations for testing new ways of relating to the land, places where the enlightened nobility practised social and environmental engineering.

The liberal intelligentsia from whom Kropotkin derived so much inspiration for his 'scientific anarchism' was not confined to social reformers. Some, like the proto-nationalist Slavophiles and Panslavs, sought to bridge the gap between the elites and the masses by emphasizing the affinity between informal discussion circles, or *kruzhki*, and Russia's village communes. A major goal of anarchist education was to cultivate in the young a love of Russia's landscapes, history, customs and language, and to nurture an appreciation for truth, honesty and hard work. For many members of the intelligentsia, the Russian Orthodox Church had long ceased to be a spiritual authority to be respected. The more radical among them considered themselves superior to the clergy, many of whom were as illiterate as the peasants, while the aristocracy tended to be apathetic about religion and their religious devotions were often merely notional. In order to eliminate disparities in education, mental habits and social dispositions, the liberal intelligentsia set up 'communes of thinkers' whose members were willing to subordinate their own tastes and passions in the interests of the common good. Writing in the 1860s, Herzen described one such circle as follows:

> They were bound by a common religion, common language and even more – by a common hatred. Those for whom that religion was not a matter of life and death gradually fell away, while others appeared in their place, and both our thought and our circle were strengthened by this free play of selective affinities and of binding shared conviction.[29]

Nevertheless, despite such liberal influences, when Kropotkin graduated from the Corps of Pages in 1862 he had not yet professed himself an anarchist. 'At that age', he commented in his memoirs, 'what else could I be but a constitutionalist?'[30] In other words he sought to reform rather than overthrow the tsarist state, believing that the tsar alone could initiate the process of reform by diverting state funds wasted on court life towards the improvement of rural life. Indeed Kropotkin was still enthralled with Tsar Nicholas II, especially following the emancipation of the serfs. As a court aide in the palace of the tsar he

> looked upon Alexander II as a sort of hero; a man who attached no importance to the court ceremonies, but who ... began his working day at six in the morning, and was engaged in a hard struggle with a powerful reactionary party in order to carry through a series of reforms in which the abolition of the serfs was only the first step.[31]

While critical of 'the foolish expenses of the court, and the sums of money which were spent at Nice to keep a squadron of the navy in attendance on the dowager Empress', Kropotkin still found time to defend Tsar Alexander from his opponents. He hoped that he might become an enlightened 'philosopher king' who could initiate social and political reform from on high.[32] This defence of the tsar could sometimes take the form of a eulogy that attributed his failings to 'the ill advice' he received from 'unreformed tribunals' and corrupt members of urban municipalities. Thus, despite his criticisms of the tsarist state and its hierarchical institutions, Kropotkin at this stage of his intellectual development was unwilling to renounce the values of the regime that had nurtured him. On graduating from military college, he served for one year as personal page to Tsar Alexander. Fascinated by the magnificence and refinement of courtly life, he subsequently recalled how his position as 'an actor in court ceremonies, in attendance upon the chief personages, offered something more than the mere interest of curiosity for a boy of my age'.[33] It was not until several years after he left the Corps of Pages that his disillusionment with the tsarist regime became so great that it caused him to lose faith in the state's developmental potential. Far from being a nineteenth-century equivalent of James Dean, in revolt against all forms of patriarchal authority, he was still steeped in the militarism of Russia's social and political life. His anarchism was never simply an individualistic revolt against expressions of authority and abuses of power. It developed instead from a mature intellectual engagement with the sciences, particularly with Darwinism and an entire range of academic disciplines.

In an overtly psychoanalytical explanation of his conversion to anarchism, George Woodcock has suggested that the young Kropotkin's experiences of the wasteful extravagances of court life were responsible for cultivating his 'innate puritanism'. It was this that caused the 'proto-anarchist' to 'shrink from the profligacy of courtly life'.[34] However it could more convincingly be argued that Kropotkin's secular puritanism and his disillusionment with court life were also products of a sustained critique of the tsarist state, and of the tsar's authority, by a man who was on the verge of become a leading anarchist intellectual. They were never simply the personal traits of a privileged youth who found the excesses of court life distasteful. Autobiographical and psychoanalytical approaches to the influences on Kropotkin's development as an anarchist are perhaps more useful in explaining what he opposed than what he supported. His anarchism derived much of its legitimacy from images of nationhood generated in the egalitarian discussion circles of young Russian intellectuals in the first half of the nineteenth century. Indeed he went a step further than most socialists in calling for the formation of anarchist communes that would remain out of reach of the authoritarian state. These were to be egalitarian communities wherein no distinction was to exist between intellectual and manual labour. While his earliest anarchist inclinations were partially distilled from his youthful experiences of militarism, patriarchy, serfdom, tsarism and general abuses of authority, they were always and essentially political in nature.

Scientific anarchism versus political violence

From the 1870s through to the opening years of the twentieth century, small groups of anarchists with no clear organizational structure, often consisting of only two or three people, were established throughout Europe and Russia. Many of their members were determined to demonstrate their utter contempt for both aristocratic and bourgeois society through acts of political violence and self-immolation, the ultimate act of political defiance. This has made it difficult to distinguish between the devoted anarchist militant who was motivated by a passion for social justice, and the shadowy psychopath whose 'voices' may have prompted him to take his own private revenge on society. Inevitably, therefore, prominent anarchists, including Kropotkin, Bakunin and Malatesta, were suspected of inspiring outrages of which they may not have approved, or even have been aware. Police agents and provocateurs regularly infiltrated these groups, setting up their own false anarchist cells in order to trap unwary activists. The French police even ran an anarchist newspaper, and the Italian government maintained agents in Paris who 'reported to their shocked and fascinated superiors lurid details of anarchist orgies devoted to the practice of free love and anarchist plots'.[35] Even by today's standards, the number of attacks on prominent political leaders from 1880 to 1914 was striking. While anarchists were by no means responsible for all of these, the techniques used were often similar to those approved by them. The assassinations of the Tsar Nicholas II in 1881, and the Archduke Franz Ferdinand in 1914, are two of the more famous examples. The murders of President Carnot of France and President William McKinley of the United States, and the assassinations of such notables as the empress of Austria, the king of Italy, the Prime Minster of Spain, and numerous unsuccessful attempts on the lives of other sovereigns, reflected an anarchist faith in the immediate and apocalyptic value of political assassination as a legitimate strategy for removing symbols of authority from the political landscape. There were those who regarded the assassination of a monarch or other powerful figure of authority as a legitimate strategy for hastening the withering away of the state. Although Kropotkin strongly rebuked those who used political violence to achieve their anarchist objectives, he believed violence was justified in certain circumstances, and that it might even be the only way to achieve revolution. Writing to an English friend in 1893, he stated:

We may say that revenge is no aim in itself. Surely, it is not. But it is *human* and all revolts have borne and for a long time will bear the character. In fact, *we* have not suffered from the persecutions as they, the workers, suffered; we who, in our houses, seclude ourselves from the cry and sight of human sufferings, *we are no judges* of those who live in the midst of all this suffering ... Personally, I hate these explosions, but I cannot stand as a judge to condemn those who are driven to despair.[36]

Thus Kropotkin believed that 'in order to conquer, something more than guillotines are required'. The revolutionary *idea*, rather than political violence, would, he argued, reduce the enemies of workers and peasants to impotence by 'paralysing all the instruments by which they have governed hitherto'. The role of the people in any revolutionary struggle, he added, 'ought to be positive at the same time as it is destructive'. Anarchists, he insisted, preferred to trust in the natural rebelliousness of the 'risen people', rather than allowing them to be led by violent revolutionaries or dissident intellectuals. However, he was equally determined to ensure that revenge 'must not be erected into a *theory*' and argued that no one had the right to incite others to political violence.[37] Nevertheless he believed that if those who experienced 'hell' in their daily lives were driven to perform 'desperate' acts to achieve some political end as a result, they should only be judged by their peers who experienced these same 'pariah's sufferings'. In a political pamphlet on anarchist morality published in 1898 he wrote:

By proclaiming our morality of equality, or anarchism, we refuse to assume a right which moralists have always taken upon themselves to claim, that of mutilating the individual in the name of social justice ... All this it must be understood, is not completely applicable until the great sources of moral depravity – capitalism, religion, law, government – shall have ceased to exist.[38]

Kropotkin's abiding fear was that anarchists, like other revolutionaries, might be forced to adopt the same methods that the state used to oppress them against the state that they sought to dismantle. Thus in *The Great French Revolution* he insisted that 'terrorism is always a method of government', and 'revolutionary government' was a contradiction in terms.[39] Yet, unlike Tolstoy and Gandhi, he did not subscribe to the view that non-violence should become a foundational principle of political action. There were times, he argued, when class warfare and political violence could be considered the lesser evil. This was why his support for the allied cause in the First World War was not inconsistent with his otherwise ambiguous views on political violence. Although he never met Kropotkin, Tolstoy, aware of his ambivalent position on violence, stated that 'His arguments in favour of violence do not seem to be the expression of his opinions, but only of his fidelity to the banner under which he has served so honestly all his life.'[40]

Print media and the legitimization of anarchism

Ten years after graduating from the military academy Kropotkin was already promoting his version of 'scientific anarchism' as a rational alternative to the political violence that was to plague anarchists on both sides of the Atlantic throughout the late nineteenth century and early twentieth. His anarchism was also a political strategy that could be used to defend the most marginalized and subordinate sectors of European society from the frontal attacks of the capitalist revolution then sweeping aside centuries-old plebeian traditions that contributed to the survival of the moral economies of peasants, craft workers and urban and rural workers. His letters to *The Times*, together with articles in such prestigious publications as the *Encyclopaedia Britannica*, *The Nineteenth Century* and *The Journal of the Royal Geographical Society* were respected throughout the academic world. Yet from the 1870s onwards Kropotkin was relentless in questioning the very structures and values of the modern state at a time when capitalism and colonialism were literally reordering the face of the earth from the steppes of Russia to the Pacific Coast of the Americas. While he eschewed religious doctrines and metaphysics and adopted the mantle of the scientist to defend the legitimacy of anarchism, he also resisted the temptations of erudite theorizing and refused to join the educational establishment. A neglected figure in most accounts of intellectual history, his teachings could be an important source of inspiration for those still opposed to contemporary expressions of authoritarian governance and globalization. His *Mutual Aid* (1902), together with William Godwin's *An Enquiry Concerning Political Justice* (1793) and Pierre-Joseph Proudhon's *The General Idea of the Revolution in the Nineteenth Century* (1851), which are still ranked among anarchism's most important texts, deserve far more attention than they currently receive.

In the closing decades of the nineteenth century he continued to make a number of important contributions to scientific journalism. He also set about outlining the principles of anarchist communism in political pamphlets, left-wing newspapers and radical periodicals. Believing that the left-wing press in much of Europe was controlled by socialists who put their faith in socialist parties advocating the takeover rather than the abolition of the state, Kropotkin now adopted the new tactic of 'the propaganda of the deed'. Henceforth his real forte would always be *'propagande par le mot'*.[41] For Kropotkin, the political pamphlet was not just a means of communication, but a weapon of class warfare. His preference for the pamphlet over the scholarly monograph was rooted in the culture of plebeian politics. More specifically, it stemmed from his conviction that left-wing books and scholarly monographs only contained 'scientific arguments in favour of socialist aspirations'. They provided no understanding as to 'how workers accepted socialist ideas, and how they could put them into practice'. He preferred political pamphlets because they were 'written for workers for whom one penny is money'.[42] They also gave Kropotkin a deeper understanding of working-class lives, including the authentic thinking of radical craft workers and the emergent working class. Thus he argued they provided insights into 'what cannot be found anywhere else – namely, the depth of thought and the moral force of the movement, the degree to which men are imbued with the new theories, their readiness to carry them out in their daily life and to suffer for them'. Kropotkin recognized that the medium was the message, and that the message essentially was political.

Political pamphlets of course also presented him with opportunities to shape radical social thought. Like the political activists and radical pamphleteers of Winstanley's England, Kropotkin regarded the inexpensive pamphlet as an 'enabling' medium that allowed him to popularize his anarchist teachings. Ever since they first began to appear in the 1870s, his pamphlets sold in the hundreds of thousands in practically every European language, especially French, English and Spanish. After their translation into Chinese and Japanese they also circulated throughout Asia, and became available in Sweden and Germany in the aftermath of the First World War. A complete bibliography of his writings, extending to more than 500 titles, was published in 1926. Kropotkin's pamphlets did not simply address issues pertinent to revolutionary struggles in his own lifetime – as Baldwin has suggested, they made 'a lasting contribution to thought in the confused conflicts which mark the long transition to a socialist economy *and to the freedoms which lie in and beyond it*'.[43] Two of Kropotkin's major works, *Paroles d'un Révolté* and *The Conquest of Bread*, initially appeared as articles in *Le Révolté*. *Fields, Factories and Workshops* began life as a series of articles in *The Nineteenth Century* between 1888 and 1890. This prestigious journal, founded by Sir James Knowles in 1877, fostered debate on major issues in modern society. Impressed with the scope of his readings and the global range of his references, a reviewer in *The Times* credited Kropotkin with 'a genuine scientific temper'. Seminal political pamphlets such as *An Appeal to the Young*, *Revolutionary Government* and *The Spirit of Revolt* also made their appearance in the popular print media. His influential pamphlet, *Anarchist Communism*, described by Baldwin as 'the simplest, clearest statement of the case for free communism', made its earliest appearance as two articles in 1887 in *The Nineteenth Century*.[44] In 1905, he penned another scholarly article on anarchism for the eleventh edition of *The Encyclopaedia Britannica*. This represented the most succinct statement ever published in the English language on the historical development and political legitimacy of modern anarchism.

From the 1870s onwards, therefore, Kropotkin set about defending the scientific legitimacy of anarcho-communism in political pamphlets and the liberal press. In 1879, eight years after the violent suppression of the Paris Commune, he founded the anarcho-communist journal, *Le Révolté*. Partially funded by his fellow geographer and anarchist, Élisée Reclus, this journal rapidly acquired a substantial readership in Switzerland and southern France, particularly in and around Lyon. Right from the start, Kropotkin filled it with scholarly articles on social and economic issues written in a style that appealed to intelligent workers. He immediately set out to make *Le Révolté* 'moderate in tone but revolutionary in substance', using it to enhance the political legitimacy of anarchism. Kropotkin, who had criticized the lack of concern for serfs and the urban poor in the tsarist Russia of his youth, now lamented the lack of any real human contact between social classes in the industrial cities of Western Europe. While the decades immediately after the Paris Commune were not the most propitious for anarchists and socialists in France and Germany, these years witnessed the emergence of a new breed of social radicals, men and women who imagined alternative ways of living and organizing social and economic life in Europe, and beyond. Thus he used *Le Révolté* to examine the origins of the state, the history of popular protest, the philosophy of anarchism and the principles of anarchist communism. Like the English socialist philosopher and poet, Edward Carpenter, he sought to develop 'a vibrant culture out of a mix of desire, need, and a resolve to ... have a fuller life in the here and now'.[45]

Just as Siberia had taught Kropotkin that mutual aid and cooperation were more important than competition and struggle in the survival of species, his encounters with working-class radicals, ex-Communards and the famous watchmakers of the Jura mountains convinced him that mutual cooperation had for centuries been a fundamental principle of social life in Europe. Although he came to these conclusions early in his career as a revolutionary activist, he did not develop their 'scientific' basis until the mid 1880s, when, settled in England, he set about unearthing the historical roots and scientific foundations of anarcho-communism. Kropotkin's life in England after 1886 was respectable and scholarly, and over the next 30 years or so he became an advisor and philosopher to the entire anarchist movement. In describing what could be termed his 'English period', Woodcock has suggested that his arrival in England 'marked the end of his life as an explorer and a revolutionary'. Thus he added:

It is true that he participated in the English anarchist movement, helping to found the periodical *Freedom* and *The Freedom Group* ... he also went on occasional lecture tours in England and even, on two occasions, in North America, and he took part in the foundation of a number of Russian exile periodicals. But these activities were sporadic, and he never again assumed the role of militant leader that he had occupied during the editorship of *Le Révolté*. Rather he tended to retire into a life of the scholarly theoretician, combining a considera-tion of the wider, sociological aspects of anarchism with a return to his former scientific interests. For long periods he lived in the seclusion of distant suburbs, where he cultivated gardens that were the envy of his neighbours and kept an open house at week-ends to a succession of visitors, including not only fellow geographers and anarchist comrades, but also English radicals and intellectuals of many types.[46]

It could equally be argued that this was the period when Kropotkin became anarchism's 'great prophetic savant', its most articulate theorist and scholar. His *Memoirs of a Revolutionist* and his monographs on anarcho-communist society, anarchist economics and anarchist development theory were readily accepted as classics in their respective genres. Unlike Godwin, Kropotkin was always proud to call himself an anarchist, despite the negative connotations that the term reacquired following the violent suppression of the Paris Commune. Whereas Proudhon distrusted revolutionaries because they could stir up 'anarchy' in the pejorative sense, Kropotkin welcomed revolution because it could liberate people's suppressed capacity for self-organization. Similarly while nineteenth-century intellectuals might rail against 'the crowd' and dread the imminent arrival of 'universal suffrage', Kropotkin was far more appreciative of the constructive potential of 'the masses'. Thus he wrote:

> give the people a free hand, and in ten days the food service will be conducted with admirable regularity. Only those who have never seen the people hard at work ... can doubt it. Speak of the organizing genius of the 'Great Misunderstood', the people, to those who have seen it in Paris in the days of the barricades, or in London during the great dockers' strike, when half a million of starving folk had to be fed, and they will tell you how superior it is to the official ineptness of Bumbledom.[47]

Unlike Tolstoy, Kropotkin spoke with an authoritative anarchist voice from within the ranks of rural and working-class radicalism. His philosophic treatment of anarchism was to transform it from an irrational reaction to the reasoned authority of the state into a rational response to hierarchical authoritarianism. Throughout his years in England Kropotkin traced the folk roots of anarchism from the slave revolts of ancient Rome, to the peasant risings of medieval Europe, to the political agitation of the Diggers in the English Revolution, to the revolt of the *sans culottes* and *Les Enragés* in the 'Great French Revolution', and to the Paris Commune of 1871.[48] The shear breadth of his thinking distinguished him from most of his anarchist contemporaries. He ranged across such diverse topics as the origins of the state, natural history, criminology and penology, social morality, the ethics of science, economic theory and the historical foundations of European society. With Bakunin's death in 1876,

Kropotkin's writings, together with those of Malatesta and Reclus, became increasingly influential in Spain, France and Italy. It was not long before his version of anarcho-communism, which stipulated that the product as well as the means of production belonged to all, became the accepted ideal of rural anarchists throughout southern Spain and Italy.

While we have little documented evidence of the impact of his writings on peasants and workers elsewhere in Europe in the 1870s and 1880s, Mintz's detailed account of the indigenous roots of rural anarchism in Spain in the opening decades of the twentieth century has shown that inhabitants of the remotest villages in Andalusia were then familiar with Kropotkin's teachings on the social history of mutual aid and cooperation. Together with such literary works as Ibsen's *Enemy of the People* and Anselmo Lorenzo's *Proletariado Militante*, Kropotkin's revolutionary writings were serialized in radical papers like *Tierra y Libertad, El Rebelde* and *La Anarquia y El Productor*. These were read by, or more often to, peasants and workers all across Catalonia, Andalusia, Extremadura and Murcia in the decades before the Spanish Civil War. *The Conquest of Bread* appears to have been a singular success in Andalusia where 'there was not an *obrero consciente*, even among the socialists, who did not know it'.[49] Here, as no doubt also in rural France and Switzerland, plebeian anarchists were highly receptive to Kropotkin's philosophy of anarcho-communism primarily because it accorded well with age-old traditions of mutual cooperation and exchange that enabled the landless poor to combat the inequalities of estate farming and challenge the moral and political authority of landlords. Kropotkin's views on mutual aid and cooperation have acquired even greater legitimacy with the recent publication of David Graeber's exploration of the historical relationships between debt and the entire fabric of social life from prehistoric times onwards. In analysing the history of money, barter, community life, marriage, friendship, greed, commerce, charity, war and government, this iconic study maintains that the informal, community-building indebtedness of 'human economies' in the past has been replaced by the mathematically precise and firmly enforced debt repayment arrangements of the present. This, Graeber argues, has contributed to widespread impoverishment and violence that very few societies have managed to avoid. A major argument of Graeber's work, and one with which Kropotkin would certainly have agreed, is that 'high trust' mutual indebtedness was a major stimulant to trade which also functioned as a social cement that bound communities together across considerable distances.[50]

While Kropotkin and Malatesta were the prime movers in the development of anarchist theory after the death of Bakunin, poor workers and peasants from the 1870s right through to the 1930s were also speaking their own language of anarchism in large areas of Europe, Latin America, China and Japan. Although not uninfluenced by these giants of anarchist theory, theirs was an anarchism that recalled earlier practices of cooperation and communal labour that had been deeply embedded in the global agricultural landscape from as early as the eighth century. Thus Spanish anarchists pointed to the fact that individuals in large tracts of pre-Christian Spain rarely owned landed property, and that land was more often than not farmed by families and entire communities. Agricultural work and harvest yields were similarly shared. Here, as in nineteenth-century Ireland and Scotland, the hereditary plots of individual families were nested within an agreed structure of community relations, and redistributed on a regular basis in order to sustain the quality of the land and the equity of yields. Similarly in the aftermath of the long-drawn-out Reconquista (c.718–1498), townships in the remoter corners of Spain were granted communal rights to encourage new settlers to repopulate lands taken from Moorish peasants and landowners. Indeed the sheer longevity of mutualism and associationism in post-Reconquista Spain goes a long way towards explaining the phenomenal strength of anarchism here long before the eruption of the Spanish Civil War. Following the split between Marx on the one hand and Bakunin and Kropotkin on the other, Spanish revolutionaries preferred the decentralized freedoms of the Russian anarchists to the revolutionary authoritarianism of Marxism, and Marxist-Leninism. In demanding the resuscitation of these networks of cooperation and exchange, plebeian anarchists all across Europe were simply seeking the restoration of primitive forms of rural anarchism and federalism that had been decimated through the privatization of property and the rise of the cash economy and landlordism in the seventeenth and eighteenth centuries. Many townships in southern Spain in particular still retained vestiges of these communal practices well into the twentieth century. Here, as in rural Russia, Ireland, Scotland, France, Italy and Poland, peasant values and rural life itself were often regarded as morally superior to estate farming and landlord systems of landholding. Goods were exchanged and frequently shared; money, always a scarce commodity, played a limited role in the daily lives of the poor; and destitute families shared their dwellings with farm animals, with many families even eating from a single common bowl of food. Social controls were exercised not through government regulation or the church and police surveillance, but through the looser though no less effective channels of gossip, public ridicule and informal practices of social censure.[51]

While Kropotkin always claimed that his anarchism was based on the scientific principles of evolutionary theory, he was also deeply impressed by the grassroots efforts of plebeian leaders to protect the autonomy of rural and working-class communities. Far from being retrogressively focused on the restoration of a lost paradise that never really existed in the first place, his politics, like those of Edward Carpenter and William Morris, reflected a deep longing for free and equal human relations that would enable individuals to develop those aspects of their character denied them under the conditions of one-dimensional capitalism. This in itself posed a major dilemma that confronted all anarchist thinkers – how to imagine an alternative free society without becoming trapped in the process of 'over-prescribing' the form that the stateless society should take. In order to avoid the narrower sectionalism of industrial working-class political protest, Kropotkin, like Carpenter, also sought out novel forms of multi-class fellowship. Thus he wished to overcome the *ennui* of urban life and once and for all end the degradation that was the ubiquitous accompaniment to urban and rural life throughout most of Europe in the final decades of the nineteenth century. To do this he had first to conceive a new 'vocabulary of desire' that made sense to the poor, one that would make the seemingly utopian anarchist alternative to capitalism somehow or other always appear imminent in the present.

The emergence of 'scientific anarchism'

Referring back to the field research he had conducted in Siberia in the 1860s, Kropotkin recalled two aspects of life that 'chiefly impressed' him during his travels in the remotest corners of Russia and Northern Manchuria. In the first place he had been amazed at 'the extreme severity of the struggle for existence which most species of animals have to carry on against an inclement Nature; the enormous destruction of life which periodically results from natural agencies; and the consequent paucity of life over the vast territory which fell under my observation'. Secondly, even in 'those few spots where animal life teemed in abundance', he failed to find, although he 'was eagerly looking for it', that 'bitter struggle for the means of existence, among animals belonging to the same species, which was considered by most Darwinists (though not always by Darwin himself) as the dominant characteristic of struggle for life, and the main factor of evolution'.[52] More than that, his observations of animal life had taught him that 'no progressive evolution of the species can be based upon … periods of keen competition'. At this stage he also began to have serious doubts as to the reality of 'that fearful competition' for food and life within each species. This was an article of faith with most Darwinists, and the dominant part which intense competition was supposed to play in the evolution of new species was repeatedly emphasized in the new writings of Social Darwinists.[53]

In his efforts to provide anarchism with scientific legitimacy, Kropotkin drew heavily on the natural sciences both to challenge Social Darwinists on their own ground and to convince his critics of the centrality of mutual cooperation to the survival of species. However, his analogies with the animal world did not mean that he derived his evidence for sociability and mutual aid from the natural sciences alone. He also appealed to popular experience, and to new research by historians, anthropologists, social scientists and geographers, in order to demonstrate that mutual cooperation was an ever-present feature of all societies. In seeking to make the sciences serve the subordinate rather than the dominant sectors of state societies, he set out to expose the ideological connotations of scientific research and to realign evolutionary theory with the cause of radical social and environmental change. Believing himself to be close to the 'pulse of the present', Kropotkin was also convinced that 'scientific anarchists' were on 'the fast-track' to the future. His writings sought to shape the way people perceived and lived in the world, and to make anarchism acceptable to whole sections of European society.[54] Turning his back on grand theory and the meta-narratives of modernity, he increasingly also turned away from direct confrontations with the authorities of the state. Like Morris and Carpenter, he was a utopian only to the extent that he regarded politics as a means to an end, the end being a radically new way of relating to and living in the world. Together with Reclus, he demanded the 'suppression of privilege and the recognition of right', because 'it pleased them not to live' if the 'enjoyments of life' were to be theirs alone. In 1884, Reclus protested against his good fortune if he could not share it with others, adding that:

> it is sweeter for us to wander with the wretched and the outcasts than to sit, crowned with roses, at the banquets of the rich. We are weary of these inequalities which make us the enemies of each other; we would put an end to the furies which are ever bringing people into hostile collision, and all of which arise from the bondage of the weak to the strong under the form of slavery, serfage and service. After so much hatred we long to love each other, and for this reason are we enemies of private property and despisers of the law.[55]

Turning his attention to the links between Darwinism and modern sociology, Kropotkin could not agree with the standard view that the 'struggle for the means of existence of every man against all other men was "a law of Nature"'. He rejected this Hobbesian view of the human condition, both because it assumed 'a pitiless inner war for life within each species', and because it made an intense struggle for existence a condition of social progress. This, he insisted, was a hypothetical proposition that had never been proven, still less was it based on 'direct observation' of organic nature. Kropotkin criticized this view of primitive men 'as wild beasts living in small isolated families and fighting one another for their food and womenfolk, till a kindly authority settled in their midst in order to enforce peace'. Such was the force of 'established prejudice', he added, that even a 'learned Darwinian' like Huxley failed to see that 'society, far from having been created by man, existed among animals long before his appearance on earth'. Thus he added:

> As long ago as those remote ages, which are lost in the dark night of the Glacial period, man lived in societies. And in these societies a whole series of institutions were worked out and rigidly observed to make possible life in common. And later on, through the whole course of human evolution, the same creative power of the nameless multitudes always worked out new forms of social life, of mutual aid, of guarantees of peace, as soon as new conditions arose.[56]

Nevertheless belief in the 'natural perversity' of man remained an item of the teaching establishment throughout Europe in the closing decades of the nineteenth century. Thus he stated:

The state in its schools and universities maintained, and continues to maintain, the same faith in the natural perversity of man. Its teachers and professors everywhere teach the necessity of having a power above man, and of implanting a moral element in society by means of punishment, inflicted for violation of 'moral law'. ... If left to themselves [they argue], human beings would revert to savagery; that without authority men would eat one another; for nothing, they say, can be expected of the 'multitude' but brutishness and the warring of each against all. Men would perish if above them soared not the elect: the priest and the judge, with their two helpmates – the policeman and the hangman. These saviours prevent, we are told, the battle of all against all ... they teach discipline, and lead men with a high hand, till nobler conceptions shall be developed in their 'hardened hearts', so that the whip, the prison, and the scaffold may be less necessary than they are today.[57]

Rather than simply turning his back on Darwinism because it 'naturalized' competition and struggle, Kropotkin adapted the inductive methodology of the new sciences to challenge the assertions of Social Darwinists. 'Applied to the whole of human knowledge', he argued, the inductive methodology of new sciences like biology, geology, zoology and comparative anatomy would enable scientists 'to build a whole conception of the universe on a scientific basis, and to cast away the prejudices that obscured it'.[58]

Even before his encounters with Darwinism, Kropotkin had been impressed with the efforts of 'plain-speaking' Enlightenment thinkers, not least the French Encyclopaedists, to provide secular explanations of the origins of moral feelings 'without recourse to inspiration from above'. However, as a result of his Siberian experiences, he could only partially agree with Diderot when he claimed that 'the consent of the nation' was the basis of all political and civil power.[59] Going one step further than Diderot, he claimed that the autonomous self-governing community should be the ultimate locus of all decision-making. Eager to avoid plebeian revolution from below, these state-centred supporters of enlightened reform had insisted that social progress should literally come from above, and that reformers had to secure the ear of the great and good before seeking widespread reforms. In refusing to recognize the role of the 'philosopher king' in the reform process, Kropotkin and his fellow anarchists claimed that the teachings of church and state alike were 'a tissue of absurdities' that kept the people ignorant and protected authority. They thus upheld scientific reason as the enemy of both faith and authority.

There were a number of reasons why Kropotkin was attracted to plain-speaking upholders of Enlightenment values like Diderot, Rousseau, Buffon, Montesquieu, Adam Smith and Francis Hutcheson. In the first place they located humans at the centre of their inquiries as they sought to trace the origins of moral feelings back to the human capacity to sym-pathetically identify with other humans, and occasionally even with other organic beings. Thus Smith's first major publication, *The Theory of Moral Sentiments*, published in 1759, was based on the writings of authors who shared his views on the importance of enlightened opinions, and an enlightened environment, to social progress and public welfare. Similarly Hutcheson's ethical theory, first outlined in his *Inquiry into the Origin of Our Ideas of Beauty and Virtue* some 30 years earlier, was a detailed discussion of the senses as the source of political and civil power and the basis for 'right action'.[60] More importantly still, as far as Kropotkin was concerned, these and other figures from the Enlightenment forged a scientific methodology from a combination of reason and empirical observation in order to provide non-judgemental accounts of the moral feelings and social customs of primitive peoples without recourse to religious scholasticism or metaphysical philosophy. Thus Rousseau traced the origins of modern political institutions to social contracts freely entered into by citizens of the state and representatives of state authority. Kropotkin was also impressed with the pioneering attempts of these writers to 'collect all knowledge scattered over the face of the earth, to present its general rules and structures to the men with whom we live and to transmit it to those who will come after us, so that the work of past centuries may be useful to the following centuries'.[61]

Beginning with observations of well-known facts about the world of nature and human society, these writers, Kropotkin argued, went on to amass a whole body of *universal knowledge* that allowed them to make informed generalizations about a wide range of social and natural phenomena. Their early scientific endeavours paid particular attention to the origins of wealth and private property, the nature of power, the sources of moral sentiments, the consequences of political oppression and the meaning of progress. What impressed Kropotkin most was the fact that they

> did not change their method when they passed from the stars and physical bodies to the world ... to the life of plants and animals, to Man and to the development of economical and political forms of human society, and finally, to the evolution of the moral sense, the religions, and so on. The method remained the same. To all branches of science they applied the inductive method.[62]

Kropotkin was clearly aware that much of what passed for 'objective' scientific knowledge in the nineteenth century was a socio-political and cultural construct. He firmly believed that modern scientists should not have 'the last word' on debates about important social and political issues, and that science could be equally, and creatively, used to legitimize anarchism and support the ideal of an anarcho-communist society. Adopting the same scientific methods as the Encyclopaedists and a minority of evolutionary theorists, he argued that Social Darwinists had distorted evolutionary theory, that they 'were on the wrong path', that nature 'teaches us a very different lesson', and that the Social Darwinian interpretation of the struggle for existence was 'nowise scientific'. The same was true of the assertions of economists who, he argued, 'tried to make us believe ... that "inequality of fortunes" [was] a law of Nature ... and that capitalistic exploitation represents the most advantageous form of social organization'.

Because they perceived the animal world as a realm of perpetual struggle, a place where half-starved creatures thirsted for one another's blood, many of these writers only succeeded in making 'modern literature resound with the war cry of woe to the vanquished, as if it were the last word of modern biology'. In so doing, Kropotkin argued, they raised the 'pitiless' struggle for personal advantages to the height of a foundational principle of the social and biological sciences. Hence it was suggested that humans had to submit to authority and struggle for the means of subsistence if they did not wish to succumb 'in a world based upon mutual extermination'.[63] To counteract these arguments Kropotkin looked to evolutionary theory in order to defend 'the perfectibility of human nature'. 'Human ethics', he suggested, evolved 'out of the sociable habits of the animal ancestors of man'. In his unfinished treatise on the historical development of ethical systems he wrote:

'Nature ... has to be recognized as the first ethical teacher of man. The social instinct, innate in man as well as all the social animals – this is the origin of all ethical conceptions and all the subsequent development of morality.' To those who felt that he placed too much faith in the perfectibility of human beings, and who mistakenly thought that he was equating sociability with love and presenting this as a factor in survival, he responded:

it is not love, and not even sympathy ... which induces a herd of ruminants or of horses to form a ring in order to resist an attack of wolves; not love which induces wolves to form a pack for hunting; not love which induces kittens or lambs to play, or dozens of species of young birds to spend their days together in the autumn; and it is neither love nor personal sympathy which induces many thousand fallow deer scattered over a territory as large as France to form into a score of separate herds, all marching towards a given spot, in order to cross a river. It is a feeling infinitely wider than love or personal sympathy – an instinct that has been slowly developed among animals and men in the course of an extremely long evolution, and which has taught animals and men alike the force they can borrow from the practice of mutual aid and support, and the joys they can find in social life. ... Love, sympathy, and self-sacrifice certainly play an immense part in the progressive development of our moral feelings. *But it is not love and not even sympathy upon which Society is based in mankind. It is the conscience – be it only at the stage of an instinct – of human solidarity. It is the unconscious recognition of the force that is borrowed by each man from the practice of mutual aid; of the close dependence of every one's happiness upon the happiness of all; and of the sense of justice, or equity, which brings the individual to consider the rights of every other individual as equal to his own. Upon this broad and necessary foundation the still higher moral feelings are developed.*[64]

In rejecting the conventional wisdom of nineteenth-century political economy, Kropotkin also taught that the integration rather than segregation of functions in society enhanced the chances of individual and collective survival. Throughout organic nature, he argued, 'the capacities for life in common grow in proportion as the integration of organisms into compound aggregates become more and more complete'. In the long run, he added, the 'fittest' communities would prove to be those that 'combine intellectual knowledge with knowledge necessary for the production of wealth'. Reinterpreting 'the struggle for existence' as the 'adaptation of all individuals of the species to the best conditions for the survival of the species, as well as for the greatest possible sum of life and happiness for each and all', he looked to evolutionary philosophy for the sources of 'moral science'. Kropotkin's reading of evolutionary philosophy suggested that 'the capacities for life in common grow in proportion as the integration of organisms into compound aggregates become more and more complete'.[65] This meant that, in the long term at least, the struggle for existence would favour those societies that managed to combine intellectual knowledge with the knowledge necessary for the production of wealth and what today we would term 'social capital'. In other words the 'fittest' would no longer include individuals whose struggle to survive forced them to specialize and pit their wits against all other members of society. Instead it would include social groups, communities and entire societies that were successful in integrating manual and intellectual labour for the production in common of life's cultural and material necessities.

Kropotkin also suggested that the more they advanced, the more human agglomerations would fragment into smaller communities as those living in the most advanced regions of these agglomerations would wish to 'start an independent life'. The latter would then convert the more backward parts of the nation by example, 'instead of imposing their opinions by law and force, or submitting themselves to the majority-rule, which is always a mediocrity-rule'. In seeking to enhance the scientific legitimacy of anarchism Kropotkin also emphasized 'the infinitesimal part' played by positive law in the moral evolution of human societies. He contrasted this with 'the immense part played by the natural growth of altruistic feelings', which began to develop as soon as social conditions favoured their growth and emergence. Mutual aid, therefore, was a major factor in human development, just as the innate moral sense of human beings was the source of all 'altruistic feelings'. In this new scenario, ethics would grow and develop from the natural growth of social cooperation in all aspects of human life. In terms reminiscent of Robert Putnam's views on the importance of social capital to community development and social cohesion, and of Pierre Bourdieu's emphasis on the role of cultural capital in differentiating late modern societies, Kropotkin maintained that the struggle for existence would no longer be merely a 'question of bread ... but a question of social economy [that would encompass] the whole field of human activity'.[66] Evolutionary philosophy, he argued, equally demonstrated that the capacity for life in common in 'organic nature' increased in proportion as 'the integration of organisms into compound aggregates become more and more complete'. While temporary divisions in manual and intellectual labour had yielded significant results in the early development of modern capitalism, these would be replaced in a 'no-government' anarchist society by the integration of intellectual, industrial and agricultural pursuits according to the capacities of individual workers and the variety of abilities available within its social 'agglomerations'. In reverting from the 'scholastics of textbooks' to the division of labour in society, Kropotkin claimed that it was now 'high time' to claim the benefits of integration. Thus while political economists insisted on strict divisions of labour within and between manual and intellectual labour, he maintained that the ideal towards which all societies were evolving was a society where 'each individual is a producer of both manual and intellectual work, and where each worker works both in the field and in the industrial workshop, where the aggregation of individuals ... produces and consumes most of its own agricultural and manufactured produce'. In the long run, therefore, societies with the best chances of survival would be those that combined manual and intellectual labour, not those 'who are now the richest because they ... have been momentarily the strongest'. Inferring 'laws of moral science' from the social needs and habits of organic nature, Kropotkin stated:

> Among animals, mutual aid is ... not only the most efficacious weapon in the struggle for existence ... but it is also the principal instrument of progressive evolution. Even in the otherwise weakest animals it guarantees longevity (and consequently accumulation of experience), security of breeding their offspring, and intellectual progress. This is why those animal species which most practice mutual aid not only better survive in the struggle for existence than those which lead an isolated life, but they also occupy a higher position in their own respective classes (of birds, insects or mammals) by the superiority of their physical structure and their intelligence.[67]

By ignoring this 'fundamental fact of nature', he added, scientists had 'stained nature with the gladiator's blood' and accepted 'an acute struggle for life within each species as an established fact which needed no proof'. As a result 'learned Darwinists' like Huxley failed to recognize that sociability among animals, and indeed humankind, was a primordial social force as old as life itself.[68]

Social reform and social administration

In Siberia, Kropotkin had been responsible for a variety of administrative and technical projects rarely entrusted to a young man of his age. Here he learned to 'manage serious enterprises and to deal with men'. Recalling his early years in Siberia he wrote: 'Having been brought up in a serf owner's family, I entered life, like all young men of my time, with a great deal of confidence in the necessity of commanding, ordering, scolding, punishing, and the like.'[69] Educated personnel, particularly men with initiative who had the capacity to act independently, were scarce in Russia's recently colonized lands in the east. This meant that his superiors regularly solicited Kropotkin's opinions on administrative reform and local government. As a young officer in a Cossack regiment in Siberia he sought to humanize relations between officers and administrators and others under his charge. On returning to St Petersburg, however, he was to dedicate his life to the overthrow of institutions that dominated the lives of people and fostered the apathy that prevented them from taking control of their own futures. He later admitted that experience taught him to regard Siberia as a station through which 'all framers of State discipline' should pass before that they began to frame their 'state utopias'. He quickly realized that officers here were less concerned with the inadequacies of military administration than with their reputations as representatives of the state. Not surprisingly, therefore, Siberia undermined any lingering faith that Kropotkin had in the efficacy of 'military and pyramidal organizations of society'. The insights he derived from conflicts of interests between the region's indigenous population and political prisoners on the one hand, and state functionaries on the other, convinced even the young Kropotkin of 'the absolute impossibility of doing anything really useful for the masses of people by means of administrative machinery'.[70] He discovered that the local state had a limited role to play in alleviating social and economic distress among semi-autonomous communities perched on the geographical and metaphorical margins of the imperial state. Yet, the further he travelled away from Moscow, the more 'civilized' and effective some sectors of local administration appeared to be. Even as early as 1862, he had observed that the upper echelons of the administration in the remoter corners of Siberia were 'far more enlightened than that of any province of Russia proper'. Arriving at Irkutsk, he found that the wave of reaction he had observed at St Petersburg 'had not yet reached these distant dominions'. The local governor, Count N.N. Muraviev, was a 'remarkable personage ... very intelligent, very active, extremely amiable, and desirous to work for the good of the country'. 'Like all men of action of the governmental school', however, was 'a despot at the bottom of his heart'.[71]

Nevertheless the count had gathered round him a number of honest young officials, including the young Kropotkin, who were anxious to improve the lot of the local inhabitants. In so doing he presided over an administration that 'was far better, far more enlightened, and far more interested in the welfare of the people than the administration of any other province of Russia'. Muraviev had also succeeded in 'getting rid of the old staff of the civil service officials who viewed Siberia as a "camp to be plundered"'.[72] However, despite their 'excellent intentions', and because they belonged to a national administrative system, the higher echelons of the local state in Siberia could only 'interfere and kill all the beginnings of local life and progress'. Thus local administrators looked with mistrust at initiatives designed by local people to alleviate social distress. Such initiatives were 'immediately paralysed by hosts of difficulties which came, not so much from the bad intentions of the administrators, but simply from the fact that these officials belonged to a pyramidal, centralized administration'. The very fact that they belonged to a government that 'radiated from a distant capital' meant that representatives of the local state looked upon everything 'from the point of view of functionaries of the government'. In other words, they thought first of all about 'what their superiors will say, and how this or that will appear in the administrative machinery'. Having concluded that the lot of the masses could not be improved by the machinations of the administrative state, Kropotkin set out in search of 'the inner springs of the life of human society'. It was then that his political convictions, if not his views on scientific anarchism, began to take shape. Thus even before leaving Siberia, he began 'to appreciate the difference between acting on the principle of command and discipline, and acting on the principle of common understanding'. The former, he argued, 'works admirably in a military parade, but it is worth nothing where real life is concerned and the aim can be achieved only through the severe effort of many converging wills'.

When the time came to leave Siberia he had already 'lost all faith in state discipline' and was 'prepared to become an anarchist'.[73] It was around this time also that he began to appreciate the 'constructive work' of the unknown masses 'which so seldom finds any mention in books, and the importance of that constructive work in the growth of forms of society'. One had to 'live with natives … to see at work the complex forms of social organization which they have elaborated far away from the influence of any civilization'. Direct observations of the contribution of social capital to the survival of indigenous communities enabled the young Kropotkin to 'store up floods of light which illuminated subsequent reading'. Thus the part played by the 'unknown masses' in the accomplishment of important historical events only became evident from direct observation. His observations on the relationship between leaders and the people also fostered a new appreciation of the role of the masses in Russian history, which Tolstoy would later portray in his monumental *War and Peace*.

Anarchists have regularly had to respond to the accusation that they 'live in a world of dreams to come, and do not see things which happen today'. In responding to this charge Kropotkin argued that they 'see them only too well, and in their true colours, and that it is what makes us carry the hatchet into the forest of prejudice that besets us'.[74] Indeed he believed that his opponents made the greatest claims on human nature in holding that it was 'the rulers, the employers, [and] the leaders who … prevented … the ruled, the exploited, [and] the led from becoming worse'. Anarchists on the other hand maintained that both rulers and ruled were 'truly spoiled by authority'. Thus in admitting the imperfections of human nature, Kropotkin made no exception between rulers and ruled. In so doing he rejected a fundamental tenet of Enlightenment philosophy which stipulated that only the best should rule the rest of society, and that the right to rule was the sole prerogative of society's most gifted members. He also maintained that all talk of 'the impracticability of socialism and the necessary slowness of evolution are of little value, because the speed of evolution can only be judged from a close knowledge of the human beings'. The more he read, the more he saw before him 'a new world', unknown to him, and 'totally unknown to the learned makers of sociological theories'. This was a world that he could know 'only by living in the Workingmen's Association and by meeting the workers in their everyday life'.[75] Divesting himself of wealth and status, Kropotkin took his position alongside poor peasants and workers, sharing their lives, and their learning, with a view to becoming a 'social seer' and a harbinger of radical social change. The egalitarian simplicity of the lives of the prisoners and peasants he met in Siberia taught him the values of humility and self-sufficiency. If in the past Siberia had been a breeding ground for Christian anarchists and utopian mystics, for Kropotkin it was the cradle in which his secular beliefs and scientific imagination were nurtured.

Together with the most advanced representatives of political radicalism, Kropotkin maintained that the ideal form of political organization was one where the functions of government were reduced to a minimum. Only then, he maintained, could the individual recover 'his full liberty of initiative and action for satisfying, by means of free groups and federations – freely constituted – all the infinitely varied needs of the human being'. The ultimate aim of society, he argued, must be 'the reduction of the functions of government to nil'. To achieve this objective, anarchists need not resort to such metaphysical conceptions as 'natural rights' and the 'duties of the state' in order to achieve 'the greatest happiness of mankind'.[76] They simply had to follow 'the course traced by the modern philosophy of evolution, studying human society as it is now and was in the past; and without either endowing humanity as a whole, or separate individuals, with superior qualities which they do not possess'. The route to an anarcho-communist future was already mapped out by 'tendencies' already existing in society. As 'aggregations' or masses of individuals, societies were always 'trying to find out the best ways of combining the wants of the individual with those of cooperation for the welfare of the species'. In their efforts to satisfy the social and economic needs of these social 'aggregations', anarchists were simply pointing in the direction that evolution was already taking society. Kropotkin also distinguished between the real wants and tendencies of human aggregations and the 'accidents', such as lack of knowledge, migrations, wars, conquests and famines, which have prevented these tendencies from being satisfied. He concluded that the two most prominent tendencies operating throughout history have been the tendency towards 'integrating labour for the production of all riches in common', and the tendency towards 'the fullest freedom of the individual in the prosecution of all aims, beneficial both for himself and for society at large'.[77]

Turning his attention to non-European societies, Kropotkin was impressed by their lack of governmental controls and the sheer number of mutual aid institutions that were products of 'the creative genius of the savage and half-savage masses during the earliest clan-period of mankind'. He insisted that it was not possible to study 'primitive mankind' without being deeply impressed by 'the sociability it has displayed since its very first steps in life'.[78] Designating those living beyond Europe as 'savages whose manners of life are still those of Neolithic man', he went on to suggest that they were 'closely bound together by an extremely ancient clan organization'. This enabled them to combine their 'individually weak forces' in order to progress and enjoy life in common. Humans, he argued, were 'no exception in nature' as they were also subject to the 'principle of mutual aid'. Like the contemporary social theorist Robert Putnam, he suggested that societies progressed when members did not rely exclusively on government but supported each other by cooperating together in the struggle for social improvement.[79] This, he argued, was a deceptively simply but neglected idea which nevertheless had profound implications for the mental health and social well being of individuals, communities and entire societies. Going one step further, Kropotkin suggested it would be 'quite contrary to all that we know of nature' if humans were an exception to the 'law of mutual aid'. It would also be contrary to nature if 'a creature so defenseless as man' found his 'protection and his way to progress not in mutual support, like other animals, but in reckless competition for personal advantages … with no regard to the interests of the species'. As far as Kropotkin was concerned, this was a proposition that was utterly indefensible because it failed to recognize the essential 'unity in nature' that rendered humans an integral part of the natural world.[80]

Despite the fact that there were 'no writers to give literary expression to social anarchism' until the publication of Godwin's monumental *Political Justice*, anarchism was a vital historic 'tendency' in European society.[81] It was particularly evident in the growth of 'free cities' in the fifteenth and sixteenth centuries, when 'free associations of workers' came together to build 'unrivalled monuments' that 'still testify to the revival of mind and the well-being of citizens'. 'Home rule' was then literally a growing need even for the smallest territorial unit or social group, while free agreement among individuals became a substitute for law and cooperation became a substitute for government. If in the past anarchism was a constructive force of the masses, by the latter half of the nineteenth century it was 'aided by the whole strength of modern science and technique'. Thus anarchists wished to 'set up institutions ... indispensable to the free development of society, in opposition to those who put their hope in laws made by governing minorities'. If the anarchist movement had its origins in 'the teaching of life itself' it was renewed 'each time it received an impression from some general practical lesson'.

The immense influence that mutual aid and sociability exercised upon the early development of humankind induced Kropotkin to extend his researches to later historical epochs. His attention was particularly drawn to Europe's medieval 'city-republics' whose influence upon modern civilization was, he argued, not yet fully appreciated. Medieval cities, he argued, were:

> not organized upon some preconceived plan in obedience to the will of an outside legislator. Each of them was a natural growth in the full sense of the word – an always varying result of struggle between various forces which adjusted and re-adjusted themselves in conformity with their relative energies, the chances of conflict, and the support they found in their surroundings. Therefore, there are no two cities whose inner organization and destinies would have been identical. Each one, taken separately, varies from century to century.[82]

His researches in medieval history seemed to confirm the centrality of 'mutual-support instincts' in European society. The craft guilds of the medieval city perfectly demonstrated the importance of 'integrated labour' and sociability in medieval civilization, and no other period of history better illustrated the constructive powers of the popular masses. As fortified villages and marketplaces, representing so many 'oases amidst the feudal forest', began to free themselves from their lord's yoke, they gradually shaped the social and spatial character of the future city. It was at this stage that many of the coastal cities of Scandinavia and the Mediterranean formulated customary maritime and commercial laws that later became models of urban organization for cities throughout Europe. The inhabitants of these early cities freed themselves from obligations to their former lords and masters through 'a series of imperceptible acts of devotion to the common cause'. Their 'liberation struggles' were directed 'by men who came out of the masses, unknown heroes whose very names have not been preserved by history'.[83]

Turning to the social composition of the medieval city, Kropotkin conceded that while the church was a powerful institution with its own political apparatus and social agenda, the corporate community of the city comprised a wide variety of classes and social ranks. To exist in such a society one had to belong to a household, a monastery, a guild or a manor. The unattached individual was condemned either to exile or excommunication. Security was predicated upon the protection of the group to which one belonged, and there was 'no freedom that did not recognize the constant obligations of a corporate life'.[84] The social contracts upon which institutions such as the family, the manor or the guild were constructed were as important as their actual physical forms. Initially at least guilds were religious confraternities formed under the patronage of a saint that accorded their members some degree of 'brotherly comfort and cheer'. They also insured them against the accidents of life, and guaranteed them a decent burial. Although they never lost sight of their religious functions, medieval guilds also pledged to stand by their members in times of need, and offered mutual succour to all their members in stressful times. Kropotkin's attention was drawn to the medieval towns and craft guilds precisely because they offered concrete examples of mutual aid and sociability in action. The members of the guild ate and drank together on a regular basis. They formulated rules and regulations for the conduct of their craft and of their members. They planned social events, including medieval mystery plays, for the edification and entertainment of both their own members and fellow townspeople. When times were good, they built chapels in honour of their patron saints, founded schools, and at the height of their power even built their own guildhalls. With their craft at the centre of their social and economic existence, the guilds constructed an entire way of life that was more or less independent of state controls.[85]

Kropotkin adopted a highly uncritical view of social relations in the medieval city and had a particularly idealized vision of the medieval guild system. Certainly craft guilds in particular started out as institutions to protect against the economic self-destruction of their members. Operating as medieval variants of modern labour aristocracies, they integrated all works of a craft into a single body where duties, promotions, profits and working hours were defined by master workers in a contract meant to govern their brother-workers' entire careers. Each guild was also to provide for the health of workers and for their widows and orphans. If, for example, a brother's house was burned down, or he lost his ship in a storm, or suffered a mishap while on a pilgrimage, all the other brethren had to come to his aid. If a brother fell ill, two brethren had to keep watch by his bed until he was out of danger. If he died they had to provide for his children, if necessary; and often as not the widow of the dead man became a sister of the guild. If the relatives of a wronged person sought revenge on a member of the guild by 'a new aggression', the brotherhood was obliged to supply him with the wherewithal to leave home, and if he chose to remain in town, 12 brothers accompanied him for his own protection.

However, guilds often had competing interests and their rules and regulations could impact adversely on those lower down the social structure of the medieval city. In towns and cities where food crafts were well organized they could function like corporations and influence the price of foodstuffs. Guilds were also alert to the dangers of unbridled competition in the medieval marketplace. In addition to controlling prices they often sought to control the quantity of goods produced so that competition would focus on the quality of workmanship. Similarly, in cities where food crafts were strong, attempts to keep down prices of basic foodstuffs were less effective than in those cities where merchant guilds were able to minimize food prices in order to lower wages. Likewise in port cities where guilds handled goods that were shipped over long distances, individual guild members sometimes tried to do business on their own and did not work in the interest of the entire guild. When guild members did manage to get away with this type of self-interested behaviour, other members were quick to follow suit.[86]

Kropotkin also envisaged the architecture of the medieval city as an organic composition that was the product of the 'natural development' of the craft-guild system. As he saw it, buildings, monuments and architectural decorations were all devised by men who knew from personal experience what artistic effects could be obtained from stone, wood or mortar. Grand medieval buildings therefore were believed to be the product of the collective experience of highly motivated and well-organized craft workers, rather than simply the 'grand idea' of any powerful individual or wealthy patron. As such, they sprang out of a medieval communal conception of brotherhood, and from a tradition of urban sociability that was fostered by the entire city. Brotherhoods of seamen, stoneworkers, metal workers and carpenters not only financed the construction of medieval buildings and monuments. They literally contributed to their construction with the result that the skills of each craft guild were abundantly evident in the final product. Less frequently were these structures the product of enslaved workers who were obliged to follow instructions from an individual overseer. Thus for Kropotkin:

The lofty tower bell rose upon a structure, grand in itself, in which the life of the city was throbbing – not upon a meaningless scaffold like the Paris iron tower, not as a sham structure in stone intended to conceal the ugliness of an iron frame, as has been done in Tower Bridge. Like the Acropolis of Athens, the cathedral of a medieval city was intended to glorify the victorious city, to symbolize the union of its crafts, to express the glory of each citizen in a city of his own creation.[87]

In tracing the archaeology of anarchism to these expressions of workers' sociability in the medieval city, Kropotkin was demonstrating the role of so-called subaltern sections of urban society in the making of their own history and landscapes. Moving forward to the eighteenth century, he also showed that at the height of the French Revolution, while the Jacobins 'did all in their power to centralize everything in the hands of government … the masses of the people, in their municipalities and "sections" … appropriated for themselves the election of judges, the organization of supplies and equipment for the army, as also for the cities, work for the unemployed [and] the management of charities'.[88]

State and political authority

We have already seen that Kropotkin regarded the states of Europe as historical creations, which from the sixteenth century onwards invaded the life worlds of the people and delegated to themselves many of the roles that were formerly the responsibility of autonomous local communities. The subsequent rise of the centralized state constituted a radical departure from the then natural tendency towards mutual aid and cooperation in medieval Europe. Once established, the modern state regarded those living within its jurisdiction as subjects of its authority. It no longer recognized the freely formed cooperative solidarities that were formerly independent of any overarching authority. For Kropotkin, the fourteenth and fifteenth centuries were a Golden Age of 'people's democracy'.[89] This was followed by two centuries of state centralization that resulted in the birth of the modern state. When the last vestiges of 'barbarian freedom seemed to disappear' from early medieval Europe, and as the continent was about to fall under the domination of thousands of petty rulers intent on establishing 'theocracies and despotic states', political life took a radically different direction. Like the cities of 'antique Greece', small and large urban agglomerations all across Europe unanimously voted to 'shake off the yoke of their worldly and clerical lords'. Fortified villages rose up against the lord's castles, defied them at first, then attacked them, and finally destroyed them. This movement for local autonomy rapidly spread from region to region, 'involving every town on the surface of Europe'. In less than a hundred years, 'free cities' had been called into existence on the coast of the Mediterranean, the North Sea, the Baltic, the Atlantic Ocean, and right down to the fjords of Scandinavia. From there it spread to the plains of Russia, Hungary, France, and Spain, and onwards to the foothills of the Apennines, the Alps, the Black Forest, the Grampians and the Carpathians. Wherever people 'united in one common idea' found or hoped to find some protection behind their town walls, they instituted their own 'co-jurations', social fraternities and 'friendship' societies. 'Boldly marching towards a new life of mutual support and liberty', they then set about changing the face of Europe, covering it with 'beautiful sumptuous buildings' that expressed the genius of free unions of free men. These they bequeathed to the following generations, along with 'all the arts [and] all the industries of which our present civilization, with all its achievements and promises for the future, is only a further development'. Thus thousands of fortified centres were built by the 'energies of village communities'. Having constructed their town walls, they quickly realized that they could also resist the encroachment of their 'inner enemies', namely the lords, as well as invading 'foreigners'. As a result, a new life of freedom began to develop within these fortified enclosures and the medieval city was born.[90]

Kropotkin's anarchism was predicated on clear-cut distinctions between the modern state and representative government. Both of these were 'ideas of a different kind'. Just as society was a product of historical forces that pre-dated the establishment of the authoritarian state, the state represented the historical centralization of governmental functions in the hands of the few. This gave rise to a plethora of legislation designed to protect property and enhance state authority. It followed from this that the modern state was 'an incubus' imposed upon society, a distorting factor that ultimately thwarted local initiative and prevented social progress.[91] In defending the legitimacy of anarchism and the 'no-government' stateless society, Kropotkin went on to emphasize the historical contingency and artificiality of the centralized state. Before submitting to the all-absorbing authority of the state, the masses of the people made a formidable attempt at restructuring society on the old basis of mutual aid and support. By the nineteenth century, however, the state alone, and the 'state's church', took care of matters of general interest. The subjects of state authority became loose agglomerations of individuals 'connected by no particular bonds' who were now forced to appeal to government to satisfy their common needs. The commercial and industrial societies that formerly organized their social and economic affairs were now treated with suspicion, while the social unions that represented the interests of the crafts and other workers were deemed unlawful. For Kropotkin, the state's absorption of social roles that were formerly the preserve of guilds, municipalities and fraternities 'necessarily favoured the development of an unbridled, narrow-minded, individualism'. As the obligations of citizens towards the state grew in number, they were relieved of their obligations to each other. The centralized, authoritarian state was born.

The new state, Kropotkin argued, quickly acquired the features of 'a society of mutual assurance between the landlord, the military commander, the judge, the priest, and later on the capitalist, in order to support each other's authority over the people, and for exploiting the poverty of the masses and getting rich themselves'.[92] It followed that each step towards economic freedom, each victory over capitalism, was a step towards 'political liberation … by means of free agreement, territorial, professional, and functional'. In *The State: Its Historic Role* (1897) the state is portrayed as only one form of political organization adopted by society in the course of history. Kropotkin insisted that 'men lived in societies without states for thousands of years before having known the State'. Village communities and urban townships flourished from the late Middle Ages right through to the Renaissance. The state's subsequent growth coincided with the emergence of 'dominant minorities' who combined the military power of warriors appointed to defend communities with the judicial power of those 'with specialized knowledge of customary law'. In time, the state developed its own cult of authority as men 'fell in love with authority' and gradually relied upon 'municipal Caesars' to solve their disputes. History had demonstrated that the state developed in order to 'prevent the direct association among men, to shackle the development of local and individual initiative, to crush existing liberties, to prevent their new blossoming – all this in order to subject the masses to the will of minorities'.[93]

Like Marx, Kropotkin also recognized that 'the political regime to which human societies are submitted is always an expression of the economic regime which exists within society'. Thus each new form of political organization would 'correspond to each new form of economic organization'. However, the relationship between the two was not that of a determining base governing a political superstructure. It was a symbiotic relationship in that the political organization of society was dialectically dependent upon its economic organization. Far from being a fatalist who was prepared to wait for the evolutionary process to dispose of the state in due course, Kropotkin believed that modern society was faced with the choice of death or renewal:

> Either the State forever, crushing individual and local life, taking over fields of human activity, bringing with it wars and its domestic struggles for power, its palace revolutions which only replace one tyrant with another, and inevitably at the end of its development there is … death! Or the destruction of States, and new life starting again in thousands of centres on the principle of the lively initiative of the individual and groups and that of free agreement.[94]

As mentioned in Chapter 1, Kropotkin's idea of the state was not unlike that of Weber who defined the state in terms of its territorial jurisdiction, bureaucratic administration and legal monopoly of force. With his emphasis on the legality of the state's monopoly of authority, Kropotkin's definition excluded colonies and other social formations that were subject to arbitrary domination. While insisting that the state was very much a creation of the sixteenth century, he nevertheless argued that the Roman Empire had all the characteristics of a super-state. He showed that ancient concepts of law and sovereignty inherited from Rome continued to exert a profound influence on the evolution of the bureaucratic and legal structures of nineteenth-century nation-states. Like de Tocqueville, he was concerned about the growing bureaucratic centralism in Europe and North America and objected to the provision of state welfare and the state administration of civil services because they sapped community initiative and ultimately led to a system of service provision that was inflexible, officious and heartless.

In criticizing both state and government, Kropotkin submitted them to the same degree of criticism that others applied to private capital. In *Modern Science and Anarchism* he argued that the state and capitalism were 'facts and conceptions which we cannot separate from each other'.[95] Throughout recent history, he added, they supported and reinforced each other to such an extent that they were now joined together by the links of cause and effect. While other nineteenth-century democrats and working-class radicals regarded universal suffrage and republican institutions as 'the last word of political wisdom', Kropotkin went a step further and submitted government and the state to deeper criticism. Having been experimented with across a wide field, representative government, he claimed, had already revealed its defects. It was obvious to him at least that these were 'not merely accidental but inherent in the system itself'. Parliament and its executive offshoots proved incapable of attending to the needs of the common people in towns, cities and rural villages dispersed throughout the country. Neither could they adjudicate between varied, and often diametrically opposed, interest groups scattered throughout the state's jurisdiction. Similarly, elections did not draw forth leaders capable of representing the entire nation, or manage, other than in a party spirit, the affairs they were compelled to legislate upon. While distinguishing between the state and government he claimed that both were oppressive and urged social reformers not to temporize with them. Representative government was always open to powerful individuals who could manipulate the electorate. Its 'inherent tendency' always veered towards centralization and the unification of state functions. Elections could not be relied upon to 'magically unearth men' who would genuinely represent the nation, while parliamentary rule was 'pre-eminently a middle class rule' and majority rule always resulted in 'mediocrity rule'.[96] For that reason, he argued, revolutionaries should not seek power but awake the consciousness of people and remind them of their fundamental goals. Socialists for their part did not fully appreciate the limitations of representative government. Convinced as they were of the necessity of economic reforms, they took no notice of the impact of government on the freedom of the individual. Too many were willing to submit society to any kind of dictatorship if this resulted in the implementation of their socialist agenda.

Kropotkin also suggested that while representative government had been useful in the struggle against autocracy, it no longer represented an ideal form of free political organization. Progress, he argued, was 'most effective when ... not checked by state interference', and future social progress lay not 'in the direction of a further concentration of power and regulative functions in the hands of a governing body, but in the direction of decentralization, both territorial and functional'.[97] While the former would foster the balkanization of the territorial state, the latter would encourage radical new forms of self-government that would return decision-making to local communities and their representatives in democratically constituted, federal institutions.

Kropotkin's defence of the 'no-government' position was predicated on two further assumptions. Firstly he believed that the growing complexity and increased integration of social and economic life would render political governance and the state increasingly difficult and ultimately render it redundant. At best this type of governance would simply become an oppressive or unnecessary source of interference in the social and economic life of modern societies. At worst it would constitute an obstacle to future progress. Secondly he suggested that demographic growth and the concentration of production in larger and larger cities would foster the further development of 'human agglomeration' and render the historic functions of government increasingly ineffective. Thus emancipation from the oppressive forces of capitalism and the state was encouraged by powerful tendencies already existing within advanced capitalist societies. These, he argued, were already facilitating the decentralization of power and government, and would ultimately contribute to the fragmentation of the territorial state into autonomous communities and townships linked together in complex new federal structures designed to maximize social and regional autonomy. Thus anarchists visualized a society wherein the mutual relations of its members would be regulated not by laws or elected authorities, but by mutual agreement between its members and by social custom and traditional habit. Such a society would no longer be 'petrified by law, routine, or superimposition'.[98] Instead, it would continually develop and readjust to circumstances in accordance with the ever-growing requirements of a free life stimulated by science, invention and 'the steady growth of higher ideals'. This would involve a radically new form of political organization that would be *'more popular, more decentralised, and nearer to the folkmote of self-government'* than representative government could ever be. In advocating radical self-government as a social ideal for the future, Kropotkin also recognized it as a progressive feature of European society in the past. It was a constructive force that fostered the development of common-law institutions to protect the majority against a dominating minority. It flourished when 'small parts of humanity broke down the power of their rulers and reassumed their freedoms'. Throughout history this type of primitive mutual associationism continually reasserted itself. In a tribute to its past achievements he described how:

> The penny bridge disappears before the public bridge; and the turnpike road before the free road. The same spirit pervades thousands of other institutions, Museums, free libraries, and free public schools; parks and pleasure grounds; paved and lighted streets, free for everybody's use; water supplied to provide dwellings, with a growing tendency towards disregarding the exact amount used by the individual; tramways and railways which have already begun to use the season ticket or the uniform tax ... all these are tokens showing in what direction further progress is expected.[99]

Even when the individual labourer appeared to reign supreme, families still had to rely on the cooperation of non-family members to clear scrubland and forests, to build roads and bridges, to save harvests and provide health care during emergencies. Even the 'inventive genius' of the captain of industry was dependent upon the energy and skills of working men and women. Or as Kropotkin put it:

> We may admire the inventive genius or the organizing capacities of an iron lord; but we must recognize that all his genius and energy would not realize one-tenth of what they realize here if they were spent in dealing with Mongolian shepherds or Siberian peasants instead of British workers, British engineers, and trustworthy managers.[100]

Notwithstanding the egotistical character of nineteenth-century capitalism, the tendency for people to cooperate in order to achieve a common goal repeatedly asserted itself, and was continually trying to 're-infiltrate' itself as a principle of public life, after an absence of four or more centuries.

4

'Scientific Anarchism' and Evolutionary Theory: Towards an Ontology of Anarchist Ethics and Altruism

The marginalization of anarchism in the social sciences

Historically, at least, it could be argued that conventional accounts of the origins and development of academic disciplines have shared with the theatre critic an obsession with the successful, particularly the success with which professional academics contributed to the political and economic development of 'their' state-societies. For these and other reasons the historians of disciplinary knowledge have generally ignored those who sat uneasily within the academic establishment, including those who for a variety of social and political reasons were excluded, or excluded themselves from, the educational institutions of their day. This latter group has certainly included the major figures of Peter Kropotkin and Élisée Reclus. Despite their very significant contributions to history, anthropology, geography and the social sciences, they have largely been excluded from, or consigned to footnotes in, most histories of disciplinary thought. Notwithstanding Kropotkin's contributions to academic knowledge, political philosophy and social theory, he has also been marginalized in many of the standard histories of political thought. Since the 1960s and 1970s, the radical social sciences have been so infused with the methodologies and conceptual categories of Marxism that they have been, to all intents and purposes, synonymous with what we might term 'academic Marxism'.[1] Thus Eric Hobsbawm, one of anarchism's harshest critics, ignoring its long historical pedigree, claimed that its roots lay in the plebeian revolutionary ferment of the 1840s, and that it attained only a slight degree of intellectual maturity in the 1860s and 1870s. Ignoring Kropotkin's enormous contribution to the theory and practice of anarchism, Hobsbawm named Proudhon ('a self-educated printer and voluminous writer') and Bakunin ('a peripatetic Russian aristocrat who plunged into it at every opportunity') as the founding fathers of modern anarchism. Completely disregarding the voluminous body of work produced by Kropotkin and Reclus between 1870 and 1920, he went on to suggest that anarchism's 'intellectual pedigree' was not 'worth drawing up as it had little bearing on the development of the actual anarchist movement'. Dismissing Bakunin as an anarchist who 'added little to Proudhon as a thinker, except an unquenchable passion for actual revolution', he concluded that the latter's 'unsystematic, prejudiced and profoundly anti-liberal theory ... [was] of no great interest in itself'. It was worthy of attention only because it 'contributed two themes to anarchist thought: a belief in small mutually supporting groups of producers instead of dehumanized factories, and a hatred of government as such, *any* government'. According to Hobsbawm, anarchism appealed only to autonomous communities of independent small craftsmen in the 1850s and 1860s who had 'not forgotten a peasant or small-town provincial childhood'. These groups, he suggested, looked on anarchism simply as a means for resisting the process of their own proletarianization and migration to the expanding and dehumanizing cities of Western Europe. In this diatribe against anarchism, Hobsbawm concluded that Bakunin, who was arguably one of Europe's most formidable anarchists, was 'not much of a thinker ... but a prophet, an agitator ... and a formidable conspiratorial organizer'.[2]

The quest for relevance that underpinned much of academic life in the 1960s and 1970s did little to rekindle an interest in the very substantial body of anarchist literature that had been produced in the latter half of the nineteenth century. While a comparatively small number of prominent leftist academics were able to foster a new radical social scientific canon within their respective disciplines, they looked to classical Marxism, rather than anarchism, for inspiration. Initially at least, this genre of 'disciplinary Marxism' was constructed deep within the universities, primarily by professional scholars and academics who had grown increasingly conscious of the epistemological crises confronting their disciplines. They were either unaware of nineteenth-century anarchism, or unwilling to be associated with a political philosophy that its critics linked only with political violence and social chaos. While the anarchist tradition was largely ignored, 'disciplinary Marxism' was disseminated through exciting lecture series, books, journals, and occasionally even television interviews with the new mandarins of academic radicalism. Many of these subsequently went on to acquire celebrity status in their respective disciplines. Whereas previously the social and environmental sciences had been broadly sub-divided into 'pure' and 'applied' branches, they now fragmented into a broadly recognizable radical/leftist tradition of scholarship and a state-centred, often 'applied' disciplinary tradition. Even within the most unlikely of disciplines, there emerged at this stage vibrant new radical schools of thought whose roots could be traced back to nineteenth-century Marxism, European socialism, feminism and environmentalism. Each school had its own small set of iconic academics whose works were tremendously influential in popularizing the social sciences and nurturing academic radicalism. To name but a few of these is to recall their disproportionate influence on an entire generation of academics since the 1960s. They have included Jürgen Habermas, Michel Foucault, Pierre Bourdieu, Anthony Giddens, Immanuel Wallerstein and Charles Tilly in sociology, Eric Hobsbawm and E.P. Thompson in history, Germaine Greer, Simone de Beauvoir and Sheila Rowbotham in feminist studies, David Harvey and Richard Peet in geography, and Frederic Jameson, Herbert Marcuse, Francis Fukuyama, Ernesto Laclau and Gilles Deleuze in critical theory and political science. Parallel to these developments within established disciplines there emerged exciting new sub-disciplinary offshoots, each headed up by a small number of highly influential academics. Thus these years also witnessed exciting new developments in postmodern studies, world-systems theory, subaltern studies, post-colonial theory, African-American studies, social movement theory, development theory and critical social theory. A number of these academics have almost inadvertently contributed to an anarchist deconstruction of the meta-narratives of modernity. They include Klaus Eder, Alberto Melucci, Henri Lefebvre and Jean-François Lyotard.

The sheer level of neglect in Kropotkin's case was compounded by a long-standing historical tendency to equate anarchism with utopianism and political chaos, and to associate anarchists with wilful acts of political terrorism. Few minorities within the radical tradition have suffered so much from an identity crisis, or have been so misrepresented, as anarchists. Writing in 1907, Errico Malatesta noted that the term 'anarchy' was 'used universally in the sense of disorder and confusion, and it is still adopted in that sense by the ignorant and by adversaries interested in distorting the truth'.[3] Despite the respect that leading anarchists like Kropotkin, Tolstoy, Reclus and Malatesta acquired from their intellectual peers, their writings have never occupied the honoured position in the tabernacle of canonical texts that the faithful reserved for the sacred texts of Marxism and Marxist-Leninism. Even today anarchists continue to suffer the consequences of their caricaturization, and indeed criminalization, by nineteenth-century opponents of anarchism. Writing well before the advent of mass media, Reclus was well aware that their enemies always found anarchists easy targets for criticism. As he saw it:

Public speakers on social and political subjects find that abuse of anarchists is an unfailing passport to public favour. Every conceivable crime is laid to our charge, and opinion, too indolent to learn the truth, is easily persuaded that anarchy is but another name for wickedness and chaos. Overwhelmed with opprobrium and held up with hatred, we are treated on the principle that the surest way to hang a dog is to give it a bad name.[4]

Certainly in nineteenth-century Europe, the political violence and the 'terrorism of the deed' perpetrated by a minority of anarchist activists were overemphasized to the neglect of the intellectual strengths of anarchism. Kropotkin, who did more than most to provide anarchism with scientific credentials, also made a number of important contributions to scientific journalism. He presented his erudite analyses of anti-authoritarianism and cooperative mutualism in the popular press, and to mixed gatherings of anarchists, socialists and working-class activists.

It could be argued that the neglect of the anarchist contribution to nineteenth-century intellectual history has been partially due to a failure on the part of professional academics to recognize the historical and geographical underpinnings of Kropotkin's 'scientific anarchism'. For many anarchism was indeed too ideological to be considered a science, and too utopian to be taken seriously. To its enemies it was quite simply an irrational, destructive social force, not a constructive political philosophy. Considered so contemptuous of the authority of the state, and state-supported schools and academic institutions, it appeared to favour political violence over and above political reason. Yet the neglect of anarchism in the history of institutionalized knowledge may also be attributed to the subjective ethos of these very disciplinary histories.

Written usually by professionals with a vast experience of teaching and research, classical histories of disciplinary thought have always been strong on chronological and biographical detail.[5] Prior to the 1970s at least, they generally paid little attention to the dialectical relationships between the historical trajectories of academic disciplines and the social and political contexts within which they developed. Written by academics who turned to history to trace the evolution of their disciplines, their authors often lacked training in the sociology and philosophy of knowledge. Not surprisingly, therefore, they produced what in effect were little more than idolatrous and internalistic accounts of academic progress written largely for professional academics. At best they emphasized the indebtedness of contemporary 'practitioners' to the 'founding fathers' of their disciplines. In so doing, they produced 'filiations of ideas' which overemphasized 'mainstreams' in the historical evolution of their disciplines, while often ignoring the wayward tributaries that did not feed into the academic mainstream, or otherwise contribute to canonical disciplinary thought. Nineteenth-century anarchism, and to a much lesser extent Marxism, are classic examples of this type of institutionalized academic neglect. While classical Marxism certainly had a profound impact on disciplinary thought throughout much of the twentieth century, anarchism received far less attention from professional academics, including those who have been responsible for the radicalization of the social and environmental sciences since the 1960s.

Despite Kropotkin's efforts to provide anarchism with a scientific basis and a rich historical pedigree, the manner in which the history of disciplines was constructed meant that his dissident and antithetical tradition of scientific anarchism was excluded from most histories of disciplinary thought and scientific ideas. Conventional historians of academic disciplines assumed that change within disciplines was an endogenous affair unaffected by the social, economic and geopolitical environments within which it occurred. This has been equally true of Kuhnian analyses of scientific revolutions since the 1960s. Ignoring the societal contexts of scientific endeavour, these have attributed revolutions in scientific thought to 'paradigm shifts' within disciplines, and largely within the confines of academia.[6] In detaching them from their societal contexts, most such histories have simply presented us with idealist interpretations of disciplinary change that treat the production of knowledge, and the elucidation of scientific theory, as the product of endogamous and largely autonomous intellectual processes. They ignore the fact that disciplines have always been socially embedded in state societies, and that scientists and academics are flesh-and-blood 'real people' who are equally embedded in very real social, political and historical spaces.[7] Thus their 'objective' knowledge and 'scientific' arguments have never been unbiased and have frequently been extremely partial. This was clearly the case in nineteenth-century Europe and North America where, as we shall presently see, geographers, cartographers, geologists, natural scientists, anthropologists and an entire generation of public administrators and policy-makers were deeply implicated in the politics and practices of state formation and nation-building. Their vulnerability to political influence, not least their thirst for recognition alongside the 'hard' sciences within the universities and other research institutions, meant that many disciplines defended nation-building and legitimized imperialism and the globalization of free enterprise capitalism. Despite its detrimental social and environmental effects on colonial society and the global ecosystem, geographers in particular were ardent defenders of ecological imperialism. Like their colleagues in anthropology and related disciplines, they were convinced that advances in the sciences in general would create a world of material abundance, social advancement and moral enlightenment. Many of these disciplines were taught in military academies, and acquired university status as well as state funding, precisely because of the services they could render to state and empire.[8] While some academics may have relied on 'the facts of nature' to conceal their partisan views behind the veil of objectivity, others openly flaunted their commitment to the authoritarian political projects of their respective states. Indeed many considered their services to the state as important as their services to the academy.

In the politically charged environments of the Darwinian half of the nineteenth century, the themes and issues that preoccupied scientists and academics were often subjects for impassioned political debate. This meant that they were also prone to change and were never beyond dispute. Even when they insisted that their research was uninfluenced by political or commercial considerations, many of Kropotkin's confrères in the educational establishment expressed their opinions on a whole range of controversial racial, social and political issues. Considered knowledgeable and well informed precisely because of their scientific training and academic expertise, their authority was called upon whenever complex issues of state governance and political authority were in dispute. While their status as academics appeared to endow them with the qualities of fairness, objectivity, wisdom and understanding, it also obscured the fact that their interpretations of nature and social change were always socially constructed within academia, and crucially also within the contested arenas of state societies structured by race and class.

Anarchism and the state-centred academy

Marxists, particularly Marxist-Leninists, have suggested that these weaknesses in the 'internalistic' approaches to the historical production of disciplinary knowledge can be exposed by highlighting the dialectical relationships between institutions of research and teaching on the one hand, and the socio-economic and political environments within which they operate on the other. This can often result in an over-simplification of Marx's teachings on historical materialism and a portrayal of scientists and academics as mere 'lackeys of the state' and instruments of state power.[9] For many indeed, this genre of economic reductionism, based as it is on a neglect of the cultural dimensions of power structures and an oversimplification of historical materialism, has become a foundational tenet of a more doctrinaire brand of Marxism. Thus not a few of his dogmatic followers have uncritically accepted Marx's assertion that:

> The ideas of the ruling class are, in every age, the ruling ideas: i.e. the class which is the dominant material force in society is at the same time its dominant intellectual force. The class which has the means of material production at its disposal has control over the means of mental production, so that in consequence the ideas of those who lack the means of mental production are, *in general*, subject to it. *The ruling ideas are nothing more than the ideal expression of the dominant material relationships*, the dominant material relationships grasped as ideas.[10]

To avoid the rudimentary reductionism and crude instrumentalism of this type of theorizing, Marxist historians like E.P. Thompson and cultural Marxists like Raymond Williams have consistently called for a recalibration of the Marxian categories of 'base' and 'superstructure', and a reconfiguration of the term 'determine', in order to deprive these categories of the mechanistic connotations that they have for Marxist-Leninists in particular. This would certainly infuse them with the dynamism of their original meaning and help to counteract the excessive structuralism involved in Marxist accounts of the complex interrelationships between ideology, science and the state. Those who have 'dogmatized' Marxism in this way would do well to heed Raymond Williams when he suggested as long ago as 1973 that 'We have to revalue "the base" away from the notion of a fixed economic or technological abstraction, and towards the specific activities of men in real social and economic relationships, containing fundamental contradictions and variations and therefore always in a state of dynamic process.'[11] Williams' cultural Marxist perspective would suggest that a more convincing dialectical approach to the social construction of knowledge should take into account the divisive nature of academic communities while simultaneously recognizing their complex and dynamic relationships with state societies. These would include not just direct links between universities and other research and teaching institutions on the one hand, and their political sponsors and funding agents on the other. It would embrace the much wider ideological milieu within which academic disciplines have operated and evolved. Such an approach would, for example, also account for the fact that the historical world of nineteenth-century academia was highly fragmented, and that many social and environmental scientists chose to remain outside academia while still conducting scientific research. Kropotkin, and to a lesser extent Reclus, who after all occupied an academic position, clearly belonged to this category. Throughout his long life, Kropotkin always maintained a highly ambivalent relationship with members of the academic community and institutions of learning. As a respected intellectual in his own right he participated in scientific discussions and contributed to some of the leading academic publications of his day. From the start, however, he never compromised his anarchist principles and always protected his intellectual independence by refusing to accept a privileged position within the ranks of the academic establishment. As a consequence, he lacked the cultural capital of the institutionalized academic, and has been almost entirely written out of the history of the European intellectual tradition.[12]

For the purposes of this discussion it may be useful to distinguish between two very broad, albeit unevenly developed and frequently diametrically opposed, traditions in the social and environmental sciences. Put simply, the 'state-centred' tradition that constituted the 'mainstream' that we have been discussing thus far has received abundant treatment in classical histories of academic disciplines. Its growth and development coincided with the rise of powerful nations that had an acute awareness of what they considered was their rightful place in the new world order. The latter half of the nineteenth century was famously marked by the ascendancy of Darwinism in the natural sciences and the encroachment of Social Darwinism in political discourse and the social sciences. Especially in recent decades, it has been widely recognized that this 'state-centred' tradition of academic endeavour contributed directly and indirectly to the rise of the surveillance state, the creation of empire, the emergence of the nation-state and the globalization of corporate capitalism. As Kropotkin was always at pains to emphasize, much theorizing in this tradition regarded the build-up and extension of state authority as a natural development that had clear parallels with natural processes operating in the biosphere and in the natural world. In so doing it legitimized state-centralization and fostered 'big-nation' nationalism in Europe and North America, while simultaneously facilitating the growth and expansion of foreign trade and the imperial expansion of metropolitan powers.[13] In the mainstream social and environmental sciences, the rise of militarism, colonialism and nationalism, accompanied as they were by the growing powers of the state, were considered not so much acts of state aggression as indications of national vigour. Thus Kropotkin was able to demonstrate that the social and environmental sciences had adopted crude formulations of Darwin's theory of evolution to mask their ideological biases and justify race thinking, state centralization, patriarchy, imperial expansion and the intensification of colonial exploitation. To his opponents, the struggle for survival was an ongoing process that was literally transforming the face of the earth and revealing exciting new ways of exploiting its natural resources. Writing as far back as the mid 1950s, J.D. Bernal suggested that this section of the academic establishment in Western Europe was merely echoing on the 'scientific' plane the prevailing and persuasive hypocrisy of bourgeois society. Thus he suggested:

Just as there were aspects of life known to exist but never mentioned, so in the social sciences references to the existence of classes or exploitation were beyond the pale. Explanations of social phenomena had to be concocted which made no allusions to these awkward facts, and if that could not be done it was better to have no explanation at all.[14]

While it may seem hardly surprising today that this state-centred tradition of scientific endeavour would not go unchallenged, in the highly charged political environments of late nineteenth-century Europe only a comparatively small minority ever considered doing so. Dissident intellectuals, including prominent anarchists of the calibre of Kropotkin and Reclus, offered their own sustained, anti-capitalist alternatives to the authoritarian state and free enterprise capitalism. These anarchists rejected the naturalization of industrial capitalism and the normalization of state authority and the capitalist work ethic. Kropotkin and Reclus in particular condemned the over-simplification of Darwin's theory of evolution and criticized Social Darwinists for uncritically defending the legitimacy of state authority and the globalization of competitive private enterprise. They were also clearly to the forefront of advanced anarchist thinkers who recognized the need to defend anarchism as a political and intellectual project. Over the course of more than 50 years, Kropotkin's writings criticized the centralization of state authority, advocated cultural pluralism, outlined radical alternatives to state education, community care and social administration, supported ecologically sound development projects, defended regional autonomy and defended the break up of nations. This was just at the time when the powerful states of Britain, the United States, France and Germany were engaged in colonial wars for imperial aggrandizement and actively involved in global acts of ecological imperialism. Free federations operating at the regional, national and global levels would, they argued, not only replace the central authority of the imperial state. They would also restore decision-making powers to local communities, thereby 'restoring the natural process of growth'. Thus Kropotkin would maintain that 'variety is life, uniformity is death', just as he would go on to emphasize that 'variety is the distinctive feature of the territory and inhabitants of all nations [and that] variety also expressed itself in a huge variety of occupations'.[15] While he opposed imperialism on the grounds that it decimated traditional societies imbued with age-old traditions of mutual aid and social cooperation, he had little quarrel with the ahistorical nationalisms of the colonial world, provided they did not advocate state centralization or introduce Western values that could further undermine the structures of indigenous autonomous communities.

Unlike Marxism, which appealed to the organized working class of England, Germany and France in particular, Kropotkin's anti-authoritarian anarchism particularly appealed to peasants and agricultural workers across southern Europe. Recent research has emphasized the global appeal of anarchism in the late nineteenth and early twentieth centuries, when anarchists were at the forefront of anti-colonial struggles in China, Japan and South East Asia.[16] While he borrowed extensively from the 'towering edifice' of Marxist socialism, Kropotkin never ignored the historical role or revolutionary potential of peasants and agricultural workers to the extent that many nineteenth-century Marxists (and later on Marxist-Leninists in particular) have often done. This was clearly an advantageous position for anarchists to maintain in an age when the industrial working class, the favoured vanguard of revolution for many Marxists and socialists prior to the emergence of Maoism in the 1950s and 1960s, was largely confined to a handful of heavily industrialized regions in nineteenth-century northern Europe. Thus, for example, in marked contrast to Marx and Engels, Kropotkin introduced the peasantry and subsistence farmers into his analysis of historical change. He was also acutely aware of the revolutionary potential of the rural poor and other subordinate sectors not directly linked to the urban working class. In an effort to understand the seeming conservatism of the rural poor in the face of working-class revolutionary activity he focused on the modes of the cultural, political and legal incorporation adopted by ruling sectors to maintain their political authority and prevent subordinate sectors like peasants, craft workers and other marginalized groups from becoming socially and politically insubordinate. In so doing he showed that ruling-class hegemony – which in authoritarian regimes like tsarist Russia, imperial China and Japan, and in monarchical Europe, permeated practically every aspect of social life – very rarely enveloped the lives of these subordinate social groups to the extent of preventing them from articulating, and defending, their own modes of work, leisure and political behaviour. Neither could the surveillance state, even under conditions of the strictest ruling-class hegemony, prohibit the oppressed from at least thinking about their own heterotopian alternative to an existing unjust social and economic reality. It could never prevent the downtrodden developing their own radically different ways of relating to each other, to nature, and to local and globalized environments. Least of all could it prevent the oppressed articulating their own ethical code, their own views on what constituted social justice, the moral economy and the 'good life'. Despite high levels of state oppression, and notwithstanding the watertight nature of the authoritarian state, there was always, as Leonard Cohen's sublime lyric 'Anthem' put it, 'a crack in everything, that's how the light gets in'.

Similarly, as Kropotkin saw it, the hegemony of ruling sectors even in the most oppressive of societies simply defined the limits of what appeared to be possible. While this limited perception of social reality may have hindered the development of alternative perspectives on social progress and historical change, there was nothing absolute, determined or inevitable about ruling-class hegemony. As a last resort, hegemony in any society could ultimately be sustained through the use of state violence and the surreptitious use of physical force and moral persuasion. Even in the more liberal state societies of Europe and North America it had to be sustained with great skill, subtlety and diplomacy, not least by the religious and educational establishment, and through the constant supervision of state institutions that were ultimately designed to protect the powerful from the powerless. This was why Kropotkin insisted on the abolition of religious authority and the transformation of teaching and scientific research from state-centred endeavours into subversive activities.

He was also alert to the fact that even in a highly authoritarian society like tsarist Russia, the hegemonic authority of the powerful rarely entailed the total acceptance by the poor of the paternalism and authority of the powerful on terms approved by the latter alone. While throughout history the oppressed appeared to accept the paternalism of the powerful upon terms set by church and state, the price for such deference was always open to negotiation. It was never predetermined, let alone immutably carved in stone or copper-fastened in draconian legal codes. The hegemony of ruling elites could often impose blinkers that prevented subordinate social groups from uniting to abolish the authority of ruling elite and establishing their own moral alternative to the hegemony of the powerful. However, as Kropotkin never ceased to argue, history showed that the hegemony of church and state alike was rarely powerful enough to completely preclude the possibility of poor people attaining consciousness of their own independent political, cultural and economic potential. This goes a considerable way towards explaining the historic appeal of anarchism to rural communities and the oppressed peasantry in Mediter-ranean Europe and in countries as far apart as nineteenth-century tsarist Russia and imperial Japan. Here, Kropotkin believed, anarchists could position themselves Janus-like at the forefront of anti-state forces and become an organic and anti-state intelligentsia dedicated to the overthrow of ruling-class hegemony and the establishment of a stateless society.

The ontological basis of anarchist altruism

Kropotkin's solidarity with those whom Fanon called 'the wretched of the earth' derived from an innate moral sense of justice, rather than from any aristocratic or philanthropic desire simply to 'do good' for those less fortunate than himself.[17] Indeed he was highly suspicious of the egotism and hedonism that underpinned nineteenth-century expressions of social philanthropy. Like so many of his educated young Russian peers in the 1870s, he had been inspired to 'go to the people' in order to bring them a step closer to a better life. As a youth in the Corps of Pages he had participated in at least one project 'to provide schools staffed by volunteers for the newly liberated serfs'. This particular altruistic venture ended in failure when it aroused the suspicion of tsarist authorities that regarded any effort to enlighten the rural poor as ultimately subversive and detrimental to the authority of the state. Despite the fact that it manifested itself at an early age, Kropotkin's altruism was never simply a sentimental Russian variant of the *noblesse oblige* that characterized European society for long periods of history. It derived instead from the intellectual and emotional energy that Kropotkin experienced as a scientist amidst the sheer profusion of life in a variety of European contexts, most especially in the rural Russia of his childhood, and in Siberia in the early 1860s. Unlike his aristocratic peers, Kropotkin's desire to 'be useful' was never simply reducible to a philanthropic impulse to alleviate poverty. Like Godwin, he believed that benevolence brought with it its own pleasures and that personal gratification ultimately derived from the gratification of others. Thus he argued:

> If a man who gives away his last shirt found no pleasure in doing so, he would not do it. If he found pleasure in taking bread from a child, he would do that but this is distasteful to him. He finds pleasure in giving, and so he gives ... When a woman deprives herself of her last piece of

bread to give it to the first comer, when she takes off her own scanty rags to cover another woman who is cold, while she herself shivers, she does so because she would suffer infinitely more in seeing a hungry man, or a woman starved with cold, than in shivering or feeling hungry herself. She escapes a pain of which only those who have felt it know the intensity.[18]

Kropotkin's ethical code rejected the religious teachings of church and state on the one hand, and the utilitarian values of the Benthamites on the other. Moral actions, he argued, were 'a mere necessity' which compelled the individual 'to enjoy the joys of his brethren, to suffer when some of his brethren are suffering'. With time they become mere habits, man's second nature, which could be gradually 'elaborated and perfected by life in society'. Thus for example we appeal to the principle of equality chiefly in 'moments of hesitation', while in 'ninety-nine cases out of a hundred' we act morally purely from habit. He subsequently summarized his ethical code for the young by exhorting them to 'spread your intelligence, your love, your energy of actions … among others'.[19] As I shall presently suggest, this also encapsulated his philosophy of knowledge and formed the basis of his educational philosophy.

One hundred years before Foucault famously asserted that 'knowledge is power', Kropotkin was alert to the 'immense power' of knowledge in achieving revolutionary social change. Following Bakunin's death in 1876, Kropotkin's theoretical writings were to give anarchism intellectual status as well as a new direction. Like Bakunin, he too wished to become a spokesman for 'the proletariat of the countryside, the outcast of history, those millions of non-civilized, disinherited, wretched and illiterates' who were still more or less 'unpolluted by all bourgeois civilization'.[20] However unlike Bakunin, the hero of the barricades and impassioned anarchist demagogue, Kropotkin's career as a revolutionary militant in the 1870s and 1880s was far less important to the anarchist cause than his celebrated writings on the state, education, social morality, regional development, mutual aid and socio-economic cooperation. His ethical code envisaged a radical democratization of education and teaching, which sought to make the sciences the 'possession of all'. He criticized academics for engaging in research and specialization literally for their own sakes, while condemning them also for their refusal to engage in the popular practice of mass politics and political organization. Like many of his socialist and anarchist contemporaries, Kropotkin had little time for the formalism of academic disciplines, preferring instead 'useful knowledge' which, he felt, could improve the lives of the socially subordinate. A full century before Paulo Freire outlined his 'pedagogy of the oppressed' for the Brazilian poor, Kropotkin, like Tolstoy, wished schools and colleges to cater to the needs of the poorest sectors of society. Reiterating Proudhon's formulation that outlined the curriculum of anarchist schools, colleges and training academies, Kropotkin stated:

> if a naval academy is not itself a ship with sailors who enjoy equal rights and receive a theoretical education, then it will produce not sailors but officers to supervise sailors; if a technical academy is not itself a factory, not itself a trade school, then it will produce foremen and managers and not workmen. We do not need these privileged institutions; we need neither universities nor technical academies created for the few; we need the hospital, the factory, the chemical works, the ship, the productive trade school for workers, which, having become available to all, will with unimaginable speed exceed the standard of present universities and academies.[21]

Popular education, he argued, could also empower the poor and the uneducated, thereby providing them with the tools to interpret and reconstruct the world about them in their image, rather than that of their rulers. The initial focal point for the newly trained masses would be rural communes (*obshchiny*), each with its own schools and training centres, and each producing the products necessary for the material and cultural welfare of society in general. These small units would voluntarily unite for purposes of cultural exchange and commerce, and without any interference from government or legal authorities. Thus anarchists would ensure that schooling would be 'merged with apprenticeship', that students would learn from practical experience, and from programmes of study devised by and for local communities of workers and peasants. This would eliminate the unnecessary separation of manual from intellectual labour in the everyday life and practices of the common people. Kropotkin, like Godwin, suggested that if men and women were to work with their hands as well as their brains for 'five hours a day from the age of twenty-five to forty-five or fifty', this would ensure the physical and material comfort of the whole of society. Having experienced the 'joys' of learning and scientific discovery, he argued that study and leisure were as important as food and shelter to the growth and development of the human spirit. Thus, just as the working lives of men and women were to be organized through cooperative associations, their leisure was to be enhanced by the proliferation of self-help and mutual-interest organizations 'reaching out into a population of fervent amateurs'. In a statement reminiscent of Herbert Marcuse's denunciation of the one-dimensionality of twentieth-century consumer capitalism, he wrote:

> Man is not a being whose exclusive purpose in life is eating, drinking and providing shelter for himself. As soon as his material wants are satisfied, other needs, which, generally speaking, may be described as of an artistic nature, will thrust themselves forward. These needs are of the greatest variety; they vary in each and every individual, and the more society is civilized, the more will individuality be developed, and the more will desires be varied.[22]

He would go on to argue that a human being should not be riveted 'for all his life to a given spot, in a workshop or a mine'. No gain was to be had from depriving men and women of such work as would bring them 'into free intercourse with nature, make them a conscious part of the grand whole, a partner in the highest enjoyments of science and art, of free work and creation'.[23] Finally, and unlike many of his aristocratic contemporaries, Kropotkin rejected quasi-racist categorizations of peasants and serfs as so much human chattel believed to be devoid of all human sentiment. In humanizing the rural poor in this manner he went several steps further than most Marxists, who simply bemoaned the backwardness of peasants and built all their hopes for revolutionary change on the backs of the urban proletariat. In the 1880s, when primary education was little more than the mechanical repetition of facts and figures, usually under the direction of stern schoolmasters, Kropotkin insisted that the purpose of education was to 'interest the child in the great phenomena of nature, to waken the desire of knowing and explaining them'. He was also convinced that an anarchist-inspired 'universal history' would avoid the national exceptionalism in nationalist histories and transcend the eurocentrism of the Western academics. For Kropotkin this was important because schools and universities maintained a dogmatic faith in the 'natural perversity of man'. Thus, he argued, teachers and professors 'everywhere teach the necessity of having a power above man, and of implanting a moral element in society by means of punishment, inflicted for violation of "moral law". If left to their own devices, they argued, human beings would revert to savagery, and society would be reduced to a state of 'brutishness' if priests, judges, policemen and the hangman did not inculcate respect for the 'nobler conceptions' of civilized behaviour.[24]

Similarly, he argued that the teaching of history should emphasize the historical contingency and artificiality of racial, social class, and indeed political and geographical boundaries. Avoiding 'national exceptionalism', with its emphasis on the cultural uniqueness of nationally defined peoples, he also wished to foster vibrant new historical imaginaries that would focus on the life-worlds of the exploited majority, regardless of distinctions of race, class, religion or gender. This was all the more important in the politically charged environments of late nineteenth-century Europe where, he argued, even the best-intentioned historian

unconsciously draws a distorted picture of the times he endeavors to depict; ... to restore the real proportion between conflict and union [anarchist scholars] are bound to enter a minute analysis of the thousands of facts and faint indications accidentally preserved in the relics of the past; to interpret them with the aid of comparative ethnology; and after having heard so much about what used to divide men, to reconstruct stone by stone the institutions which used to unite them.[25]

Where young men were called upon to support the nationalist and imperialist objectives of their respective nation-states, Kropotkin urged geographers, social scientists and historians in particular to teach their students that

we are all brethren, whatever our nationality. Geography must be – in so far as the school may do anything to counterbalance hostile influences – a means of dissipating ... prejudice and of creating other feelings more worthy of humanity. It must show that each nationality brings its own precious building stone for the general development of the commonwealth, and that only small parts of each nation are interested in maintaining national hatreds and jealousies.[26]

Criticizing the educational policies of the state for promoting militarism and fostering imperialism and chauvinistic nationalism, he called on teachers everywhere to alert their students to the evils of 'national self conceit'. Thus he argued:

> The small differences we notice in the customs and manners of different nationalities, as also the differences of national character which appear especially among the middle classes, make us overlook the immense likeness which existing among the labouring classes of all nationalities ... It is the task of geography to bring this truth, in its full light, into the midst of the lies accumulated by ignorance, presumption and egotism.[27]

In contrast to the Social Darwinists, he sought to demonstrate that the historical record contained ample evidence of the triumph of international and inter-tribal cooperation over the sectionalist interests and authoritarian ethos of the modern state and the individualist ethos of modern capitalism. Thus a critique of nationalism was implicit in his opposition to industrial capitalism and the centralization of state authority. As far as Kropotkin was concerned, nationalism was just another state-sponsored ideology, promoted by the intelligentsia, to serve the national interests of the state and cater to the needs of industrial capitalism. Nationalism as he saw it advanced the class interests of the national bourgeoisie, while simultaneously fostering the global supremacy of White nations. Not surprisingly, therefore, the nationalist intelligentsia, and especially nationalist academics, performed important propagandistic functions in the geopolitical environment of nineteenth-century Europe. In the aftermath of the French Revolution, particularly following the national uprisings of the 1830s, the political and academic establishment literally nationalized the socio-geographical and historical imaginations of their people. Thus they revered the *volk* traditions of their nations, recounted the exploits of national heroes, emphasized the centrality of ethnic heritage to the cultural survival of their people, and provided strong historicist and quasi-racist justifications for the nation-building objectives of the national bourgeoisie. By the 1870s, the belief that nations, like individuals, had a right to be free rather than be ruled either by monarchs or foreign leaders had become a central tenet of European liberalism. Throughout the last quarter of the nineteenth century this evolved into a foundational principle of political thought in Western Europe. It was then that an assortment of new ideas about the authority of the state and the rights of people to govern themselves had so gripped the minds of the masses that they coalesced into what Gramsci termed a 'material force'.[28] Nationalist ideology came to dominate the social thinking of an entire historical bloc, uniting national society from within and maintaining its political grip on all social classes.

Kropotkin's critique of Social Darwinism was to become a 'principle pole of opposition' to these hegemonic ideas.[29] However, rather than prioritizing the development of theory over the practical task of organizing and politicizing the masses, he called on anarchists to maintain an intimate and active relationship with the poor, and to immerse themselves in the popular practice of peasant and working-class politics. He was particularly critical of radical intellectuals whose preoccupation with theoretical debates and ideological issues meant that they were detached from the day-to-day lives of the rural poor and working-class people. From sophisticated debates about social policy and lofty philosophizing about history and the nature of social progress, he turned to the mundane task of raising the political consciousness of peasants and workers and called on fellow anarchists to teach them how to read and write. In *An Appeal to the Young*, written in 1899 when the youth of Europe were being encouraged to submit to the moral and political authority of their social and intellectual superiors, he asked:

> In what respect does the philosopher, who pursues science in order that he may pass life pleasantly to himself, differ from the drunkard there, who only seeks the immediate gratification that gin affords him? The philosopher has, past all doubt, chosen his enjoyment more wisely, since it affords him a pleasure far deeper and more lasting than that of the toper. But that is all! Both one and the other have the same selfish end in view, [namely] personal gratification.[30]

Coming of age of the anarchist scientist

By the 1870s Kropotkin was clearly identifying with those who sought to become spokespersons for the rural poor who, following the abolition of serfdom in 1862, were being forced to move to the cities or condemned to lives of poverty and social exclusion in the comparative isolation of the countryside. However, rather than turning his back on the sciences to become an anarchist activist, he was to spend the remainder of his life putting anarchism on a scientific footing and presenting his own anarchist critique of hegemonic Darwinian explanations of social progress and the development of state authority. In so doing, he demonstrated that scientific knowledge had been socially constructed and was always susceptible to ideological manipulation. He also suggested that it was entirely possible to reconstruct disciplinary knowledge and use the deductive reasoning of science to bolster the political legitimacy of the stateless society. Yet his version of scientific anarchism drew criticism from many of his fellow anarchists. Emma Goldman not only castigated his aforementioned deafening silence on the issue of women's liberation and sexual freedom – she also accused him of being overly ascetic and too 'bookish'.[31] While recognizing that Kropotkin's writings were a powerful theoretical defence of the stateless society, Malatesta felt that he was inclined 'to use science "to support his social aspirations"'. He further criticized him for taking anarchism to intellectual heights from which it was difficult to discern any meaningful role for the 'insurrectionary deed' and anarchist propaganda.[32]

Kropotkin's formal conversion to anarchism has been traced to his meetings with the young anarchist schoolmaster, James Guillaume, and the independent-minded watchmakers of the Jura villages in the early 1870s. His renunciation of state service at this stage practically coincided with his father's death, leaving him freer to follow the dictates of his emerging revolutionary consciousness. By the early 1870s, he had been in contact with the International Workingmen's Association. He was already on the way to becoming one of anarchism's most persuasive philosophers when anarchism was the dominant force in the self-consciously internationalist European Left. In Zurich he mixed with working-class radicals, took part in heated discussions about the Franco-Prussian war, and read 'furiously for entire nights' about social anarchism and class struggle in other European countries. Describing the political awakening that resulted from these experiences he wrote: 'The more I read the more I saw that there was before me a new world, unknown to me, and totally unknown to the learned makers of sociological theories – a world that I could know only by living in the Workingmen's Association and by meeting the workers in their everyday life.'[33] On moving to Geneva he regularly attended meetings of the radical Jura Federation, where he encountered many ex-Communards from the Paris Commune. Writing years later about the meetings he attended in Masonic Halls in the city, he recalled that he

> much preferred to be in the environment of the workers themselves. With a glass of sour wine, I sat long into the evening at some table in the hall among the workers, and soon became friendly with some of them, particularly with one stonemason who had deserted France after the Commune. ... Now I could observe the life of the movement [the International] from the inside and better understand how the workers themselves saw it.[34]

Even before this, especially during the period he spent in Siberia and Finland, he had become convinced that his life lay outside the military establishment, and outside academia. Siberia, he wrote, had brought him:

> into contact with men of all descriptions; the best and the worst; worst; those who stood at the top of society, and those who vegetated at the bottom – the tramps and the so-called incorrigible criminals. I had ample opportunity to watch the ways and habits of the peasants in their daily life, and still more opportunities to appreciate how little the State administration could give them, even if it were animated by the very best of intentions.[35]

After having observed the conditions in the prisons and the penal colonies of Siberia, he was horrified at the indifference of centralized autocratic government and its provincial outliers in places like Siberia. He became even more disillusioned when he realized that political indifference in St Petersburg and political corruption in Siberia had conspired to frustrate local efforts to improve the lives of convicts and the indigenous population of poor peasants. At this stage also, he came to abhor the brutality, corruption and incompetence of state functionaries, while appreciating the natural good sense, initiative and capacity for spontaneous cooperation of the 'uncivilized' inhabitants of this frozen outpost of imperial Russia. In Siberia, Kropotkin recognized that administrative structures tended to paralyze the 'excellent intentions' of even the most benign administrators, just as they could kill local initiatives and thwart grassroots efforts to improve social and economic life. Because they ultimately identified with a pyramidal, centralized administrative system that 'radiated from a distant capital', administrators tended to examine everything from the point of view of state-centred functionaries and government officials.[36] Following his meetings with members of the International Workingmen's Association, Kropotkin became increasingly convinced that organized groups of independent craft workers, skilled tradesmen, peasants, poor schoolteachers and the urban working class possessed the political consciousness and power that he hoped to instil among the peasants and workers of his own country. Referring specifically to the watchmakers he met in the Jura Mountains, he wrote:

> The very organization of the watch trade, which permits men to know one another thoroughly and to work in their own houses, where they are free to talk, explains why the level of intellectual development in this population is higher than that of workers who spend all their life from early childhood in the factories. There is more independence and more originality among petty trades ... The clearness of insight, the soundness of judgment, the capacity for disentangling complex social questions, which I noticed among these workers ... deeply impressed me ... But the equalitarian relations which I found ... appealed even more strongly to my feelings.[37]

The egalitarian relations that he observed among these workers, not least their 'independence of thought and expression', appealed 'even more strongly' to his emerging anarchist imagination. Recollecting this period years later, he described how 'when I came away from the mountains, after a week's stay with the watchmakers, my views upon socialism were settled; I was an anarchist'.[38]

Having turned down an academic post offered to him by the Russian Geographical Society, Kropotkin returned to St Petersburg where he became involved in the revolutionary struggle to abolish the autocratic regime of tsarist Russia. Recognizing 'the immense power' of scientific knowledge, he set about constructing the intellectual edifice of scientific anarchism. Far from abandoning scientific research for an insecure and perilous career as an anarchist activist, he continued to draw on his Siberian experiences in order to develop a radical alternative to Social Darwinism and the state-centred and positivist paradigms that were then dominating the social and environmental sciences in many centres of learning in Europe and North America. In particular, he attacked Thomas H. Huxley's portrayal of 'nature red in tooth and claw', deeming this to be a caricature of the natural world that was being used to provide a quasi-scientific justification for competitive struggle and authoritarian rule.[39] Huxley had been the professor of natural history at the Royal School of Mines in London since 1854. He was to become the foremost expounder of Darwinism in Britain from the 1870s right through to his death in 1895. He was particularly revered within the scientific community for having fused Darwinian evolutionary theory with anthropology, providing a deeply deterministic and racist perspective on 'man's place in nature'. This was the title of one of his most famous works, published in 1863, the year after the young Kropotkin graduated from the Corps of Pages. Huxley's Social Darwinian views received their greatest exposure in his paper, 'The Struggle for Existence and its Bearing on Human Society', published in 1888. This prompted Kropotkin to write a reply, and in 1890 he set about publishing a series of detailed essays in *The Nineteenth Century* on mutual aid among animals, among 'savages', among 'barbarians', and among the inhabitants of the medieval city. These would later form the basis of his most effective and renowned work, *Mutual Aid: A Factor of Evolution*, which was finally published in book form in 1902. He first encountered the concept 'mutual aid' in a paper by the Russian zoologist K. Kessler that was first published by the St Petersburg Naturalist Society in 1880. Kessler had been Dean of St Petersburg University and developed his ideas on mutual aid in a lecture he delivered in January of that year, a few months before his death. 'As a zoologist of old standing', he protested against 'overrating the importance' of the term 'the struggle for existence', which had been borrowed from zoology and was widely used in the 'sciences which deal with man' to portray nature as 'a pitiless struggle for existence'.[40] Thus it was Kessler, not Kropotkin, who first pointed out that the more individuals of a species 'keep together, the more they mutually support each other ... the more are its chances of the species surviving [and] making further progress'. 'All classes of animals, especially the higher one', Kessler argued, 'practice mutual aid'. In terms later adopted by Kropotkin to stress the importance of mutual aid as a factor in the survival of species, Kessler would go on to state:

I obviously do not deny the struggle for existence, but I maintain that the progressive development of the animal kingdom, and especially of mankind, is favoured much more by mutual support than by mutual struggle … All organic beings have two essential needs: that of nutrition and that of propagating the species. The former brings them to a struggle and to mutual extermination, while the needs of maintaining the species bring them to approach one another and to support one another. But I am inclined to think that in the evolution of the organic world – in the progressive modification of organic beings – mutual support among individuals plays a much more important part than their mutual struggle.[41]

Statements such as these demonstrate that Social Darwinism was never as strongly developed in tsarist Russia as it was in the state societies of Western Europe and North America. Kropotkin would adopt the 'principle of mutual aid' as a foundational tenet of European anarchism, and a central principle of his scientific anarchism.

The biological basis of social morality

It was in *Mutual Aid* that Kropotkin developed his thesis that the 'intellectual faculty' in animals and humans was 'eminently social' and that it fostered the communication skills and imitative behaviour that enabled species to learn from experience. As we have seen, he argued that mutual aid and free cooperation between humans reached their apogee in the rich communal life of Europe's medieval cities. Despite attempts by the coercive institutions of state to eliminate cooperation and replace voluntary organizations with state-managed agencies, the mutual aid tendency in society survived right down to the late nineteenth century in countless interstices of European and colonial society. Historical research had shown that even the most coercive and well-organized state had not managed to eliminate the mutual aid tendency and human sociability. Having stressed their centrality to the evolutionary process, Kropotkin then proceeded to demonstrate that human propensities towards mutuality and cooperation were the foundation of all social ethics.

Again and again, he reiterated the importance of 'intimate co-operation among members of each level of living things as a fundamental factor in their survival'. Thus he suggested that an innate moral sense expressed itself in the natural needs of all animals, including humans, as they struggled together to survive and evolve. Rejecting the authoritarian moral codes of church, state and the intellectual establishment alike, he argued that their dogmatic claims to truth should never displace the intrinsic sense of justice that permeated mutually supportive urban and rural communities in Europe and pre-capitalist societies elsewhere. Altruism, he argued, was rooted in this innate moral sense of humanity, which was also to be the basis of anarchist morality. Because he considered the moral sense that underpinned social behaviour to be ultimately instinctive, artificial laws or government regulation must not hamper it. Laws, he argued, perverted man's natural moral sense and hindered social progress. They were also no match for the innate sense of justice, which, despite the ravages of capitalism and the atomization of society under capitalism, could still be found within rural communities and working-class districts throughout Europe and North America. Thus he argued:

> The millions of laws which exist for the regulation of humanity appear upon investigation to be divided into three principal categories: protection of property, protection of persons, protection of government. ... Half our laws – the civil code in each country – serve no other purpose than to maintain this appropriation [of property], this monopoly for the benefit of certain individuals against the whole of mankind ... And a great many of our criminal laws have the same object in view, their end being to keep the workman in a subordinate position towards his employer, and thus affording security for exploitation.[42]

In writing voluminously on the role of mutual aid in the survival of societies, the nature of anti-capitalist and anti-statist ethics, the political economy of anarchist society, and the need for spontaneity in the revolutionary process, Kropotkin estranged himself from the leading Marxist and other revolutionary parties of his day. These, he argued, were inherently elitist and dictatorial, and sought to replace one form of state control with another that posed even greater risks to local initiative and local autonomy. He insisted that human beings perform at their best when they are in a position to 'apply their varied capacities to several pursuits'.[43] In a prescient statement in which he foretold the threat to individual liberties posed by fascism and Bolshevism, he claimed that in a society organized on anarchist principles:

man would not be limited in the free exercise of his powers in productive work by a capitalist monopoly, maintained by the State; nor would he be limited in the exercise of his will by a fear of punishment, or by obedience towards individuals or metaphysical entities, which both lead to depression of initiative and servility of mind. He would be guided in his actions by his own understanding, which necessarily would bear the impression of a free action and reaction between his own self and the ethical conceptions of his surroundings. Man would thus be enabled to obtain the full development of all his faculties, intellectual, artistic and moral, without being hampered by overwork for the monopolists, or by the servility and inertia of mind of the great number. He would thus be able to reach full *individualization*, which is not possible, either under the present system of *individualism*, or under any system of State socialism in the so-called *Volkstaat* (popular State).[44]

Thus Kropotkin the scientist insisted that the stateless society was not so much a utopian aspiration as an evolutionary 'imperative', and 'immanent historical reality'. Viewed thus, anarchism was the 'creative force of the masses' that had devised common-law institutions in order to defend themselves against an authoritarian minority. It originated among the people, and would preserve its moral and creative potential only so long as it remained a movement of the people. As he saw it, anarchism refused to be hampered by 'the metaphysics of Hegel, Schelling and Kant, the expositions of Roman or Canonical law, [the moral authority] of learned professors of State law, or the political economy of metaphysicians'. As a constructive force of the people it endeavoured to protect and extend the mutual aid institutions that were indispensable to the free development of society, in opposition to 'those who put their hope in laws made by governing minorities'. Anarchists, he added:

conceive a society in which all the mutual relations of its members are regulated, not by laws, not by authorities, whether self-imposed or elected, but by mutual agreement between members of that society, and by the sum of social custom and habits – not petrified by law, routine, or superimposition, but continually developing and continually readjusted, in accordance with the ever-growing requirements of a free life, stimulated by the progress of science, invention and the steady growth of higher ideals.[45]

He also believed that anarchism could revolutionize attitudes towards public morality and social behaviour, thereby undermining the role of church and state as the main arbiters of moral conduct. The moral code of scientific anarchism was rooted in the sociability of human society, rather than in any supernatural belief systems or metaphysical doctrines. With his characteristic tendency to rely on man's natural propensity towards social responsibility, Kropotkin further suggested that society, unlike government, was a natural phenomenon. If the artificial restrictions imposed upon society by laws and state regulations were removed, men and women would act responsibly. In arguing thus he ignored the fact that individuals are often conditioned to depend upon the state and may be reluctant to take responsibility for their own actions once the state is dismantled. Recognizing that a minority of 'asocial' individuals may reject the beneficial effects of work, he claimed that society had the right to use moral condemnation and public opinion to compel them to recognize their social responsibilities. Thus Kropotkin, like Godwin, was not immune from the temptations of self-righteousness. He claimed that solidarity and communal work 'strengthened the species in the fight for the maintenance of their existence against the adverse powers of nature'. His innate Puritanism, which was rooted in secularism rather than religion, made him a strong defender of the beneficial qualities of 'attractive work', which he, like William Morris, considered essential for the success of an anarchist society. This is especially clear from the following statement in which he discusses the plight of an imaginary 'useless man' in any future anarchist society:

If you are absolutely incapable of producing anything useful, or if you refuse to do it, then live like an isolated man or like an invalid. If we are rich enough to give you the necessities of life we shall be delighted to give them to you ... You are a man, and you have a right to live. But as you wish to live under special conditions, and not leave the ranks, it is more than probable that you will suffer for it in your daily relations with other citizens. You will be looked upon as a ghost of bourgeois society, unless friends of yours, discovering you to be a talent, kindly free you from all moral obligations by doing all the necessary work for you.[46]

In keeping with his holistic view of nature, Kropotkin also demonstrated that the organic world of plants and animals, and the 'inorganic' physical universe, were all subject to the same organizing principles. For that reason they experienced more or less identical cycles of growth and decay. The entire world was susceptible to revolutionary 'vibrations', which in turn brought about progressive evolutionary – and when times were propitious, revolutionary – social change. The evolutionary principles of growth and decay that were so clearly discernible in nature were equally discernible in human history. Everywhere one looked, the universe was in a perpetual state of flux. Far from being the natural tendency towards which all phenomena gravitated, harmony in nature, and in human society, 'was nothing more than the equilibrium established at one point of time by the adventitious arrangement of forces'.[47] Thus a constantly changing equilibrium is preferable to a social life regulated by the fixed laws of church, state and the academic establishment. With everything in a constant state of change, it followed that there was little need for static social hierarchies to maintain discipline and control the evolutionary process either in human society or in the animal kingdom. Having stressed the dynamic character of harmony in the 'no-government' society, Kropotkin went on to argue:

> Anarchism is the name given to a principle or theory of life and conduct under which society is conceived without government – harmony is such a society being obtained, not by submission to authority, but by free agreements concluded between the various groups, territorial and professional, freely constituted for the sake of production and consumption, as also for the satisfaction of the infinite variety of needs and aspirations of a civilized being.[48]

Despite the intensification and centralization of the authority of the nation-state, and notwithstanding the competitive ethos of modern capitalism since the sixteenth century, Kropotkin demonstrated that the mutual aid tendency had continually reappeared and reasserted itself in society. Even in the latter half of the nineteenth century it was still manifesting itself in the 'infinity of associations which... embraced all aspects of life [and had taken] possession of all that is required by man for life'.[49] In criticizing Social Darwinists, Kropotkin maintained that evolutionary theory did not support the contention that competitive struggle and the authoritarian state were in any way inevitable, let alone essential or permanent features of human society. Instead, the sheer resilience of mutual aid and social cooperation pointed in the direction of a stateless society comprising myriads of autonomous 'micro-societies' nested within mutually beneficial federal structures. Social progress was predicated on the resolution of conflict and the triumph of cooperation, rather than class warfare or the permanent dialectical synthesis of opposing social forces. As a necessary strategy for the *preservation of the welfare* and progressive *development* of every species, the mutual aid instinct was what Darwin described as 'a *permanent instinct*'.[50] As such it was '*always at work* in all social animals, and especially in man'. Because it evolved out of the 'very beginnings of the evolution of the animal world', it was 'deeply seated in animals, low and high', and more powerful even than the instinct of maternal love, as 'it is present in such animals as the mollusks, some insects, and most fishes, which hardly possess the maternal instinct at all'. Thus Darwin correctly viewed the instinct of 'mutual sympathy' as one that was '*more permanently* at work in the social animals than even the purely egotistic instinct of direct self-preservation'. This led Kropotkin to argue that the study of human society revealed 'laws of moral science' and that these were predicated on the 'social needs and habits of mankind'. Ethical codes and social morality, he suggested, derived from the day-to-day biological needs of socialized individuals in communities, while the social instincts were as equally innate in humans as they were in all other social animals. Humans, he argued, were embedded in nature, just as individuals are also members of society. 'Man did not create society, society has existed before man' – this became an axiomatic principle of scientific anarchism. In human society as in the animal world, the 'law of mutual aid' was 'the law of progress'. Unlike the Social Darwinists, Kropotkin did not subscribe to the view that man was 'naturally aggressive': 'Man has always preferred peace and quiet. Quarrelsome rather than fierce, he prefers his cattle, land, and his hut to soldiering.' The idea of good and evil, moreover, 'has thus nothing to do with religion or a mystic conscience. It is a natural need of animal races. And when founders of religions, philosophers, and moralists tell us of divine and metaphysical entities, they are only recasting what each ant, each sparrow practices in its little society.'[51]

Viewed thus, nature dictated that humans were essentially moral beings whose sociability enhanced their collective sense of justice. In the end, their just actions were transformed into social habits ingrained in the daily praxis of learning how to live, learn, work and socialize together. Humans, he maintained, had their own conception of 'good' and 'evil', their own faith in the 'gradual triumph of the good principle'. These were so deeply ingrained in human nature that they could become a reliable basis for a new secular morality. Thus Kropotkin claimed that the modern world needed a 'realistic moral science' free from superstition, religious dogmatism and metaphysical mythologies. This new morality, he added, must also be infused with the 'higher feelings' and 'brighter hopes' that had inspired those who placed their trust in the achievements of modern science. Such a moral science, he added, is 'what humanity is persistently demanding', and was eminently achievable in the scientific environment of late nineteenth-century Europe. For the first time in history, humankind had reached 'a point where the means of satisfying its needs are in excess of the needs themselves'. Modern science, he argued, had achieved a 'double aim':

On the one side it has given to man a very valuable lesson of modesty. It has taught him to consider himself as but an infinitesimally small particle of the universe. It has driven him out of his narrow, egotistical seclusion, and has dissipated the self-conceit under which he considered himself the center of the universe and the object of the special attention of the Creator. It has taught him that without the whole the 'ego' is nothing; that our 'I' cannot even come to a self-definition without the 'thou.' But at the same time science has taught man how powerful mankind is in its progressive march, if it skillfully utilizes the unlimited energies of Nature.[52]

While acknowledging the need for a sceptical approach to the ethical authority of the sciences, Kropotkin was convinced that evolutionary theory contained the elements of a system of ethics. Thus he recognized that a fecundity of will and thirst for action would be morally deficient if accompanied by a poverty of feeling and an intellect incapable of creation. Similarly, 'mental fertility' that was devoid of a 'well developed sensibility' will bring forth 'such barren fruits as literary and scientific pedants who only hinder the advance of knowledge'. Properly formulated, however, the new ethic advanced by scientific anarchism would respond to the needs of the present day. The greatest happiness of the greatest number, Kropotkin insisted, was now possible and was no longer a mere Utopia. Moreover, the prosperity and happiness of no nation-state or social class could ever be based, even temporarily, upon the degradation of other classes, nations or races. For Kropotkin, therefore, the problem confronting those who wished to develop a code of ethics suitable for the new scientific age was to ensure that *morality* was grounded in the international world of present-day realities. Morals, he argued, should never be 'transcendental', as the idealists desired, but must 'be real'. Moral satisfaction, in other words, was to be found in this life, and not in 'some form of extra-vital condition'. While moral values and ethical codes may be in a permanent state of flux, they must always be embedded in human sociability and mutuality rather than in the coercive strictures of either church or state. It followed from this that human beings were not only naturally moral – they were also morally progressive. Moreover, their innate sense of justice and morality would become more refined, and comprehensive, with the development and evolution of civilization itself. Thus Kropotkin believed that the human capacity to sympathize, and empathize, with the sufferings of others increased the more intense and delicate our moral senses became. Hence he argued:

> The more powerful your imagination, the better you can picture to yourself what any being feels when it is made to suffer ... The more you are drawn to put yourself in the place of the other person, the more you feel the pain inflicted upon him ... the more will you be urged to act so that you can prevent the pain, the insult, or injustice.[53]

He believed that the sheer historical resilience of the human tendencies of mutuality and sociability had rendered them the most enduring features of the evolutionary process in human society and organic nature in general. He also claimed that the limited success of ethical systems since the Enlightenment suggested that humans were never satisfied with a naturalistic *explanation of the origins of the moral instinct*. They required *justification* for why they should accept any particular explanation of the origins and future direction of moral codes. Thus simply to trace the origin of moral feelings, or to point to the causes that have contributed to the growth and refinement of the moral sense, was not enough. People needed to have a criterion for judging the moral instinct, to know where it will lead them. More importantly they needed to be assured that their moral code will not 'result in the weakening of the race and its ultimate decay'. Thus Kropotkin maintained that the purpose of ethics 'is not to advise men separately [but] rather to set before them, as a whole, a higher purpose, an ideal which, better than any advice, would make them act instinctively in the proper direction'. Just as 'mental training' accustomed people to perform 'an enormous number of mental operations almost unconsciously', the aim of ethics was 'to create such an atmosphere in society as would produce in the great number, entirely by impulse, those actions which best lead to the welfare of all and the fullest happiness of every separate being'. This, he argued, was 'the final aim of morality' and to reach it people must free their moral training from any self-contradictions that it might contain. Kropotkin's reading of human and natural history suggested 'the permanent presence of a *double tendency*', pointing in one direction towards the greater development of *sociality*, and in the other towards a consequent increase in the utter intensity of life. This resulted in an increase of happiness for *individuals*, while simultaneously contributing to the physical, intellectual and moral development of society as a whole.[54] To promote the further development of these natural social tendencies is the practical mission of all anarchists. Because the moral sense is so intimately linked with the mutual aid tendency and sociability, society cannot evolve, or even survive, without it.

Anarchism and anti-foundational radicalism

For Kropotkin mutual aid, justice and morality were not simply abstract metaphysical concepts. They were 'consecutive steps of an ascending series, revealed to us by the study of the animal world and man'. They constituted an *organic necessity* 'which carries in itself its own justification, confirmed by the whole of the evolution of the animal kingdom, beginning with its earliest stages, ... and gradually rising to our civilized human communities'. Therefore the idea of good and evil exists within humanity itself, and regardless of the degree of intellectual development they may have attained, or the degree of prejudice and personal interest prevailing in society at large, humans have always defined 'good' as that which is useful to the individual and to society, and 'evil' as that which 'is hurtful to it'. Anarchist morality urges that we consciously '*do* to others what we would have them *do* to us in similar circumstances'. In concluding that 'All of the conscious and deliberate actions of humans have the same source', Kropotkin went to suggest that:

'Those that are called virtuous and those that are designated as vicious, great devotions and petty knaveries, acts that attract and acts that repel, ... all are performed in answer to some need of the individual's nature. All have for their end the quest for pleasure, and the desire to avoid pain.'[55]

In outlining a code of ethics independent of state sanction or legal obligation, Kropotkin claimed that altruism ultimately derived from an awareness of the sociability and sheer profusion of life on earth. Anarchist morality seeks the free development of every individual's faculties in the plenitude of social existence. What we admire in a truly moral man is 'his energy, the exuberance of life which urges him to give his intelligence, his feeling, his action, asking nothing in return'. Therefore, the strength of anarchism resides in its deep appreciation of the value of human faculties and passions, and in the fact that it ignores none of these faculties. Thus he argued: 'The feeling of solidarity is the leading characteristic of all animals living in society ... In all animal societies solidarity is a natural law of far greater importance than the struggle for existence, the virtue of which is sung by the ruling classes in every strain that may best serve to stultify us.'[56] For social anarchists in particular this resulted in 'an overflow' of feelings of fellowship for others that were accompanied by a profound intensification of emotional and intellectual energy. To seek pleasure and avoid pain was, for Kropotkin as for all Benthamites, the 'general line of action' in human society and the natural world. If humans once ceased in their quest for that which is agreeable to the individual and the community, society itself would disintegrate into a state of anarchy in the pejorative sense. Under these conditions social life would become impossible and death would befall all forms of organic life. In proclaiming themselves anarchists, Kropotkin's followers were also disavowing 'any way of treating others in which we should not like them to treat us'. They were also declaring that they would 'no longer tolerate the inequality that has allowed some among us to use their strength, their cunning or their ability after a fashion in which it would annoy us to have such qualities used against ourselves'. Viewed thus, equality in all things was 'the synonym of equity' that came to define the anarchist's every deed.

For Kropotkin also, good deeds and elevated ideals spurred humans on to achieve even greater things. Thus he argued, once the human being

> catches a glimpse of how lovely life might be if better relations existed among men, he feels in himself the power to succeed in establishing these better relations with those he may meet on his way. He conceives what is called an ideal. ... Life is vigorous, fertile, rich in sensation only on condition of answering to this feeling of the ideal. Act against this feeling, and you feel that your life bent back on itself. It is no longer at one, it loses its vigour. Be untrue often to your ideal and you will end by paralyzing your will, your active energy. Soon you will no longer regain the vigour, the spontaneity of decision you formerly knew. You are a broken man.[57]

Whereas Kropotkin regarded mutual aid as a fundamental factor of evolution, Huxley argued that the life of 'primitive' man was 'a continuous free fight', and that strife was an eternal feature of primitive society. Strife indeed was not merely a condition of progress for Huxley – it was also inevitable. Writing at the height of Europe's 'scramble for Africa', and at a time when the Native American civilizations of North America were all but obliterated, Huxley contributed to the naturalization of colonial warfare by reducing it to

> the same level as a gladiator's show. The creatures are fairly well treated, and set to fight – whereby the strongest, the swiftest and the cunningest live to fight another day. The spectator has no need to turn his thumbs down, as no quarter is given. He must admit that the skill and training displayed are wonderful. But he must shut his eyes if he would not see that more or less enduring suffering is the mead of both the vanquished and the victor.[58]

Kropotkin criticized this portrayal of nature as 'a field of unrestricted warfare', chiefly because it rendered struggle and strife the basis of social existence, and seemed to provide scientific legitimacy for Nietzschean claims that modern civilization was witnessing the end of morality and the rise of a new species of amoral 'supermen'. In a remarkable series of observations based on his own researches and those of other scientists, he challenged Huxley's view of nature as 'red in tooth and claw'. Turning to the natural world, he suggested that 'species that live solitarily or in small families are relatively few, and their numbers are limited'.[59] They are either species that are in decline, or their solitary existence is the result of artificial conditions created by human destruction of the balance of nature. Mutual aid, he argued, was fundamental to the survival and progressive development of more successful species, including humans, and was the most important factor in their evolution. In a paradigmatic statement on the role of cooperation and mutual aid in the entire evolutionary process he wrote:

Life in societies enables the feeblest animals, the feeblest birds, and the feeblest mammals to resist, or to protect themselves from the most terrible birds and beasts of prey; it permits longevity; it enables the species to rear its progeny with the least waste of energy and to maintain its numbers albeit at a very slow birth-rate; it enables the gregarious animals to migrate in search of new abodes. Therefore, while fully admitting that force, swiftness, protective colours, cunningness, and endurance to hunger and cold, which are mentioned by Darwin and Wallace, are so many qualities making the individual or the species the fittest under certain circumstances, we maintain that under *any* circumstances sociability is the greatest advantage in the struggle for life. Those species which willingly abandon it are doomed to decay; while those animals which know how best to combine have the greatest chance of survival and of further evolution, although they may be inferior to other in *each* of the faculties enumerated by Darwin and Wallace, except the intellectual faculty.[60]

His Siberian experiences also made Kropotkin deeply suspicious of Malthusian teachings on the relationship between food supply and population growth. It was in Siberia that he first became aware of 'the overwhelming importance in Nature of what Darwin described as "the natural checks to over-multiplication"'. He suggested that the Malthusian doctrine of overpopulation described demographic conditions in capitalist societies, and only then where the balance between resources and population in those societies was artificially disrupted. So-called 'overpopulation' reflected the consequences of a global division of labour peculiar to industrial capitalism.[61] In Siberia Kropotkin had gained a scientific understanding of the importance of struggle and competition to the evolutionary development of all species, including humans. Even in the harsh Siberian environment he discovered that competition never attained the same level of importance as mutual aid and cooperation in the survival and evolution of species. Instead of overpopulation and struggle he found that 'paucity of life' was the most distinctive feature of that immense part of the globe that he called Northern Asia. Here Kropotkin was brought face to face with the bountiful character of nature, which further caused him to have 'serious doubts ... as to the reality of that fearful competition for food and life within each species which was [such] an article of faith with most Darwinists'.[62]

Kropotkin's assault on Social Darwinism was only partially premised on the political and economic attractions of small, self-governing communities as alternatives to the centralizing, collectivizing and competitive tendencies of the state and modern capitalism. It was also predicated on the legitimacy, and political desirability, of cultural pluralism. Thus he clearly recognized the potentialities and ethical authority of syndicalism, the new trade unionism, and other national and international expressions of rural and working-class solidarity then emerging in some of the most advanced societies of the Western world. Rather than rejecting Darwinism or ignoring Social Darwinian defences of the competitive ethos of capitalism, he plumbed the depths of Darwinian natural science in order to fuse anarchism with evolutionary theory and thereby draw out its more radical and antithetical implications for the advancement of the stateless society. He encouraged anarchists to turn to the long-standing nineteenth-century tradition of apolitical 'associationism' and to tackle social questions by building support for radical social change from the ground up. Thus he identified an entire range of already-existing self-help organizations, including the cooperative movement, Masonic lodges, building societies, credit unions, agricultural societies, rural self-help organizations, workers confraternities, charitable organizations and craft guilds, all of which were to become building blocks of the stateless society. Rather than manipulating these or co-opting their leaders in order to enhance the political power of anarchists, he insisted that associationism and the preservation of mutualism were ends in themselves rather than the means to a state-centred end. While recognizing the potential of trade unionism to become a powerful modern expression of associationism, he believed that unions should function like real communities. Thus he called on the trade unions, which already had strong linkages with local communities and their immediate hinterland, to provide for the social welfare and cultural and educational needs of their communities, rather than simply becoming a base for national political parties. Support for these local solidarities as opposed to national organizations and the *nationalist state* was to distinguish the reformist left from grassroots anarchists in places as far apart as Barcelona and the American Northwest in the late nineteenth century and early twentieth.

Not the least of Kropotkin's achievements was the fact that he managed to keep the possibility of the stateless society alive in a triumphant age of chauvinistic nation-building. As a historically grounded expression of radical empiricism, his conception of the anarchist society was based both on historical examples of mutual aid and cooperation on the one hand, and on immanent tendencies in late nineteenth-century societies that continued to point in the direction of mutual support, cooperation and self-help on the other. As such it countered the utopianism of philosophical anarchism, the egotism of individualist anarchism and the pessimism of bourgeois realism. As a vehicle for modern 'anti-foundationalist' thought and action it recognized the ideological fault line separating 'practical' or social anarchists from 'individualist' anarchists. Thus it distinguished between the 'individualist' and 'philosophical' anarchism of existentialist writers like Max Stirner (1806–56), and 'practical anarchists' for whom anarchism was a political means to an end that must in principle always remain uncharted and undefined. The dilemma confronting Kropotkin and all rebels was how to imagine an alternative to the state and modern capitalism 'without becoming trapped in a prescriptive construct' that would place new restrictions on social and economic liberties.[63] Thus he was acutely aware of the many 'discomfiting historical instances' that illustrated just how easily political ideals could become canonized. Recognizing that radical protest could also become ossified and end in 'repressive dystopias', he opposed everything that contributed to the institutionalization of authority. While keeping his anarchist utopia in his mind's eye when proposing practical changes to the existing social order, Kropotkin insisted that the anarchist alternative to the modern state was never a utopian impossibility but was always 'in some sense immanent in the present'.[64] Thus his scientific anarchism was fundamentally opposed to the collectivizing tendencies of modern capitalism that categorized people as workers or employers, ranked societies in racial hierarchies on the basis of putative differences in intelligence and developmental potential, and allocated them to discrete national and ethic groupings. In an effort to circumvent the rigid absolutism of this narrow perspective on the capacity of peoples to engage in historical change and achieve social progress, Kropotkin conceived of the social as 'pluralistic'. Borrowing from Darwin's theory of mutation and Proudhon's notion of social reciprocity, he further suggested that societies were not 'ready made' social entities that anarchists could take for granted. Nor were they ideal social 'types' for which they could plan. For Kropotkin, Darwinism had much wider political and philosophical repercussions than was recognized by those who reduced it to a set of entrenched scientific principles that proved, and approved of, competition and natural selection as the only basis for progress in the natural world and human society. As he himself showed, it had other wide-ranging philosophical and political implications that pointed to the role of mutual aid and seemingly chance happenings in bringing about radical social change. Against the Social Darwinists over-emphasis on competition and struggle, he insisted that evolutionary change was a generative and *ungoverned* process involving the addition of social variations occurring at the 'vibrant interstices' of unfettered social, economic and cultural exchange.[65] This is another way of saying that the anarchist society is an unplanned 'historical happening', the product of ungoverned hybridizations that literally unify a whole variety of seemingly unconnected events both in the raw material of social experience and in the social consciousness of peoples. It is a complex mosaic embodied in real people, in their value systems, cultural traditions, social customs and political ideals:

> That is why anarchism, when it works to destroy authority in all its aspects, when it demands the abrogation of laws and the abolition of the mechanisms that serve to impose them, when it refuses all hierarchical organization and preaches free agreement, at the same time strives to maintain and enlarge the precious kernel of social customs without which no human or animal society can exist. Only instead of demanding that those social customs should be maintained through the authority of a few, it demands it from the continued action of all.[66]

Unlike other societies, therefore, the anarchist society was never to be embodied in the centralized authority of the state, let alone in any fixed authoritarian structures or institutional forms. Thus for Kropotkin, there could be no anarchist catechism, dogma or libertarian creed. While advocating social anarchism, which he equated with 'scientific anarchism', he was aware of the sheer variety and dynamism of nature. Nothing in nature was preconceived, all was the result of 'collisions and encounters'. Equilibrium that can take millions of years to establish can be shattered by a 'sudden redistribution of force' or by a 'momentary rupture of the equilibrium'. Harmony thus appears as nothing more than

> a temporary adjustment established among all forces acting upon a given spot – a provisionary adaptation. And that adjustment will only last under one condition: that of being continually modified; of representing every moment the resultant of all conflicting actions. Let but one of those forces be hampered in its actions for some time and harmony disappears. Force will accumulate its effects, it must come to light, it must exercise its actions, and if other forces hinder its mani-festation it will not be annihilated by that, but will end by upsetting the present adjustment, by destroying harmony, in order to find a new form of equilibrium and to work to form a new adaptation.[67]

For Kropotkin, all anarchists had one common characteristic that separated them from the rest of humankind. This uniting point was their negation of the principle of authority in social organizations and their opposition to all constraints imposed by institutions founded on principles of authority. This more than anything else accounted for anarchism's originality, dynamism, spontaneity and vitality. Thus Kropotkin's critique of the state was predicated upon a prior critique of the intellectual authority of the academic establishment. His critique of the state-centred politics of the left and right alike represented a timely and intellectually sustained assault on the foundational tenets of authoritar-ian philosophy and state-centred science. As an anarchist he not only set out to rewrite the history of social progress from the bottom up. He also demonstrated that government, whether monarchical or democratic, was a top-down affair that was always anchored in a set of antecedent beliefs or 'founding principles' that extolled the advantages of political authority and identified statelessness with social chaos and even barbarism. Thus anarchism in this wider sense did not simply imply opposition to the state and political leadership. It also entailed a radical, but not necessarily violent, disavowal of all 'first principles' of political authority. As such it dispensed with the necessity for the modern state, and attacked the foundational principles of religious authority, monarchical rule, Western democracy and state-centred socialism.

5

Kropotkin's Anarchism and the Nineteenth-Century Geographical Imagination: Towards an Anarchist Political Geography

Race, state and nation and the politics of geographical exploration

There was little about Kropotkin's privileged upbringing in the rural hinterland of nineteenth-century Moscow to suggest that he was to become Europe's foremost anarchist theorist. Everything about his educational background, not least his military training, his boyhood travels and geographical expeditions in Siberia, Arctic Russia and Scandinavia, seemed to prepare him for a successful career as an army officer, most likely with high-ranking regional administrative responsibilities. Failing that, he could have opted for a career as a conventional Russian geographer with specialized interests in physical geography and physiography. Certainly when he graduated from military school in the early 1860s he could have selected a career in any branch of military service. While still in his twenties, however, he turned down the opportunity of a 'glorious post' in a government ministry. Instead, as we have seen, he took up a position in an obscure Cossack regiment in the remote recesses of Eastern Siberia. This, he believed, would be infinitely preferable to 'a boring two years' of university lectures delivered by 'various fools'.[1] As we have also noted, however, the years Kropotkin spent in Siberia sharpened rather than blunted his geographical imagination. Even aside from the geographical reports on expeditions that he undertook as an army officer, his writings on evolutionary theory, medieval history and social anthropology all testify to the fact that he possessed a sophisticated geographical imagination. His research interests in zoology and natural history, together with geographical fieldwork in Siberia and Northern

Asia, were the very stuff that turned many a nineteenth-century army officer and explorer into a professional geographer.

Intimations of a geographer-in-the-making are also scattered throughout Kropotkin's *Memoirs*. The first section of this work in particular is filled with geographical insights. Thus with the sharp eye of a social geographer in the making, he described his childhood years in the Old Equerries' Quarter of Moscow, and on his father's estate to the south of that city, at a crucial watershed in the evolution of modern Russia. The second section recounts his experiences as a student in the military academy of the Corps of Pages, and also contains valuable material on his training in field research and cartography. The third section of his memoirs reads like a nineteenth-century travel narrative. Filled with detailed descriptions of fieldwork and geographical expeditions, it also demonstrates Kropotkin's intimate knowledge of the physical and human geography of Siberia, Manchuria and Central Asia. Kropotkin arrived in Siberia shortly after Bakunin's cousin Count Murav'ev-Amurskii had added large tracts of this vast region to imperial Russia. Referring specifically to his descriptions of Siberia, Colin Ward has argued that few writers have so accurately conveyed a 'sense of inhabiting not a country but an immense continent'.[2]

To appreciate Kropotkin's radical contribution to the history of geographical exploration one has to understand the racist geopolitical and indeed geographical motivations that impelled many nineteenth-century explorers to undertake arduous expeditions to some of the remotest corners of the world. The category of 'race' was then widely used as a form of social debasement and moral denigration that allowed White explorers and empire-builders to justify their colonial expansion and ascribe social and economic inferiority to whole swathes of the global population. It also signified a sense of belongingness and superiority by fostering quasi-biological constructs of peoples which when used pejoratively reflected negative tendencies of dissociation and exclusion. Not surprisingly, therefore, 'race', like the far more benign category 'ethnicity', had a powerful hold on European political and academic discourse in the Darwinian half of the nineteenth century. Used thus, race not only signified a set of physical characteristics and phenotypical traits that contributed to the 'simianization' of entire peoples. It also suggested an amalgam of derogatory and highly fictitious properties that 'fixed' peoples as inferior or superior, and set colonial societies, and especially peasants, workers and other marginalized social groups, apart from their metropolitan superiors. As such it was used to police the boundaries between the 'civilized' worlds of Europe and North America and the 'barbaric' world beyond. It was thus never simply an ideological category or theoretical device that could be used in an abstract fashion to define peoples. Ruling elites across Europe and North America regarded the racial inferiority of entire sectors of global society as something that could be explained away in environmental terms, as a more or less a permanent state of affairs. Viewed thus, their racial inferiority was deemed to be beyond the power of enlightened leaders to control or ameliorate. Racism therefore became an important element in justifying the formation and reproduction of free and un-free social relations of production. It not only provided a quasi-scientific justification for the 'unfreedoms' of oppressed peoples – it also gave states power to deny the poor access to the corridors of power. When combined with nationalism this type of racism bolstered the 'racial purity' of White homelands by outlawing racial mixing and controlling population movements between the colonial world and metropolitan society, and between 'backward' rural enclaves and centres of urban refinement. Anarchists were to show that the roots of this type of state-centred race thinking were also traceable to a wide range of nineteenth-century Western attitudes that linked culture and progress to ideals of self-improvement through orderliness, cleanliness and deference to authority.

The racist and state-centred agenda of nineteenth-century exploration is an important factor in understanding the young Kropotkin's drift towards anarchism in the 1860s. Traditional accounts of geographical exploration focused on the courageous efforts of a handful of intrepid, and predominantly male, explorers who satisfied national pride by planting their nation's flag at the outer limits of the 'civilized' world. In recounting epic tales of human endurance, these accounts celebrated the success of heroic individuals who struggled against unimaginable odds to open up the world's wildernesses to Western science. While national rivalry and geopolitical considerations clearly influenced their decision to extend the limits of geographical knowledge, those who participated in these expeditions were also committed to scientific research as a means to advance national interests. Thus the Scottish-born geologist and geographer Roderick Murchison, who had been born into a well-estab-lished family of Highland landowners and was appointed President of the British Association for the Advancement of Science in 1846, regarded David Livingstone as the ultimate Victorian explorer.[3] If Livingstone's Scottish roots, impoverished upbringing and missionary zeal appealed to Murchison the patriotic Scot, his determination to expand the boundaries of British science and the empire appealed to Murchison the scientist.

In an entry on geographical exploration in the *Encyclopaedia Britannica* in 1898, Clement Markham, a polar explorer and President of the Royal Geographical Society, insisted that geopolitical and commercial considerations should go hand in hand with military conquest and the pursuit of knowledge in all state-sponsored expeditions. The British explorer Richard Burton recalled stories of fellow explorer Henry Morton Stanley as a 'man who shot Negroes as if they were monkeys'. At the dusk of the nineteenth century, many Europeans had come to regard Africa as the White Man's Graveyard, a continent where their men-folk succumbed to tropical diseases and died because they could not adapt to tropical and sub-tropical environments. It was famously also a place where men went to die in wars against Africa's native inhabitants in order to prove their manhood. Francis Galton, President of the Royal Geographical Society and the founding father of the pseudo-science of eugenics, looked on geographical exploration as a means of awakening the British navy from the 'sloth of routine' that would 'save it from the canker of prolonged peace'. He also favoured well-educated young naval officers over hardened amateurs when selecting leaders for important expeditions, and believed that officers, rather than scientists, should be the leaders of such expeditions. A powerful advocate of polar exploration, he felt that expeditions to remote regions would test the endurance of officers and toughen them up in preparation for war.[4] Like many of those in the military and geographical establishment of Great Britain he considered geographical exploration as considerably 'more wholesome than petty wars with savages'.

In an age when travel literally made geographers out of men, while women were expected to dutifully remain at home and raise their families, the exploits of Nietzschean *übermensch* like Scott, Shackleton and Amundsen certainly boosted national morale. Kropotkin criticized this genre of Nietzscheanism for fostering a 'spurious' form of bourgeois individualism that thrived on lackeyism and a servile respect for authority and the cult of the superhero. In a letter to Max Nettlau in 1902, he claimed that the individualism so respected by the military and naval establishment, and which he associated with 'the beautiful blond beast', was based on 'foolish egoism'.[5] It could not exist unless the masses were oppressed and cowed into a state of submission where they could only admire the heroic deeds of their social superiors. This type of hero-worship, he argued, actually belittled the individual. It did not inspire anyone, let alone offer 'anything great and inspiring' to the masses of people.[6] Without denying the effectiveness of the great explorers in attracting the attention of the masses through their exploits and adventures, he had little faith in men who might be 'a hero of a moment'. The individuality that Kropotkin respected attained its greatest development not in the heroic explorations of larger-than-life individuals like Scott, Amundsen and Shackleton, but in the more mundane workspaces of peasants and workers who cooperated in their daily tasks to satisfy their social needs. Yet polar explorers like Amundsen and Scott, both of whom were contemporaries of Kropotkin, provided the military establishments of Europe with idealized role models that lesser men were expected to emulate, particularly in times of war. Explorers and adventurers of this ilk were national heroes, celebrities who demonstrated the manly virtues of courage, competition, intelligence and authoritarian leadership in critical times and trying environments. They gained heroic status by undertaking epic journeys out into the unknown, and coming back with heroic tales of great discoveries. In overcoming insurmountable odds, they were also responsible for setting new standards of human excellence and endurance in the competitive world of nineteenth-century capitalist society.

The history of geographical exploration in Russia is peopled with such heroic individuals, among whom Kropotkin deserves to be listed. In his memoirs he wrote:

My extensive journeys ... taught me how little man really needs as soon as he comes out of the enchanted circle of conventional civilization. With a few pounds of bread and a few ounces of tea in a leather bag, a kettle and a hatchet hanging at the side of my saddle, and under the saddle a blanket, to spread at the camp fire upon a bed of freshly cut spruce twigs, a man feels wonderfully independent, even amidst unknown mountains thickly clothed with woods or capped with snow. A book might be written about this part of my life.[7]

It was while engaged in these state-sponsored expeditions that Kropotkin collected the data he subsequently used to refute Social Darwinian claims about the role of competition in the making of 'superheroes' and the survival of species. In criticizing the geopolitical agenda of state-sponsored expeditions and refusing to function as a passive agent of the tsarist state, Kropotkin subverted the *raison d'être* of this type of geographical exploration in the Darwinian half of the nineteenth century.

Charged like his fellow officers with the responsibility for extending the state's influence to the remotest corners of the Russian Empire, Kropotkin's geographical explorations in Siberia and Northern Asia undoubtedly expanded the boundaries of scientific knowledge. However, unlike his confrères in Russia's military and scientific establishment, he adapted geographical exploration to new purposes, using it to challenge the state-centred assertions of the academic establishment and question the very legitimacy of the state. For the political and geographical establishment, Siberia was a place that held in its icy grip the answers to a plethora of questions about Russia's geography, geology and climate.[8] For Kropotkin, on the other hand, it had demonstrated the crucial importance of sociability and mutual cooperation to the survival of species, including humankind itself. If establishing the configurations of river systems and mountain ranges were major concerns of the imperial state, the social and environmental effects of state actions on the fragile landscapes and indigenous population of Siberia were soon to become the young Kropotkin's main concern.

The success of his geographical explorations can certainly be measured in the conventional manner, as testing the limits of human endurance in one of Russia's harshest environments. However it can also be calculated in terms of the painstaking field research that contributed to the development of anarchist geography and environmental science, which completely refuted the state-centred views of Russia's academic establishment. If his Siberian experiences tested Kropotkin's patience with military life and the bureaucratic state, they also helped him to undermine the basic tenets of Social Darwinism and environmental determinism. But he was also well aware of the pleasures of geographic research at this stage of his career. This is clear from his assessment of the excitement of scientific discovery. Extolling the pleasures of scientific research, he wrote:

There are not many joys in human life equal to the joy of the sudden birth of a generalization, illuminating the mind after a long period of patient research ... Out of the wild confusion of facts and from behind the fog of guesses – contradicted almost as soon as they are born – a stately picture makes its appearance, like an Alpine chain suddenly emerging in all its grandeur from the mists which concealed it the moment before, glittering under the rays of the sun in all its simplicity and variety, in all its mightiness and beauty. And when the generalization is put to a test, by applying to it hundreds of separate facts which seemed to be hopelessly contradictory the moment before, each of them assumes its due position, increasing the impressiveness of the picture, accentuating some characteristic outline, or adding an unsuspected detail full of meaning. The generalization gains in strength and extent; its foundations grow in width and solidity; while in the distance, through the far-off mist on the horizon, the eye detects the outlines of the new and still wider generalization. He who has once in his life experienced this joy of scientific creation will never forget it; he will be longing to renew it; and he cannot but feel with pain that this sort of happiness is the lot of so few of us, while so many could also live through it – on a small or grand scale – if scientific methods and leisure were not limited to a handful of men.[9]

Deeper stirrings of a geographical imagination

Kropotkin's field researches in Siberia, Finland and Manchuria had already gained him a reputation in geographical circles by the late 1860s. His account of the glacial geography and physiography of the Asian landmass was a pioneering work of physical geography that could take its place alongside similar studies of the physical geography of nineteenth-century Europe and North America. In writing up his memoirs in his fifties, he recalled:

All sorts of valuable materials relative to the geography of Russia passed through my hands in the Geographic Society, and the idea gradually came to me of writing an exhaustive physical geography of that immense part of the world. My intention was to give a thorough geographical description of the country, basing it upon the main lines of the surface structure which I began to disentangle for European

Russia; and to sketch in that description the different forms of economic life which ought to prevail in different physical regions. Take, for instance, the side prairies of Southern Russia, so often visited by droughts and failures of crops. These droughts and failures must not be treated as accidental calamities: they are as much a natural feature of that region as its position on a southern slope, and the rest; and the whole economic life of the southern prairies ought to be organized in prevision of the unavoidable recurrence of periodical droughts. Each region of the Russian empire ought to be treated in the same scientific way, as Carl Ritter treated parts of Asia in his beautiful monographs.[10]

In the spring of 1864, and contrary to military regulations, Kropotkin was already publishing articles exposing the despotic nature of the local state and social administration in Siberia. These early writings provide detailed social and geographical descriptions of the harsh living conditions in this remote outpost of imperial Russia. Yet it was at this stage also, when he had not yet turned towards anarchism, that he called for regional surveys of Eastern Siberia with a view to assessing its suitability for future colonization by settlers from European Russia. Although he found it increasingly difficult to reconcile his concerns for local farmers, hunters, herdsmen and political prisoners on the one hand, with his duties as an officer and state official on the other, Kropotkin was not yet prepared to abandon military life. Instead he chose to progressively disengage from his official duties in order to devote more time to the study of the region's physical geography and natural history. At one stage, he took part in a state-sponsored expedition to carve out an alternative route across a triangular enclave of Manchuria that thrust deep into south-eastern Siberia. An older route had added several hundred miles to the journey from Chita, the administrative capital of the region, to Vladivostok on the shores of the Sea of Japan. Founded in 1860, this port, then known as the Lord of the East, had been a primitive fishing and whaling centre throughout much of the eighteenth century. In 1872, shortly after Kropotkin had left Siberia, it was chosen as the strategic base for the Russian Pacific Fleet. Hence opening a new route that would link it to the interior of Russia was of the utmost importance.

Throughout his final years in Siberia, Kropotkin also conducted detailed scientific surveys of the natural history of Siberia. In 1866, under the auspices of the Imperial Geographical Society of Russia, he explored south-central Siberia in order to collect data on the region's geology, physical geography and glacial history. The following statement outlining his own motives for taking part in this expedition makes it clear that it was intended purely as an exercise in physical geography:

> To discover the true, leading principles in the disposition of the mountains of Asia – the harmony of mountain formation now became a question, which for years absorbed my attention. For a considerable time the old maps, and still more the generalization of Alexander von Humboldt, who after a long study of Chinese sources, had covered Asia with a network of mountains running along the medians and parallels, hampered me in my researches, until at last I saw that even Humboldt's generalizations, stimulating though they had been, did not agree with the facts.[11]

Kropotkin's 700-page report on the geographical exploration of the remote Olekminsk-Vitimsk of Siberia, undertaken in the mid 1860s when he was still in his twenties, became a 'desk book' study for an entire generation of Russian geographers and geologists. On the basis of these extensive field observations and cartographic exercises he had succeeded in outlining a theory that explained the structural delineation of this region's mountain ranges. In research findings that were at variance with those of Humboldt, the leading authority on the subject, he established that all of northern Europe had once been covered by an ice cap. Contrary to conventional geographic wisdom, he suggested that the landmass of Eurasia had been subjected to a prolonged period of desertification. His research further suggested that layers of moving glaciers had traversed large tracts of northern Europe, including Russia, leaving behind a heavily glaciated landscape.[12] While modern geographers and geologists now consider this conventional wisdom, in Kropotkin's day it was scientific heresy.

The 1860s were undoubtedly years of intensive geographical exploration in Siberia and Manchuria. Much of this was carried out under the aegis of the Imperial Geographic Society of Russia, founded in St Petersburg in 1845. The Society played an active role in the national life of the country and many of its members, not least its founding father, K.I. Arsenyev, had strong research interests in the regional and economic geography of Russia. Academic geography in Russia at this stage was newly constructed by Arsenyev and his colleagues, men whose diverse research interests were not unlike those of the young Kropotkin. These men, many of them hardened explorers and army officers, had come together to establish an institutional framework for the presentation and discussion of geographical research. In addition to geographical exploration, the Society also promoted studies in the geology, meteorology, hydrography, anthropology and archaeology of Russia. From 1845 to 1917, a period which almost exactly spanned Kropotkin's life, the Society published no less than 400 volumes of scientific papers and academic works on specialized topics that collectively came to be known as 'the geographical sciences'.[13] As an important channel for scientific ideas from Western Europe, including the geographical works of Carl Ritter and Alexander von Humboldt, it is hardly surprising that the Imperial Geographic Society attracted widespread support from Russia's political establishment. Not unlike its counterparts in Victorian Britain and post-Napoleonic France, the Society fostered the development of commercial geography, sponsored geographical exploration and actively supported the extension of state authority to the outer limits of its empire. In its view, the purpose of science was to establish 'the empire of mankind'. Hence the world was not just to be 'made known' through scientific endeavour – scientists had to master and manage it in the interests of the state and use it in the service of humankind. Not surprisingly, therefore, the Society attracted the attention of many of those who sought the national unification of Russia under the hegemony of the industrial bourgeoisie and a reinvigorated aristocracy.

However, the Imperial Geographic Society was also home to a small number of young reformers who insisted that geography should not simply be concerned with academic matters, or dedicated solely to the advancement of national interests. This group insisted that geographical fieldwork and exploration should be used to advance social reform in a country still in the grip of an autocratic ruler and a conservative oligarchy. Kropotkin clearly belonged to this school of thought. Thus he would urge geographers, and other scientists, not to divorce themselves from the political and economic life of the Russian peasantry, but to throw themselves into the cause of social liberation by adopting the role of spokesmen for the oppressed. Unlike his aristocratic peers, he was not prepared to stand aside while the country's peasants and ex-serfs were driven into the factories and slums of expanding cities, jettisoned as social cast-offs, and sacrificed to the twin causes of state-centralization and capitalist modernization. His interest in physical geography coincided with a revival of the Russian state's interest in its polar regions. This had largely been forced upon the Imperial Geographic Society between 1869 and 1871 when a handful of 'bold Norwegian seal-hunters' had quite unexpectedly opened the Kara Sea off the coast of Northern Siberia to coastal navigation. To the extreme astonishment of Russia's rulers and the embarrassment of its geographical establishment, it was discovered that these polar waters, which had once been 'confidently' described as 'an ice cellar permanently stocked with ice', had now been 'entered by a small number of Norwegian schooners'. Kropotkin's 'Arctic Report' was to lead to his appointment as leader of a reconnoitring expedition to polar Russia, a position that he declined when he chose instead to study esker formations in Finland.[14] Addressing the Teacher's Guild Conference in Oxford almost 20 years later he would confirm that he could not 'conceive of Physiography from which Man has been excluded'.[15] Even while conducting research on glacial landscapes, he was always aware that these had also been inhabited by human beings, whose very survival depended upon their ability to cooperate.

The geographic works which Kropotkin considered most in tune with the regional diversity and natural majesty of a nineteenth-century world under attack from the forces of global capitalism were Humboldt's *Cosmos* (1849–58) and Élisée Reclus' monumental *Geographie Universelle* (1876). The latter is to anarchist political geography what *Das Kapital* is to Marxist political economy. In praising Reclus' magnum opus, Kropotkin maintained that it was 'a description of the earth so thoroughly intermingled with that of man, that if man were taken out ... the entire work would lose ... its very soul'.[16] Inspired by works such as these, he set out to put anarchism on a scientific basis. In stressing the logical links between the modern philosophy of the natural sciences and modern anarchism, he sought to integrate the moral with the material dimension of reality, and to make this his conception of geography. Here again, he viewed geography as a practical and engaged intellectual endeavour that could and should render 'important service' to humankind.

Kropotkin's early interests in geography developed at a time when Russian geographers had largely avoided the Social Darwinism that had so bedevilled geography in Germany and America in the closing decades of the century. Thus Russian geographers and social scientists were far less impressed with environmental determinism and evolutionary theory than their counterparts in Britain and North America. For that very reason they were also largely unaffected by the schismatic tendencies that afflicted the environmental sciences in these two power houses of Social Darwinism. Following the abolition of serfdom in 1861, many of those attached to the liberal wing of the Imperial Geographic Society dedicated themselves to improving the lot of poor peasants and liberated serfs. While they were certainly familiar with evolutionary theory and the developmental concepts of Darwin, Spencer and Marx, they tended to write highly evocative regional monographs that were rich in lyrical flair and local colour. In shying away from evolutionary theory, Russian geographers adopted an extremely pragmatic and functional approach to their discipline. Many were more concerned with the human impact of economic change on Russia's natural environments than with the putative effects of environmental factors on social and economic development. These were being highlighted by Social Darwinists elsewhere in Europe and North America at the time. Thus V.V. Dokuchaiev, who had been appointed the first professor of geography at the university in St Petersburg in 1885, had strong research interests in soil geography and agricultural development.[17] Nevertheless, like their counterparts in Britain and Germany, Russian geographers were also nurtured in an environment of militarism, colonial expansion and racism. Their elitist concern with the role of geography in the economic modernization of Russia drew them into the orbit of state formation and empire-building. Moreover, if Russian geographers tended to reject some of the more extreme forms of environmental determinism, Russian historians were not slow in emphasizing the role of environmental factors in shaping the national character of Russia.

Kropotkin's memoirs contain little of the introspection and soul-searching religiosity of Tolstoy. Instead Kropotkin comes across as methodical, hardworking, intensely serious, self-confident and absolutely certain that his own opinions were correct. As a late-Victorian moralist who was 'devoted to plain living and high thinking', he was always more concerned with 'ideas and characters' than with 'faces or voices'. As anarchism's most prominent intellectual, he would continue to maintain close contacts with the scientific community, especially the Royal Geographical Society of Great Britain and Ireland, throughout his long life. It was even rumoured that he was offered the professorship of geography at Cambridge, on condition that he renounce his anarchist beliefs.[18] Even while writing articles for the revolutionary *Bulletin de la Federation Jurassienne* in the mid 1870s, Kropotkin continued to act as the correspondence editor for the English science journal *Nature*. His fellow geographer and friend, James Scott Keltie, who was later to become the President of the Royal Geographic Society, was the then editor of this journal. Kropotkin regularly wrote articles on geophysics, physical geography, natural history and climatology, and addressed geographical societies in Britain, France and North America. While deeply involved in revolutionary politics as an anarchist organizer, he also maintained a strong commitment to geographic research. Indeed his science journalism allowed him to re-establish what was to become a lifelong dual commitment to the refined world of the geographic establishment and the revolutionary world of anarchist agitation. Thus when most of the anarchist opponents of tsarism were forced underground by state authorities in the 1870s, Kropotkin openly attended meetings of the Imperial Geographic Society of Russia in order to outline his research findings on the glacial history of Eastern Siberia.[19]

While imprisoned in the high-security St Peter and Paul fortress in St Petersburg, he completed his two-volume account of the formation of the major mountain ranges of Asia and the glacial geography of Finland and Central Europe. Permission to study and write in prison had been granted largely because of pressure from colleagues in the international scientific community, including some of Europe's most prominent geographers.[20] In his memoirs he would recall that this was the one factor that made his imprisonment more tolerable. Nevertheless while his academic peers in the educational establishment recognized his contributions to physical geography and the earth sciences, they completely ignored his contributions to anarchist geography and the environmental and social sciences.

Thus it was largely his long-standing association with professional geographers, and not least his contributions to physical geography, that brought Kropotkin, and indeed Reclus, to the attention of academics in Britain, France, Germany and Belgium. In an obituary of Kropotkin published in the *Geographical Journal* in 1921, written by Scott Keltie, Secretary of the Royal Geographical Society (RGS) between 1892 and 1915, it was stated:

This is not the place to deal in detail with Kropotkin's political views, except to express regret at his absorption in these seriously diminished the services which otherwise he might have rendered to geography. Kropotkin's contributions to geography are records of his great explorations in Eastern Siberia and the discussion of the great problems they suggested to him, and his investigations into the glaciology of Finland. He was a keen observer, with a well-trained intellect, familiar with all the sciences bearing on his subject; and although his conclusions may not be universally accepted, there is no doubt that his contributions to geographical science are of the greatest value.[21]

Keltie had befriended Kropotkin shortly after he arrived in England in 1876. They shared a long and valued association, and Keltie recalled that Kropotkin had 'made himself at home' in the offices of the RGS, where he was involved in many of its activities. He translated and published papers on the geography of Russia, and regularly refereed papers submitted for publication in the society's prestigious *Geographical Journal*. What is remarkable about Scott's professional assessment of Kropotkin is that it is strikingly similar to that of his biographers, George Woodcock and Ivan Avakumović. These two anarchist historians also suggested that Kropotkin's conversion to anarchism was directly responsible for terminating his promising career as 'an original geographer'. After Siberia, they argued, Kropotkin 'would undertake no journeys or explorations … he wrote … many articles in English and foreign scientific magazines and delivered lectures … But he ever expanded his knowledge in an original way, or used it for the production of further geographical theories.'[22]

All three of these writers failed to recognize the geographical under-pinnings of Kropotkin's writings on a whole range of topics, including human ecology, regional development, social autonomy and the political organization of space. While the anarchist historians may be excused for not recognizing his efforts to expand the imagination of disciplinary geography, it is less easy to excuse his professional colleague and prominent geographer, Scott Keltie, for not recognizing Kropotkin's role in radically developing the scope, as well as outlining the social functions, of the discipline of geography in the late nineteenth century. As Breitbart has staunchly maintained, 'Kropotkin's most important and original con-tributions to geography … came *after* he escaped from prison in Russia and went into exile.'[23] Indeed, contrary to the view of Keltie and his colleagues, Kropotkin did not forego a career in professional geography in order to devote his life to anarchism. As an anarchist theorist he criticized Social Darwinism for its scientific shortcomings, and resolutely exposed the ideological underpinnings of academic geography, history, political economy, anthropology, sociology and political science.

In seeking to expand the range and political roles of geographical inquiry, he set about constructing an antithetical, counter-hegemonic science of social and environmental relations, which, he hoped, would contribute to the development of a more equitable and stateless society. Nevertheless, unlike his fellow anarchist and geographer, Élisée Reclus, Kropotkin never received a Patron's Medal from the RGS.[24] That his portrait, which had been commissioned by the Society in 1904, still hangs in its London headquarters is testimony to his social status as a valued associate of the RGS. But it was never intended as a mark of respect for his contributions to anarchist geography and the social sciences. Moreover, Kropotkin never missed an opportunity to express his opposition to the elitist character of the RGS. The Society once organized a banquet at which the assembled guests paid homage to his contributions to the physical geography of Russia and Northern Asia. Protocol demanded that the occasion should commence with a toast to the Queen. In keeping with his anarchist principles, Kropotkin refused to pay homage to the monarch.[25] Despite his close associations with many members of the RGS, he also declined an offer to become an official Fellow of the Society. Both these incidents illustrate the ambivalence between 'responsibility and respect' that characterized Kropotkin's relationship with the academic world throughout a life that was more or less equally devoted to the advancement of science and his brand of 'scientific anarchism'. His resentment at the royal patronage of scientific institutions did not prevent him forming close working relationships with professional academics. Neither did it impinge upon his commitment to research that would enhance the scientific legitimacy of anarchism.

Kropotkin and the nineteenth-century geographical canon

Given the fact that Kropotkin's anarchism was formulated in a period of intense international and imperial rivalry, it is hardly surprising that he also articulated a radical political geography of nation and empire to act as an alternative to the centralization of political and economic power in the latter half of the nineteenth century. Thus Kropotkin's writings on economic development and human ecology outlined a radically different ecology and political geography for a new world order that was increasingly under the domination of Western powers. A strong defence of ecological diversity and cultural pluralism underpinned his critique of state-sponsored capitalism and imperial expansion. As we shall see, he strongly condemned the commodification of nature and labour in an age of heightened nation- and empire-building. Like his fellow geographer and anarchist, Élisée Reclus, Kropotkin was an ardent defender of 'people power' who fought for local autonomy and cherished all forms of regional and ecological diversity. In *Fields, Factories and Workshops* he outlined the basis of anarchist regional policy. His writings on food production and agricultural reform, outlined chiefly in this volume and in *The Conquest of Bread*, still have direct relevance to current debates about food security and sustainable development. In challenging the uneven development of capitalism and the over-concentration of economic and cultural capital in the urbanized core areas of metropolitan society he laid the basis of the anti-globalization movement.

All of this makes radical geography's Marxist orientation since the 1960s all the more surprising. In his day, Kropotkin was a respected physical geographer, an esteemed explorer, and a respected intellectual who also made important contributions to scientific journalism between 1870 and 1920. Nevertheless, until recently, only a handful of geographers – including Myrna Breitbart, Bob Galois, Richard Peet and Gary Dunbar – have sought to re-establish the links between the radical geography of the 1970s and the anarchist tradition of the nineteenth century. In so doing they certainly rescued Kropotkin and Reclus from the dust heaps of academic history, and made significant contributions to anarchist geography in their own right. However, unlike many Marxist academics, they never managed to muster sufficient followers to form anything like a substantial school to counteract the preponderant influence of Marxism on the theory and practice of radical geography. Indeed, Richard Peet, a deservedly highly respected radical geographer who was also receptive to anarchist geography in the 1970s, devoted less than a page of his otherwise insightful history of geographical thought to a discussion on Kropotkin's contribution to the discipline.[26] He remains a marginal figure in most standard accounts of political geography, with the notable exception of the work of Gerry Kearns, who has recently contrasted

Kropotkin's writings on the state with those of the imperialist geographer Halford Mackinder.[27]

In an extremely sardonic, and brief, summary of Kropotkin's contribution to academic geography, David Hooson describes him as 'one of the most colourful part-timers in Russian geography in the latter half of the 19th century'. Hooson's account of the history of pre-Soviet geographical thought at least recognized that Kropotkin's 'lifelong scientific interest remained essentially geographical'. However, according to Hooson, he was 'deflected towards politics by urgent convictions and what he saw as the plight of his fellow-countrymen'. Throughout the 30-odd years he spent in England, Hooson argued, Kropotkin was primarily 'engaged in the promotion of his own brand of anarchism', but had also 'succeeded in building a considerable reputation in geography, particularly in the (somewhat monarchical!) Royal Geographical Society'. Noting that he 'wrote for *The Times* and other journals on such topics as the progress of Russian expeditions and the trans-Siberian railway', Hooson acknowledged that Kropotkin had 'developed his own interesting, if vulnerable, theories of the "Dessication of Asia"'. Hooson also conceded that the 'many articles on Russia' which Kropotkin submitted to the *Encyclopaedia Britannica* were 'usually very comprehensive in their demographic, economic and historical, as well as physical, facts, with full bibliographies of the Russian literature which retain their interest today'. He patronizingly concluded that Kropotkin was 'an exceptionally prolific writer' on a range of topics 'un-related' to geography, and that his 'love both for geography and for Russia never left him in exile'.[28]

Writing 50 years after his death in 1921, the American geographers Preston James and Geoffrey Martin were still consigning Kropotkin to a footnote in their 'in-house' account of the history of geographical ideas. Having noted that he 'never held a university post' they simply described him as 'a member of the Russian aristocracy' who was 'a devoted anarchist and close friend of the French geographer-anarchist Élisée Reclus'. Recognizing his 'lifelong interest in the study of geography', and his association with the Royal Geographical Society from 1876 to 1917, they claimed that 'most of what Reclus had to say about Russia came from Kropotkin'. Reclus fared somewhat better than Kropotkin in this history of geographical thought, which nevertheless contained only six references to his voluminous life work. Thus it was noted that Reclus had been a disciple of Alexander von Humboldt, who in turn had been a student of 'the great German teacher of Geography, Carl Ritter'. James and Martin also noted that Reclus was the Director of the Institut Geographique at Université Nouvelle in Brussels between 1894 and 1905. They described his magnum opus, *L'Homme et La Terre*, as a 'descriptive, systematic geography' written 'in the Ritter manner, with a preponderant emphasis on physical geography'. Finally they noted that Reclus had been

> identified by the French government as one of the leading promoters of anarchism ... In 1892 he was appointed as professor of comparative geography at the University of Brussels in Belgium. Because of his continued activity as a revolutionary anarchist, his appointment was cancelled. One reason for his immunity from any penalty other than banishment from France was his standing as a scholar and the resulting efforts of European scholars to give him protection ... His major work was the completion of a major work of the kind that Ritter had started. His nineteen-volume 'new universal geography' was, in a sense, the last echo of the classical period when one scholar could present all available knowledge about the earth as the home of man. Reclus took great care with the clarity of his writing. Unlike Ritter's *Erdkunde*, which is well known for its numerous obscure passages, Reclus' work was easy to read and understand ... His standing as a scholar was given further support by numerous other writings, including a detailed description of the history of a stream and a similar work on a mountain.[29]

However, Reclus has received far more sympathetic treatment from the radical geographer Bob Galois, who has claimed him as one of nineteenth-century Europe's most prolific geographers. Measured quantitatively, indeed, his output may even have exceeded that of Humboldt, one of the founding fathers of modern academic geography. Unlike many professional geographers of his day, Reclus, like Kropotkin, was compelled to live largely by his pen for long periods of time. Indeed this may help to account for the sheer volume of his published work. Unlike Kropotkin, he did manage to hold down a position as a professor of geography, albeit in the final 11 years of his academic life. Yet his monumental *L'Homme et La Terre*, published between 1868 and 1869, laid the foundations of social geography and established Reclus' international reputation as a geographer. While many of his geographical works would now be considered unduly descriptive and somewhat journalistic, they nevertheless reiterated a deep concern about global disparities in the distribution and utilization of the earth's resources, at a time when most academics put their faith in the free market to solve the problems of global poverty and social inequality. Like Kropotkin, Reclus also urged geographers to devise an alternative geographical organization of the global economy in order to achieve a more equitable redistribution of the earth's riches. Writing at a time when political leaders considered Malthusian population theory the conventional wisdom of the day, Reclus argued that mal-distribution of wealth rather than overpopulation was at the root of global poverty. Recognizing his continued relevance today, the political decentralist Kirkpatrick Sale has described Reclus' geographical works as 'unflinchingly scientific', claiming that his writings on the 'human-nature interaction' outlined the geographical principles of modern-day bioregionalism and environmentalism.[30]

Nevertheless, steeped as they were in the empiricist tradition of 'fact finding' and fieldwork, professional geographers like Hooson, Scott Keltie, Preston James and Geoffrey Martin perceived academic geography as an apolitical discipline whose roots were firmly planted in such 'objective' sciences as geology, physical geography, zoology, climatology and physiography. They never considered either Kropotkin's or Reclus' writings on anarchist geography, regional development, social anthropology and political theory as anything other than 'deflections' and ideological diversions that had no bearing on their geographical research. For these authors, as for the majority of Kropotkin's academic contemporaries, geography was simply a discipline that let the facts speak for themselves. As such, they insisted, it had no room for philosophical conjecture or normative speculation. To these writers, as indeed to the majority of geographers today, Kropotkin was simply a minor figure in the evolution of physical geography whose 'obsession' with anarchism 'diminished' the services he might otherwise have rendered to the academic discipline of geography.

Anarchism versus state-centred academic geography

To understand why Kropotkin did not choose the professional path of academic geography it may be useful to briefly examine the research agendas and political background of academic geography and related disciplines when they were institutionalized in the universities and military academies of Britain, France, Germany, Russia and the United States in the closing decades of the nineteenth century. Having been presented with a number of opportunities that clearly could have resulted in a promising and highly successful career as a physical geographer, Kropotkin consciously struggled with, though in the end did not agonize over, the decision not to follow the path of the career geographer. He reflected that:

> It often happens that men will pull in a certain political, social or familiar harness simply because they never have time to ask themselves whether the position they stand in and the work they accomplish are right; whether their occupations really suit their inner desires and capacities, and give them the satisfaction which everyone has the right to expect from his work. Active men are especially liable to find themselves in such a position ... Life goes, and there is no time to think, no time to consider the direction one's life is taking. So it was with me.[31]

Fundamental to his reasons not to opt for an academic career in a discipline which he clearly loved was his steadfast refusal to become implicated in the nation-building and state-centred projects of his professional counterparts. Throughout his career as an anarchist theorist, Kropotkin was equally critical of both the ethos and the ethics of mainstream or state-centred geography. This was a geographical tradition that had been intimately woven into the social and political fabric of nineteenth-century aristocratic society. It had its roots in patrician circles and gentlemen's clubs in Britain, France and Russia in the late eighteenth and early nineteenth centuries. Right from the start, theirs was a tradition of research and geographical exploration that catered to state interests and attracted widespread support from privileged members of class-structured societies who were also interested in developments in natural history and social philosophy. Formalized geographical societies were established in London in 1830, in Paris in 1831 and in St Petersburg in 1845. Their members were predominantly 'men of learning' who also belonged to that stratum of aristocratic society that Veblen labelled 'the leisure class'. To paraphrase Veblen, they tended to 'live by the industrial community rather than in it', at least prior to the 1850s and 1860s, and their relations with the commercial world of capitalism were 'of a pecuniary rather than an industrial kind'.[32] Thus an obsession with natural history, geographical exploration, foreign travel, athletic sport and the martial arts character-ized the membership of amateur geographical societies in the lead-up to their institutionalization in the universities and military academies of Europe.

Throughout the 1830s and 1840s in particular, geographical societies tended to have a high preponderance of clergymen, naval officers and members of the landed gentry. By the 1860s and 1870s, however, the social profile of these societies changed dramatically as they began to attract increasingly large numbers of merchants, explorers, colonial administrators, industrialists, army officers and missionary clergymen. At this stage geography was closely linked with 'soft' subjects such as natural history, map-making, archaeology and anthropology, and with 'hard' sciences such as geology, zoology, comparative anatomy and botany. Whilst the discipline of geography acquired university status in a number of universities between 1860 and 1890, a geographical education had already been an important component of the curriculum of the leading military academies of Europe and North America. Indeed it acquired its status at a time when the bourgeoisie of Britain, France, Germany and the United States became increasingly convinced that advances in the sciences, as well as the arts, would create a world of material plenty, social progress and moral enlightenment. Driven by an impulse to control nature, regulate space and promote the global triumph of commerce and capitalism, disciplines like geography, botany, zoology and geology also became deeply pragmatic and highly technocratic. By the latter half of the nineteenth century, this contributed to the global 'commodification' of plants, animals and environments, as geographers and other environmental scientists classified immense quantities of factual information, much of it amassed by explorers and through state-sponsored geographical expeditions similar to those in which the young Kropotkin was engaged in the 1860s.[33] Henceforth 'applied disciplines' like geography, geology and cartography became closely identified with the military establishment, colonial elites and colonial administra-tors, and with the bureaucratic agencies of expansionist nation-states. Adopting environmental determinism as their foundational philosophy, geographers now began to attribute variations in global patterns of social and economic development to racial and environmental factors. In the militaristic environment of mid nineteenth-century Europe it was widely recognized that schools and colleges had an important role to play in the development of competitive individualism and the ethos of militarism. Wars, it was suggested, were waged as much with maps and scientific know-how as with conventional weaponry. Thus it was suggested that Germany's victory over France in the Franco-Prussian War of 1870–71 was attributable to 'skilful military movements performed by an army thoroughly acquainted with the geographical features of the country over which was moved'.[34] In the contested terrains of the colonial world, the geographical training received by young cadets at the military academies was often crucial to the delineation of political boundaries and the resolution of boundary disputes. Thus in a paradigmatic paper, 'Geographical Knowledge and Boundary Disputes', published in the *Geographical Journal* in 1899, Sir Thomas Holdich, a British expert on boundary problems who was also a contemporary of Kropotkin, insisted that geography should be of practical use in resolving boundary disputes. In 1884, only 20 years after Kropotkin began his military service in Siberia, Holdich was the leader of a team of geographers responsible for demarcating the boundary between Russia and Afghanistan. He became superintendent of 'frontier surveys' in colonial India from 1892 to 1898, and later went on to delineate the political boundaries between Chile and Argentina.

Many of the 'founding fathers' of modern geography and cartography were contemporaries of Kropotkin who went on to become highly respected members of Europe's political and academic establishment. Far from inhabiting the ivory towers of academia, however, they were deeply implicated in the practical politics and 'realpolitik' of their respective nations. Thus, for example, the writings of prominent geographers such as Alexander von Humboldt (1769–1859), Carl Ritter (1779–1859), Roderick Murchison (1792–1881), Friedrich Ratzel (1844–1904), Clements Markham (1830–1916), Ellsworth Huntington (1876–1947), Karl Haushofer (1869–1946) and Halford Mackinder (1861–1947), to name but a few, were highly influential well beyond the narrow confines of academia. Mackinder was a Member of Parliament, as well as the British High Commissioner for South Russia and the chairman of the Imperial Shipping Committee and the Imperial Economic Committee. His *Democratic Ideals and Reality: A Study in the Politics of Recon- struction*, published in 1919, was widely read and continued to have a profound influence on geopolitical thought throughout the first half of the twentieth century.

Some academics, not least those who had successfully headed up geographical expeditions to remote corners of the world, were considered minor celebrities in their day. Their geographical works, especially their travelogues, were widely read and helped to create a nineteenth-century variant of modern-day celebrity culture. Thus Simon Bolivar considered Baron von Humboldt 'the true discoverer of South America' who 'had done more good for America than all her conquerors'. Humboldt's most recent biographer has claimed that 'no other European had a comparable influence on the intellectual culture of nineteenth-century America'. A friend of Goethe and Schiller, Humboldt was considered by some to be 'as famous as Napoleon'. Similarly, the palaeontologist Stephen Jay Gould has described him as 'the world's most famous and influential intellectual [who exerted] enormous influence over the lives and thoughts of an entire generation'. 'No one', he added, 'did more to change and enhance science in the first half of the nineteenth century than Alexander von Humboldt, the cardinal inspiration for men as diverse as Charles Darwin, Alfred Russell Wallace, Louis Agassiz and Frederic Church.'[35] Carl Ritter, another immensely influential earth scientist who was professor of geography at Berlin from 1827 to 1859, was also the director of studies at the Military School. He laid the foundations of modern 'scientific' geography with his widely read work, *Die Erkunde*. Published in 1817, this was a pioneering study in environmental determinism and as such became a foundational text for Social Darwinists who sought to provide scientific justification for the global supremacy of the White races.

Friedrich Ratzel, a prominent German geographer and renowned Social Darwinist, pushed the boundaries of 'applied geography' to new limits by promoting geopolitics as indispensable tool of statecraft. In so doing he not only politicized geography, but also adapted it to the state-centred agendas of empire-builders and nation-builders. In his paradigmatic essay, 'The Territorial Growth of States', published in 1899, Ratzel promoted an organic theory of the state that compared nation-states in particular to organisms requiring *lebensraum* (i.e. 'living space') in order to develop. Thus he maintained that states, specifically the White nation-states of the northern hemisphere, were like 'living organisms'.[36] Their growth and development could not be endangered by restrictions on their access to resources and territory. Hence he suggested that the progress of nations was dependent upon on the expansionist capabilities of their citizens as they set out to take control of territory and exploit resources on a national global scale. Viewed thus, the ability of White settlers to survive the challenges involved in the exploration and settlement of wilderness areas and the colonial world indicated their racial and national virility.

Later in life Ratzel would defend this facile comparison between states and living organisms by suggesting that it was intended not so much as a scientific hypothesis as an illuminating metaphor to arouse the geographical imaginations of impressionable students. Nevertheless, in the second volume of his monumental *Anthropgeographie*, published in 1891, Ratzel fused geography with anthropology to create a state-centred geographical 'science' that documented the influences of physical geography and environment on the growth or failure of racially defined peoples.[37] It is important to emphasize that he came to geography precisely when Kropotkin was developing scientific anarchism as an alternative to the state-centred Social Darwinism that permeated many corners of academia outside Russia from the 1870s onwards.

Ratzel was not content with defending 'natural' competition between nations as an optimal stratagem for ensuring the social and economic survival of the 'fittest' nations. He also maintained that the 'militarization' of nation-states as a result of arms spending and the enhancement of their naval power would ultimately improve international security while simultaneously ensuring the global triumph of competitive private enterprise. Thus he lauded the achievements of explorers and geographers, and all those who helped powerful states to keep a firm grip on their national territory and their colonial possessions while also asserting power and authority in a global arena. All those who threatened the territorial integrity of either the nation or the empire were considered enemies of the state. Hence national separatists and ethno-nationalist minorities in the nation states of Europe, and national liberation movements in the colonial worlds of India, Africa and South East Asia were considered balkanizing forces because they threatened the cohesion of the nation and the unity of an imperial world. They were particularly derided for doing so at a time when statesmen, military leaders and captains of industry were all demanding national unity at home and colonial stability abroad. Claiming the world for these 'lords of humankind', Social Darwinists like Ratzel and his followers defended strong government in the colonial world and a minimum of state interference in the advanced nations of the metropolitan world as an optimal strategy for global development.[38] Thus their Darwinism had all the hallmarks of an anarchism of the rich and powerful. As a foundational philosophy of late nineteenth-century political conservatism, it promoted a quasi-secular worldview that was devoid of any concern for the poor, and almost completely lacking in religious piety, sentimentality or any emotional attachment to the powerless and the underprivileged. It was also devoid of any reverence for customary authority or cultural tradition. Neither in the colonial world, nor in what has come to be known as 'Old Europe', did Social Darwinism of this genre have much respect for historical continuity. Instead Darwinists, many of whom were celebrated geographers and social scientists, considered pre-capitalist societies as politically backward social formations that were doomed to failure. For Kropotkin, these same societies deserved to be protected, particularly if they were infused with the ethos and practice of mutual aid, or if they possessed sufficient cooperative spirit to provide for the material and cultural needs of their underprivileged members. As so many obstacles to the untrammelled expansion of competitive free enterprise, Kropotkin's opponents, on the other hand, suggested that these societies could justifiably be swept aside by the modernizing forces of transformative colonialism and competitive individualism under the auspices of authoritarian governments.

There was, however, no conspiracy on the part of the state to 'institutionalize' the disciplinary canon of one section of the geographical establishment at the expense of '*ex cathedra*' pioneers of radical social and environmental science like Kropotkin and Reclus. Far from being mere 'lackeys' of the state, professional academics willingly performed a whole range of services in the national interest. Thus they regarded themselves, and were widely regarded by their political and cultural confrères, as public officials who worked for the public good and helped define the national interest. In other words they were 'statesmen' in the true meaning of the term, men who literally constituted the scientific, cultural and intellectual establishment of their respective nations. Like Kropotkin's father, and several of his uncles, theirs was a tradition of state service that ultimately had its roots in the European Enlightenment and extended back to the closing decades of the eighteenth century. This was a period when social philosophers, many of whom could more accurately be described as human geographers, began to draw analogies between transformations in human society on the one hand, and the changing world of nature on the other. From the 1830s onwards these thinkers also drew comparisons between the Industrial Revolution and the French Revolution. If the former fundamentally altered ways of thinking about the economy, society and the natural environment, the latter had radically altered the political boundaries and political landscapes of large tracts of Europe and its colonial appendages. This was also a time when 'catastrophic theory' entered geology, climatology and physical geography, appealing to an entirely new generation of young academics who had grown accustomed to violent convulsions in European society.

At this stage also there were clear parallels between intellectual trends in the sciences and the arts on the one hand, and social and political thought on the other. Seemingly abstract concepts like 'classicism', 'romanticism' and 'medievalism' filtered through to the 'softer' disciplines of history, geography, archaeology and anthropology where they had a profound effect on European's perceptions of their place in the world. By the second half of the century, Darwinian concepts like 'the survival of the fittest', 'natural selection' and 'the territorial imperative' began to sweep away static notions of space, time and human nature itself.[39] By the 1870s, the institutionalization and professionalization of the social and environmental sciences contributed to their nationalization, and to an acute fragmentation of the new disciplinary knowledge. Disciplinary divisions and sub-divisions now began to appear in academia, where they frequently mirrored the divisions of labour in the world of industrial capitalism. Concerns over efficiency, marketability, profitability and the national interest, all of which were so apparent outside academia, became increasingly evident within the world of academic disciplines. This in turn enhanced the state-centred expertise of professional academics, and no doubt further improved their political and social standing in their respective societies.

Referring to educational changes in mid nineteenth century Europe, Hobsbawm suggested that 'the progress of schools and universities measured that of nationalism, just as schools and especially universities became its most conspicuous champions'.[40] What Hobsbawm failed to note was that nationalism had also contributed to the development of 'national schools' of geography, history, archaeology, anthropology and political economy in Britain, France, Prussia and Russia from the 1850s onwards. With the onset of a new spirit of academicism towards the end of the century, distinctions were increasingly drawn between the superior 'pure' sciences and the more mundane 'applied' sciences. This resulted in the sciences, particularly the 'earth sciences', becoming even more concerned with the advancement of the national interests of the state. Western perceptions of progress and civilization infiltrated disciplines like geography, anthropology and archaeology and became the 'necessary furniture' of nation-states and empires in countries as far apart as colonial India and North America.[41] This resulted in even greater efforts to legitimize state authority and to portray authoritarian nation-states as the only alternative to a neo-Hobbesian world of social disorder, racial conflict and political chaos. The 'enlightened' sectors of these societies took to nation-building partly as a response to the threat of social revolution erupting within the ranks of the rural and urban poor.

Not surprisingly, therefore, many of those employed in universities and in military academies were convinced they were working for the eventual benefit of 'a vast and inert mass of ignorant and misled common people, which would no doubt welcome liberation when it came, but could not be expected to take much part in preparing for it'.[42] Like their enlightened counterparts in industry and commerce, they believed that the historical evolution of 'their people' was a socially progressive moral force that was as uncontrollable and spontaneous as the evolutionary development of living organisms. They also developed an obsession with the national psyche and the national ego, and concentrated their geographical focus on the territories and natural resources of their nation and its imperial appendages. In his *Physics and Politics*, Walter Bagehot (1826–77), editor of the influential *Economist* magazine, summed up the 'nation-centredness' of many his contemporaries when he suggested that 'We cannot imagine those to whom nationalism is a difficulty; we know what it means, when you ask us, but cannot very quickly explain or define it.' The Spanish-born Harvard philosopher and poet, George Santayana, expressed this sentiment more forcefully when he suggested that 'Our nationality is like our relations to women: too implicated in our moral nature to be changed honourably, and too accidental to be worth changing.'[43] Statements like these littered the writings of cultural nationalists and nationalist academics in the latter half of the nineteenth century. Indeed the works of scientists and academics could sometimes acquire national importance and were ranked alongside those of poets, novelists and journalists who fostered nationalist 'renaissances' across Europe and the Americas throughout much of the period.

With the exception of a small number of marginalized figures, including Kropotkin and Reclus, few scientists or academics were courageous enough to challenge the 'naturalness' of nationalism or the inviolability of state authority. Those who rejected the idolatrous inter-pretations of 'their people's' history, including those who refused to accept their nationalistic prognoses for future progress, ran the risk of being branded unpatriotic at best and traitorous at worst. Thus legal categories originally intended for those guilty of crimes against the state could now be applied to the intellectual opponents of nation-building and the nationalist bourgeoisie. The term 'traitor' could also be levelled against an entire range of political activists, including international socialists and national separatists who threatened the territorial integrity of the nation-state. More than all of these, however, anarchists were subjected to this type of vitriolic criticism because they rejected the state as well as the nation. Indeed one reason why Kropotkin was so reviled by his aristocratic peers in the political and educational establishment was that he placed the interests of 'lesser peoples' such as peasants and the urban poor of Europe, as well as the inhabitants of the historic 'Third World', above those of industrial capitalists and the global bourgeoisie. Considered misguided because they wished to replace the competitive ethos of modern capitalism with the communitarian values of peasants and workers, Kropotkin, Reclus and their anarchist followers were widely criticized for defending the 'moral economies' of these sectors of national and global society from the champions of modern capitalism.

If England gave Darwinism to the world, Social Darwinism was at its most prevalent in the United States, where it was readily received not least by the pioneers of corporate capitalism.[44] The sheer scale of its enterprises and the pace of social and economic change in the United States meant that concepts like 'struggle for survival' and 'survival of the fittest' would be revered as foundational principles of American free enterprise. The country's entrepreneurial spirit and work ethic, together with the low level of governmental interference in social and economic affairs, regularly impressed visiting scientists and political leaders alike. Ratzel visited the United States and Mexico in 1874–75, some 15 years after the publication of Darwin's *Origin of Species*. He was particularly impressed with the achievements of settlers of German origin in the

American Midwest and Southwest, who, he contended, had enhanced the social, economic and cultural life of America as a whole. In studies of settler life in the interior of the country, he claimed to discern the emergence of a discernible pattern in the contact between 'expanding' peoples on the one hand, and pre-capitalist 'retreating' societies on the other. In an iconic statement that explicitly legitimized the aggressive expansion of free enterprise capitalism, he argued:

A superior people, invading the territory of its weaker savage neighbours, robs them of their land, forces them back into corners too small for their support, and continues to encroach even upon this meagre possession, till the weaker finally loses the last remnants of its domain, is literally crowded off the earth ... The superiority of such expansionists consists primarily in their greater ability to appropriate, thoroughly utilise and populate territory.[45]

In another statement that also had clear implications for minority peoples and indigenous communities throughout America and continental Europe, it was suggested that: 'Evolution needs room but finds the earth's surface limited. Everywhere old and new forms of life live side by side in deadly competition; but the later improved variety multiplies and spreads at the expense of the less favoured types. The struggle for existence means a struggle for space.'[46]

Using 'scientific' methods derived from the natural sciences, particularly zoology and comparative anatomy, Ratzel then engaged in a 'non-hypothesis-testing form of positivism which enabled him to popularise geographical explanations of state behaviour'. This led him to formulate historical and geographical 'laws of nature', which, he believed, governed the diffusion of such disparate living entities as plants, animals and peoples. These 'laws of nature' could then be used to justify ethnic cleansing and racial oppression in the colonial world. They also underpinned 'scientific' explanations for the successful adaptation of White minorities to the rural environments of North America, Australia and colonial Africa. In arguing thus, Social Darwinists carried evolutionary theory much further into the social and physical sciences and into the world of nation-building and imperial expansion than Darwin ever intended. Ellen Churchill Semple, who had studied under Ratzel at Leipzig, has suggested that the sheer fecundity of his geographical imagination often left little room for testing the validity of his 'scientific principles'. Writing in 1911, she recalled:

> He enunciates one brilliant generalization after another. Sometimes he reveals the mind of a seer, throwing out conclusions which are highly suggestive, on the face of them convincing, but which on examination prove untenable … He took a mountain-top view of things, kept his eye always on far horizons, and in the splendid sweep of his scientific conceptions sometimes overlooked the details near at hand. Herein lay his greatness and his limitations.[47]

Nevertheless, it was 'scientific' generalizations such as these that provided many Western governments with a geographical code of state practice that legitimized nation-building and imperial expansion. Geographers like Friedrich Ratzel and Karl Haushofer in Germany, Isaiah Bowman and Ellsworth Huntington in the United States, Halford Mackinder in Britain, and the environmental determinist Thomas Griffith Taylor in Australia, together with their numerous disciples inside and outside academic geography, made extensive use of modelling and statistical techniques to give their theorizing the semblance of scientific objectivity. Thus three years after the death of Kropotkin, Ellsworth Huntington used his presidential address to the Association of American Geographers to argue that 'the pinnacle of geographic achievement' would be achieved whenever scientists could explain geographic variations in 'human character' by reference to climatic and environmental factors.

Huntington's concern for the status of geography and the many 'scientific' associations that he helped to establish was matched only by his concerns about issues of race, class and gender as they affected American society. Despite onerous professional commitments and a voluminous output of academic texts and peer-reviewed academic papers, Huntington was deeply involved in over 50 professional and political organizations in the United States. From 1934 to 1938 he was President of the Board of Directors of the American Eugenics Society. One of his most important works was *The Pulse of Asia*, which was published in 1907 and purported to explain the history of human progress by outlining it geographical context. In *Civilization and Climate*, published in 1915, he made abundant use of cartography and statistical techniques to prove that the growth and decline of civilizations were ultimately determined by climatic factors. His *World Power and Evolution*, published in 1919, was widely acclaimed in the United States and Western Europe as a classic on modern political geography. Like Kropotkin, he published many of his 242 research papers in academic journals and in popular periodicals.[48] Unlike Kropotkin, however, Huntington believed it was the duty of professional academics to support the state and inform government. A major exponent of climatic determinism, he maintained that socio-biology could explain social and economic disparities within American and global society. Also unlike Kropotkin, he believed that the 'natural' leaders of developed nations, and by extension the entire world, should be drawn from the military-industrial and educational establishment of Western Europe and North America. He was particularly concerned about the effects of mass immigration on White Anglo-Saxon America. An early advocate of immigration controls, he called for strict measures to limit the number of immigrants entering the United States from impoverished and ethnically diverse regions in Eastern Europe and Russia. He also believed that miscegenation posed a threat to the racial and moral fabric of White America. He vehemently opposed liberal demands for a relaxation of immigration controls, arguing that this would 'dilute' the national character of White Anglo-Saxon America and introduce 'weaker strains' into the body politic of American society. Believing that only the best should rule the rest of society, he castigated professional middle-class women for not living up to their 'social responsibility' by producing sufficient numbers of 'well-bred' children to counterbalance the masses of children born to 'coloured', 'genetically inferior' working-class mothers. An advisor to the Australian government in the run-up to the First World War, he warned against the dangers of Black immigration to that country, and suggested that other White nations could do worse than follow their 'intelligent' example by closing their borders to the impoverished and 'racially inferior'. For the United States he recommended 'a stringent and effective regulation of immigration so that for ten or twenty years we may be sure that we are admitting none except those whose *inherent capacities make them fit to share our citizenship*'.[49]

Whereas Kropotkin looked to pre-colonial and medieval history for evidence that mutual aid and social cooperation were factors in survival and evolution, Huntington was drawn to world history because of the alleged weaknesses that he perceived in the philosophical and methodological approaches of historians and other academics. The study of history, he maintained, required an intimate knowledge of the dynamic influence of climatic and environmental factors on the rise and fall of civilizations. Those who ignored these were, he argued, 'unscientific'. While recognizing the importance of ambition, competition, scientific achievement and 'constructive statesmanship' to the survival of White civilization, he criticized fellow scientists and academics for according only a minor role to geographic factors in the success, and failure, of historic societies. Thus he argued that historians in particular were 'so impressed with the importance of economic considerations, or *purely human matters* such as ambition, religious ardour, mechanical invention, constructive statesmanship or scientific, literary and artistic achievement, that they feel that other subjects are scarcely worthy of consideration'.[50]

Science for Huntington, as indeed for Kropotkin, was most emphatically a quantitative exercise in deductive reasoning. However, his model of human behaviour was far from simple, and he certainly did not subscribe to the view that individuals lacked autonomy and were mere playthings of powerful environmental and biological forces. Nevertheless, while many would agree that Kropotkin could be placed at the 'soft' end of this continuum because of his optimistic faith in human ability, Huntington has usually been placed at the opposite 'hard' end. This was not a position of which he would have approved. As an internationally recognized scholar and professor of geography at Yale University, Huntington regularly warned against any oversimplification of the role of environmental factors in global patterns of development and underdevelopment. He insisted that scientists should always expect to have their hypotheses submitted to the rigours of empirical tests, and that the sciences in general should also have sound empirical foundations. While historians, archaeologists and anthropologists have criticized his inadequate grasp of world history, social scientists have accused him of engaging in intricate 'curve-fitting' exercises in order to correlate climatic-environmental conditions with the 'mental achievements' of different racial groupings in global society. It could, however, be argued that Huntington's real weaknesses lay elsewhere. The ideological kernel at the heart of his 'scientific' explanations for variations in global patterns of development and underdevelopment legitimized massive abuses of power in the global as well as the national arena. Indeed, after Huntington, the 'laws of nature' were used to justify ethnic cleansing, racial segregation, patriarchy, class conflict, social hierarchy, immigration controls, White supremacy and, ultimately, the racialization of scientific discourse.

Anarchist geography and the quest for social relevance

The foregoing discussion on the institutional functions of academic disciplines is central to any radical reappraisal of Kropotkin's position in the history of disciplines such as geography, anthropology, cartography and environmental science. It is to be hoped that it will also help in any reinterpretation of his criticism of state-sponsored academia and its disciplines. It may also explain why he was always so determined to provide anarchism with an intellectual pedigree and scientific basis. Kropotkin's entire life history testifies to the inadequacies of economic reductionism in accounting for the origins and development of scientific thought. As we have seen, everything about his privileged upbringing pointed in the direction of a life in the service of the tsarist state. Even after his disillusionment with courtly life in St Petersburg and his subsequent disillusionment with military life and social administration in Siberia, he could well have opted for a prestigious academic position and gone on to become a member of Russia's scientific elite. He was not yet 30 when he turn down the post of secretary of the Physical Section of the Imperial Geographic Society. That he chose not to take up a career in the physical sciences had more to do with the ethos and ethics of the academic establishment than with his own personal views on the joys of scientific research and academic life. Following his rejection of an academic career, Kropotkin brought his long-held desire to 'do useful work' to his political career as an anarchist activist and as an anarchist scientist and political geographer. At a time when the sciences in general and the social and environmental sciences in particular were the domain of the privileged, Kropotkin argued that it was the responsibility of all socially concerned scientists to serve the socially subordinate in combating poverty, social injustice and political oppression. As someone who was particularly opposed to the ethos and ethics of disciplines like geography, history, social science and anthropology, he outlined a new moral code, and an anarchist philosophy of praxis, that was politically and philosophically at odds with the academic establishment of his day. As a secular anarchist, and unlike many of his peers within academia, his ethical code was also devoid of the metaphysical influences that continued to inform social theory in an era of scientific revolutions.

Kropotkin's own views on the ethics of academic research developed initially from his observations of convict life and social administration in Siberia. He would later recall that Siberia had taught him the attractions of federalism, and in a 'Letter to the Workers of the World' which he wrote towards the end of his life he predicted the break-up of imperial Russia:

> Imperial Russia is dead and will never be revived. The future of the various provinces which composed the Empire will be directed towards a large federation. The natural territories of the different sections of this federation are in no way distinct from those with which we are familiar in the history of Russia, of its ethnography and economic life. All attempts to bring the constituent parts of the Russian Empire, such as Finland, the Baltic Provinces, Lithuania, Ukraine, Georgia, Armenia, Siberia and others, under a central authority are doomed to failure.[51]

It was in Siberia also that Kropotkin first began to distinguish between the innate morality of the political prisoners and impoverished peasants on the one hand, and the rigid morality of church and state on the other. For Kropotkin, representative government, the highest achievement of nineteenth-century political democracy, was synonymous with manipulation, fraud and corruption. Writing in 1887 he believed that it had already 'accomplished its historical mission' by giving 'a mortal blow to court-rule' and awakening 'public interest in public questions'.[52] Yet Kropotkin's opposition to the official 'scientism' and Social Darwinism of his day did not stop short at his critique of 'official ethics' of church and state. It also extended to the ideological role of academics in legitimizing state authority and facilitating the development of competitive free enterprise capitalism. Thus he was strongly opposed to the institutionalization of systemic knowledge in elitist colleges, universities and other centres of learning. While conducting research on the glaciated landscapes of southern Finland in 1871, he admitted that he had been forced to think 'a great deal … about social matters' and came to the conclusion that, satisfying as it was, this type of research was largely irrelevant to peasants who struggled to survive through difficult times in these challenging environments. This was to have a decisive influence upon his subsequent refusal to become a professional geographer.

Kropotkin's sojourn in Finland certainly provided him with ample opportunities to contemplate his future role in society, forcing him to choose between the privileged life of the physical scientist and the difficult and dangerous life of the anarchist activist. He once recalled that it was while walking from one gravel-pit to another in southern Finland with his geologist's hammer on his shoulder that he became acutely aware of the 'immense amount of labour the Finnish peasant spends in clearing the land and breaking up the hard boulder clay'. While he appreciated the importance of the American farm machinery and new methods of soil fertilization then being introduced into this corner of Finland, he went on to question

the use of talking to this peasant about American machines, when he has barely enough bread to live upon from one crop to the next; when the rent which he has to pay for this boulder clay grows heavier and heavier in proportion to his success in improving the soil ... He gnaws at his hard-as-a-stone rye-flour cake, which he bakes twice a year; he has with it a morsel of fearfully salted cod and a drink of skimmed milk. How dare I talk to him of American machines, when all that he can raise must be sold to pay rent and taxes? He needs me to live with him, to help him to become the owner or the free occupier of that land. Then he will read books with profit, but not now.[53]

It was while he was engaged in this research that Kropotkin, who was then still in his late twenties, was offered the prestigious position of secretary of the Physical Science branch of the Imperial Geographical Society of Russia. Incapable of envisaging the physical landscape without describing the difficult conditions of the peasants and other workers who were its impoverished custodians, he declined the offer for the following reasons:

Science is an excellent thing. I knew its joys and valued them perhaps more than many of my colleagues did. Even now as I was looking on the lakes and hillocks of Finland, new and beautiful generaliza- tions arose before my eyes ... a grand picture was rising and I wanted to draw it, with the thousands of details I saw in it; ... to open new horizons for geology and physical geography ... But what right had I to these joys when all around me was nothing but misery and struggle for a mouldy bit of bread; when whatsoever I should spend to enable me to live in that world of higher emotions must needs be taken from the very mouths of those who grew the wheat and had not bread enough for the children? From somebody's mouth it must be taken, because the aggregate production of man still remains so low. Knowledge is an immense power. Man must know. But we already know much! What if that knowledge – and only that – should become the possession of all? Would not science itself progress in leaps and cause mankind to make strides in production, invention, and social creation, of which we are hardly in a condition now to measure the speed? The masses want to know: they are willing to learn; they *can* learn. There, on the crest of that immense moraine which runs between the lakes, as if giants had heaped it up in a hurry to connect the two shores, there stands a Finnish peasant plunged in contemplation of the beautiful lakes, studded with islands, which lie before him. Not one of these peasants, poor and downtrodden though he may be, will pass that spot without stopping to admire the scene. Or there, on the shore of the lake, stands another peasant, and sings something so beautiful that the best musician would envy him his melody for its feeling and meditative power. Both deeply feel, both meditate, both think; only give them the means of getting leisure. This is the direction in which, and these are the kind of people for whom, I must work. All those sonorous phrases about making mankind progress, while at the same time the progress makers stand aloof from those whom they pretend to push onwards, are mere sophisms made up by minds anxious to shake off a fretting contradiction. So I sent my negative reply to the Geographical Society.[54]

Kropotkin believed that geography, as a holistic and interdisciplinary subject, should also be an emancipatory discipline. As the 'great integrator of knowledge' it could help to forge the common bonds shared by workers and peasants across national and racial boundaries. He strongly criticized state schools and colleges whose teaching methods were making 'attractive and suggestive' subjects like history and geography among 'the most arid and unmeaning of subjects'. The same could be said, 'with almost the same words, and with but a few exceptions, with regard to Physics and Chemistry, to Botany and Geology, to History and Mathematics. A thorough reform of teaching in all sciences is as needful as a reform of geographical education.' He added:

Surely there is scarcely another science which might be rendered as attractive for the child as geography, and as powerful an instrument for the general development of the mind, for familiarising the scholar with the true method of scientific reasoning, and for awakening the taste for natural science altogether. Children are not great admirers of Nature itself as long as it has nothing to do with Man. The artistic feeling which plays so great a part in the intellectual enjoyments of a naturalist is yet very feeble in the child. The harmonies of nature, the beauty of its form, the admirable adaptation of organisms, the satisfaction derived by the mind from the study of physical laws, – all these may come later, but not in early childhood. The child searches everywhere for man, for his struggles against obstacles, for his activity. Minerals and plants leave it cold; it is passing through a period when imagination is prevailing. It wants human dramas, and therefore tales of hunting and fishing, of sea travels, of struggles against dangers, of customs and manners, of traditions and migrations, are obviously one of the best means of developing in a child the desire of studying nature. Some modern 'pedagogues' have tried to kill imagination in children. Better ones will understand what a precious auxiliary imagination is to scientific reasoning.[55]

Not surprisingly, therefore, Kropotkin also believed that geography had a powerful role to play in 'dissipating the prejudices in which we are reared with regard to the so-called "lower races"'. As such it could challenge the *mission civilatrice* of European nations where students were taught 'from their tenderest childhood ... to despise "the savages", to consider the very virtues of pagans as disguised crime, and to look upon the "lower races" as upon a mere nuisance on the globe'. Thus he argued that one of the greatest achievements of modern ethnographic studies was to 'demonstrate that these "savages" have understood how to develop highly in their societies the same humane sociable feelings which we Europeans are so proud to profess'. Despite the poor record of state schools and colleges in overcoming racial prejudice, the teaching of geography and history in particular, he argued, could 'do much to raise the moral development of the majority to the high level reached by a few'. Political leaders in late nineteenth-century Europe had 'understood the necessity of a reform as soon as the so-called "practical" interests of colonization and warfare were brought to the front'. It was, he argued, now high time to discuss the reform of geographical education and an 'earnest discussion will necessarily show that nothing serious can be achieved in this direction unless we undertake a corresponding, but much wider, general reform of all our system of education'.[56] Freed from their Eurocentric prejudices, disciplines like geography, history and anthropology could also relate 'life-tales of self-devotion, of love for humanity, not invented but real, not distant but near at hand, which we ... see every day around us'. As a means of making education a joyful rather than a dreary experience, teachers of geography and history could relate the folklore and customs of other nations in such a way as to inspire the imaginations of students of all ages. Thus he suggested that no Greek myth could 'supersede the finely artistical, the chaste, the highly humanitarian myths and songs of ... Lithuanians or Finns'. The folklore of all nationalities contained 'such artistic, such vigorous, such broadly human tales, that one cannot see without regret our children fed on Greek and Roman traditions, instead of making them familiar with the treasures concealed in the folklore of other nationalities'. Having consulted the works of progressive ethnologists and geographers he recognized that there was 'a broad place for a separate, most important science, and not merely for a *graphy*, but for an *ology*'. Thus the geographer of the future, he argued, would 'tax many kindred sciences' collecting research data, and he foresaw that 'many specialities' would develop as a result of this. Some of these would be 'more closely connected with history', while others would be linked with the physical sciences. Only geography, however, could 'cover *all* this field at once and ... combine in *one* vivid picture all separate elements of this knowledge: to represent it as an harmonious whole, all parts of which are consequences of a few general principles and are held together by their mutual relations'.[57]

Kropotkin's commitment to reform in the structure, substance and teaching methods of geography, and of the sciences in general, was not unrelated to his wider criticisms of the fragmentation of knowledge and compartmentalization of social life in the disjointed, uneven world of capitalist modernity at the end of the nineteenth century. In works such as *The Conquest of Bread* and *Fields, Factories and Workshops*, and in pamphlets such as *What Geography Ought To Be* and *Anarchism: Its Philosophy and Ideal*, he outlined his anarchist alternative to the state-centred political geography of the academic establishment. In these and other writings he reiterated his criticisms of the social hierarchies and iniquitous class divisions of industrial capitalism. These, he argued, were radically accentuating the unnatural division between manual and intellectual labour, and between town and country. In so doing they retarded social as well as personal development, and ultimately inhibited socio-economic progress. He also believed that the fragmentation of work practices under conditions of industrial capitalism greatly enhanced the commodification of labour. In transforming work from a cooperative practice into a competitive process, this fostered the development of increasingly authoritarian structures of workers' surveillance and managerial control. With labour no longer an expression of workers' sociability and cooperation, management and machinery dictated the rhythms and character of working life, both on the land and in towns and cities. This gave rise to a 'starvation of the spirit', which, in Kropotkin's eyes, was every bit as serious as material deprivation in that it further suppressed all expressions of individualism and throttled the very lives of working people. In criticizing the competitive ethos of capitalism, and not least its social and environmental consequences, Kropotkin also rejected arguments that attributed the atomization of labour and the decimation of community life to market forces and economic 'laws'. Thus he maintained that there was nothing 'natural' about the decline of traditional communities in rural Europe or in its urban centres. To attribute the decimation of community life to 'economical law' was, he added, a 'grim joke'. Just as one could not describe the death of soldiers on the battlefield as a 'natural' event, one could not describe the death of urban or rural villages as an inevitable consequence of mechanization or industrialization.[58] Thus Kropotkin railed against divisions between town and country with the same force that he condemned iniquitous class divisions, including distinctions between manual and intellectual work. They all encouraged feelings of powerlessness among workers, and ignored the need for sustainable development and ecological balance. These social and spatial divisions fostered alienation, encouraged the centralization of authority, and contributed to an undue degree of specialization in the market for manual and intellectual labour.

Anarchism and the decentralization of power and production

In *Fields, Factories and Workshops* – a foundational and prophetic account of his new version of anarchist geography that began life as a series of articles between 1888 and 1890 – Kropotkin outlined his criticisms of the social and geographical consequences of processes of capitalist modernization that had been operating since the late fifteenth century. This work set out to debate the central question of modern economics, namely 'How should we produce the necessities of life?' Reprinted again at the end of the First World War, it was principally concerned with the deterioration of the quality of life, and of urban and rural environments, under monopoly capitalism. It also raised important questions concerning global food security and the sustainability of energy supplies in an age of rapid urbanization. *Fields, Factories and Workshops*, therefore, developed into a treatise on the causes and consequences of the over-centralization of productive processes and the consequent dehumanization of manual and mental labour. In response, it presented the anarchist alternative to the compartmentalization of life and work in late nineteenth-century capitalist societies. New sources of energy, especially electricity and wind power, meant that the centralization of power production was no longer necessary. Similarly, the concentration of industrial production in large units and in urban areas was no longer essential. Thus, he argued: 'There is absolutely no reason why these and like anomalies should persist. The industries must be scattered all over the world; and the scattering of industries amidst the civilized nations will be necessarily followed by a further scattering of factories over the territories of each nation.'[59]

In this text Kropotkin also took issue with Adam Smith and other advocates of the division of labour. He was likewise critical of the international division of labour in the emerging global economy. Because they were 'dazzled with the results obtained by a century of marvelous inventions', conventional economists and political leaders 'proclaimed the necessity of dividing the whole of humanity into national workshops having each of them its own specialty'. Long before the emergence of the 'People Before Profit Movement', he criticized 'the narrow conception of life which consisted in thinking that profits are the only leading motive of human society, and the stubborn view which supposes that what has existed yesterday would last forever'. In criticizing the over-specialization and fragmentation of work under conditions of advanced capitalism, he believed that many had already perceived that there is no advantage for the community in riveting human beings for all their lives to a given occupation or profession. This only deprives men and women of such work as would bring them into a much wider, and freer, relationship with the world, one that would make them 'partners' in the enjoyment of science, culture and the arts.[60]

Nations, too, he argued, were refusing to become specialized, as each one sought out 'a compound aggregate of tastes and inclinations, of wants and resources, of capacities and inventive power'. The new spatial order envisaged by anarchists would result in each nation becoming 'her own agriculturalist and manufacturer; each individual working in the field and in some industrial art; each individual combining scientific knowledge with knowledge of a handicraft – such is, we affirm, the tendency of civilized nations'. This, he suggested, was no longer a utopian dream:

> Already now, our food consists, even in modest households, of produce gathered from all over the globe. Our cloth is made out of fibres grown and wool sheared in all parts of the world. The prairies of America and Australia; the mountains and steppes of Asia; the frozen wildernesses of the Arctic regions; the deserts of Africa and the depths of the oceans; the tropics and the lands of the midnight sun are our tributaries. All races of men contribute their share in supplying us with our staple food and luxuries, with plain clothing and fancy dress, while we are sending them in exchange the produce of our higher intelligence, our technical knowledge, our powerful industrial and commercial organising capacities! Is it not a grand sight, this busy and intricate exchange of produce all over the earth which has suddenly grown up within a few years?[61]

In their day, texts like *Fields, Factories and Workshops* and *The Conquest of Bread* were considered blueprints for 'a new economy'. They recognized that 'the energies used in supplying the needs of human life, and the increasing scale of these needs, were not inexhaustible'. Writing in 1918, Bertrand Russell regarded *Fields, Factories and Workshops* as a new departure in anarchist social planning and a new direction in anarchist economic theory. 'Socialists and anarchists in the main', he wrote,

> are products of industrial life, and few among them have any practical knowledge of food production. *The Conquest of Bread* and *Fields, Factories and Workshops* are very full of detailed information and, even making allowances for an optimistic bias, I do not think it can

be denied that they demonstrate possibilities in which few of us would otherwise have believed.

Some 50 years after *Fields, Factories and Workshops* first appeared, Herbert Read believed that its 'deductions and proposals' remained as valid 'as on the day when they were written'.[62]

In that publication, Kropotkin also discussed the role of scientific innovations and modern technology in the decentralization of industrial and agricultural production at a whole variety of spatial levels. More specifically he examined the possibility of using scientific techniques and new technologies to recreate the traditional organic links between town and country on the one hand, and between intellectual and manual labour on the other. Like Reclus, he argued that the organic and 'naturally collectivist' communities of pre-capitalist Europe, where the absence of rigid divisions between town and country meant that people lived in greater harmony with their environments, had been severed by the twin forces of nation-building and capitalist modernization. Similarly in the colonial world, imperial expansion and the privatization of global resources had decimated small-scale societies and led to their forceful integration into a hierarchical world order increasingly under the control of market forces and White metropolitan nations. Right from the start, Kropotkin set the tone of his discussion of an anarchist alternative to the political economy of capitalism in terms that would be echoed by Harry Braverman's critique of the degradation of working conditions under industrial capitalism. Thus he outlined 'the advantages which civilized societies could derive from a combination of industrial pursuits with intensive agriculture, and of brain power with manual work'. Indeed Kropotkin's response to the degradation and minute subdivision of the labour process was to argue that

> the reduction of the worker to no more than a source of undifferentiated labour power ... is the essential feature of one historically specific mode of production. The ends achieved by the system are an astounding proliferation of certain goods, a concentration of political and economic power in fewer and fewer hands, and a relative impoverishment – despite so-called high standards of living – of the working population.[63]

This resulted in the helotization and degradation of the labour process. Similarly, the intensification of this type of 'degraded' work stultified workers through a 'habitude of endlessly repetitive activity', thereby cutting the worker off 'from the possibility of self-respect and political initiative in his quality of man and citizen'. Like Henry George and Harry Braverman, Kropotkin recognized the contradictions of a system of production that resulted in one third of the population of the United States being ill-fed, ill housed and ill-clothed. The decentralization of agriculture and the development of a mixed economy were his solutions to the seeming paradox of capitalist development at the end of the nineteenth century. The environmental and social effects of these were a central feature of his defence of the mixed economy, just as smaller and decentralized units of production were considered favourable to personal development because they would substitute individual initiative for regimentation, and ultimately influence the kind of political organization that workers would support. In practice, the regimes in question had substituted for the consent of the governed the principle of 'virtual representation' that parliament invented for the benefit of the American colonies.[64]

He further suggested that Europe had the capability to fundamentally transform industrial and agricultural production by laying the foundations of a new world order consisting of multiple semi-autonomous 'micro-societies' bound together within mutually agreed federal structures. Thus he argued:

> The scattering of industries over the country – so as to bring the factory amidst the fields, to make agriculture derive all those profits which it always finds in being combined with industry … and to produce a combination of industrial with agricultural production – is surely the next step … This step is imposed by the very necessity of producing for the producers themselves; it is imposed by the necessity for each healthy man and woman to spend part of their lives in manual work in the free air.[65]

Moreover, his reasons for advocating the decentralization of industry were quite different from contemporary arguments in favour of regional policy and the dispersal of industry. For Kropotkin 'the scattering of industry' was a means to an end – that end being the creation of a stateless society.

In modern industrial societies, on the other hand, regional policy has been used as a strategy for legitimizing state authority by bolstering support for government through the creation of employment opportunities in disadvantaged areas and in political constituencies where such support might otherwise be weak. Particularly since the 1960s, governments have been big investors in and important regulators of socio-economic activity in all modern state-societies. Hence their regional policies can have very considerable impacts on spatial variations in levels of economic activity and the standards of social well being of their citizens. Indeed, a growing body of literature in political geography and political science now sees political parties as rational agents of the state that operate like profit-maximizing capitalists when they use regional policy to *legitimize* their control over state authority in spatial as well as socio-political contexts. This is why governments are often compelled to consider their political futures, as well as the wishes of their electorates, when formulating and implementing policies that may have powerful regional and socio-economic consequences.[66] For Kropotkin on the other hand, the 'scattering of industry' and other forms of economic activity was a means to enhance regional autonomy and the authority of local actors, thereby reducing the attractions of 'big government' and central authority. This was because any additions to the autonomy of local communities and the regions were to come at the expense of the central authority of the state. This in turn would lead to the progressive weakening of central government's authority in the spatial arena.

Finally, for Kropotkin, the 'scattering of industry over the country' was also a means for achieving conditions of ecological balance and improving the quality of life for workers by bringing the benefits of sustainable economic activity to cultural deserts and economic backwaters. Indeed, there was literally a world of difference between his arguments in favour of regional industrialization and those who advocated the dispersal of industry in capitalist societies. In state capitalist societies, access to abundant supplies of cheap and unskilled labour, together with the avoidance of environmental regulations, have been crucially important to the success or failure of industrial regional policy. This was the complete reverse of Kropotkin's arguments in favour of regional and local autonomy.

In *The City in History*, first published in 1961, Lewis Mumford was impressed with the visionary quality of Kropotkin's views on sustainable development and the organic economy:

KROPOTKIN AND THE ANARCHIST INTELLECTUAL TRADITION

Almost half a century in advance of contemporary economic and technical opinion, [Kropotkin] had grasped the fact that the flexibility and adaptability of electronic communication and electric power, along with the possibilities of intensive biodynamic farming, had laid the foundations for a more decentralized urban development in small units, responsive to direct human contact, and enjoying both urban and rural advantages.[67]

Mumford praised Kropotkin for emphasizing the organic links between town, cities and countryside prior to the rise of powerful industrial cities in the nineteenth century. He demonstrated that townships in colonial New England were socio-economic and political organizations that enclosed groups of towns, villages and hamlets nested in the surrounding countryside. These, he argued, achieved a balanced economy, were relatively self-sufficient, and possessed a high degree of local autonomy. They performed the functions of local government, including the provision of schools and the maintenance of roads. Historically at least, the inhabitants of these New England townships recognized the need for 'decentralized facilities'. Unlike the abstract political system of state-centred political democracy that emerged from the late eighteenth century onwards, their townships were organically rooted in the urban and rural landscape.

Influenced by Kropotkin's writings on mutual aid and the guild structure of medieval cities, Mumford demonstrated how towns and villages in early colonial America were also laid out in the manner of Kropotkin's medieval European villages:

At one end were barns and sheds, at the other end, the factories and workshops; on either side lay the orchards, the vineyards, and the gardens; while in the areas between the communities carefully planted forests provided a large part of the lumber needed for their furniture-making industry ... The architecture of these villages, and their general layout, a comely, straightforward brick vernacular, was superior to the usual run of buildings in the second half of the nineteenth century; it vied with that of earlier Shaker communities in everything but architectural inventiveness.[68]

In keeping with Kropotkin's defence of the viability of the small community, Mumford went on to suggest that, despite their small-town scale, these were practical, common sense advances in urban development. They operated successfully in their rural settings and could have made a major contribution to city building in the eighteenth and nineteenth centuries, when they were obliterated through the centralization of political power and the massive concentration of economic activity in the amorphous, sprawling cities of the coal age. Mumford described the early colonial towns as centres of 'ecotechnic culture' because they utilized water and wind power to generate energy and achieve a balanced economy. He went so far as to claim that they could have competed with coal and iron. They even maintained a decentralized socio-economic and political regime long enough to take advantage of the discovery of electricity and the production of light metals. Kropotkin depicted these types of communities as 'organisms bubbling with life'.[69] They developed in different ways in different places, depending upon environmental and geographical conditions, the nature of external commerce, and the degree of resistance to external influence. All of these factors gave each community its own distinct character, history and social geography. This was the type of urban-rural landscape that, with the aid of modern science and technological innovations, Kropotkin wished to resurrect out of the ashes of a decadent capitalist modernity. In terms again reminiscent of Marcuse's critique of the one-dimensionality of modern capitalism, he argued that anarchists alone had the ability to construct this qualitatively new society in a stateless form.[70] He further suggested that there were no technical reasons why machines should not be distributed between several establishments, and called for the application of science to agriculture in order to raise production and reduce the number of workers in the agricultural sector.

Stressing Kropotkin's influence upon urban planning since the nineteenth century, Peter Hall has also shown that his writings in particular, together with those of Reclus and Proudhon, underpinned much of Patrick Geddes' futurist vision of a 'neotechnic order' for the modern world. Like Kropotkin in particular, Geddes 'took the position that society had to be reconstructed not by sweeping governmental measures like the abolition of private property, but through the efforts of millions of individuals: the "neotechnic order" meant "the creation, city by city, region by region, of a Eutopia"'.[71] At first glance his rural background, and his strong preference for regional as opposed to national strategies for social and economic development, seemed to predispose Kropotkin to distrust the metropolitan culture of an emerging capitalist modernity. That said, he would by no means have approved of the strict rural ethos and authoritarian structure of modern-day groups such as the Amish. His communes of the future were to be urban as well as rural. They were never conceived as simply territorial agglomerations, and were intended to be set up in such a way as to facilitate social groupings of equals that had neither boundaries nor frontiers. Ideally they would also dispense with the urban-rural divide, developing a symbiosis of both the urban and the rural. Hence Kropotkin was always deeply impressed with the latest innovations in technology and wanted his 'bubbling' urban and rural communities to take full advantage of such developments. Whereas Tolstoy grew to detest Moscow and urban life in general, and in his early years was forever running off to the family estate at Yasnaya Polyana, Kropotkin belonged to that generation of young Russians who did not wish to live 'half lives' of gambling, socializing, hunting and estate-man-agement. For many talented young men and women of this generation the rural mansion and family estate were 'stifling cages' that thwarted their political and intellectual ambitions.[72] Thus he had responded eagerly to the revolutionary tradition of Paris from 1789 to 1871, and valued cities for their radicalism and social diversity. Far from being 'anti-city', his version of scientific anarchism was underpinned by a strongly defended historical thesis that defended urban lifestyles. While he opposed urban squalor, he was always prepared to champion new forms of urban living that would give free rein to human capabilities. Even as a young man in Moscow he had visited a number of the city's factories and was impressed by the 'poetry of the machine'.[73] When in England he visited several small cutlery workshops in Sheffield and 'was fascinated by the survival of older forms of production amidst the giant factory system'. He also thought workshops had a vitality and flexibility that was worth saving, despite poor working conditions. In an article published in *The Nineteenth Century* in October 1888, under the title 'The Industrial Village of the Future', he began to outline his arguments in favour of participatory democracy and small-scale cooperatives that were developed 10 years later in *Fields, Factories and Workshops*.[74]

Kropotkin's researches into patterns of urban life in Europe led him to conclude that a 'communalist' revolution in the twelfth century had resulted in a proliferation of village communities and urban confraternities. These, he argued, managed to retain their liberties right throughout the medieval period by fending off 'nascent kinglets', despotic monarchies and their theocratic allies. Their hard-earned liberties had found fertile soil in the medieval city, where each urban village, or parish, was the domain of self-governing guilds. This was a spatial arrangement where each city comprised 'a union of streets, parishes, and guilds [that] held its plenary assembly in the grand forum, and … elected its judges and had its banner to rally the militias of the guilds and districts'. As a miniature 'free state' each city dealt with other cities as a sovereign entity in its own right, developed relations with whomever it wished, and 'concluded alliances either nationally or outside the national territory'.[75] In extolling the freedoms of the medieval city, Kropotkin argued that:

> In those cities, under the shelter of their liberties acquired under the impulse of free agreement and free initiative, a whole new civilization grew up and attained such expansion that the like has not been seen up till now … Never, with the exception of that other glorious period of ancient Greece, had society made such a stride forwards. Never in two or three centuries, had man undergone so profound a change nor so extended his power over the forces of nature.[76]

He suggested that the liberties that had underpinned social life in the medieval city reasserted themselves in the Paris Commune, one of the most profound challenges to the capitalist organization of urban space in modern times. Led by Proudhonist anarchists, the Communards had managed to articulate a discordant decentralized vision of urban life that was radically opposed to the compartmentalization of urban space and the hierarchical control of urban life in Paris after Haussmann's attempts to render the city a plaything of monopoly capital. Thus the Commune contained within it shades of 1848 Revolution now re-enacted in the capitalist city. As Harvey has suggested, it 'was wrought in part out of a nostalgia for the urban world that Haussmann had destroyed … and the desire to take back the city on the part of those dispossessed by Haussmann's works'.[77] For Kropotkin, however, it was much more than this. Whereas Proudhon tended to fear social revolution because it might lead to 'anarchy' in the pejorative sense, Kropotkin welcomed it because it liberated the people's suppressed capacity for self-organization.

Thus it was in the midst of the Commune that a much older principle of authority re-emerged. This allowed social groupings to form that relied on their own initiative and spontaneity rather than giving in to being ruled by those who claimed to represent them. Thus, Kropotkin showed that the Communards were not simply reacting against the 'Haussmanni-zation' of Paris since the 1850s. They represented an anarchist tradition of urban resistance to authoritarian rule that had its origins in the medieval city. Kropotkin saw the medieval cities of Europe as being divided into 'sectors' or parishes that radiated outwards from the citadel or the cathedral until they reached the city ramparts. Each of these sectors was inhabited mainly by an 'art' or trade, with new trades – the 'young arts' – occupying the suburbs, which in due course would also be enclosed within the fortified walls of the city as it expanded outwards. Each street or parish was a distinct territorial unit that shared many of the charac-teristics of the village communities that had resisted encroachments of state authority since at least the twelfth century.[78] Thus, each urban village within the city had its popular assembly, forum, tribunal, militia and the symbols of independent local authority. Each city was 'federated' with other small communities and 'sub-towns' that were arranged around the 'mother city', each maintaining its own way of living and working, and resolutely defending its social and cultural independence.[79] It was this version of urban life, which, according to Kropotkin, the Communards of Paris were seeking to resurrect in the interstices of a late nineteenth-century capitalist modernity. He went on to suggest that in 1871:

the people of Paris, who have overthrown so many governments, were only making their first attempt to revolt against the governmental system itself; consequently they let themselves be carried away by the fetish worship of governments and set up their own. ... The Commune itself, the child of a period of transition, born beneath the Prussian guns, was doomed to perish. But by its eminently popular character it began a new series of revolutions, by its ideas it was the forerunner of the social revolution. Its lesson has to be learned, and when France once more bristles with communes in revolt, the people are not likely to give themselves a government and expect that government to initiate revolutionary measures.[80]

Viewed thus, the Paris Commune represented a transitional phase in the evolution of a radically reinvigorated expression of urban modernity that had its roots in the spatial structure of the medieval city, and took its inspiration from the defenders of medieval urban liberties. Thus Kropotkin wished to arrive at the anarchist city of the future after revisiting the cities of the medieval past. The communes of the next revolution, he argued, would not only 'break down the state and substitute free federation for parliamentary rule' – they would once and for all part ways with that rule to become anarchist communes within a much wider anarchist society.

Like Proudhon, Kropotkin also believed that modern cities had come to symbolize the artificiality of capitalist society. He attributed the debased quality of urban life in advanced capitalist societies to the predominance of factory production and heavy industry in particular. As far back as Proudhon, anarchists' regional loyalties and opposition to large-scale manufacturing industries had predisposed them to distrust the metropolitan culture and social degradation of large cities. To Kropotkin, therefore, cities came to represent not just the artificiality of modern life but their political, cultural and socio-economic dominance. Indeed his opposition to social hierarchies appears to have been matched by an opposition to the hierarchical structure of the world of cities, where provincial town and small cities of several thousand inhabitants occupied one end of a continuum that extended all the way to teeming 'urban agglomerations' of millions of people. However, even more so than Proudhon, Kropotkin combined respect for peasant values with an awareness of the liberating and cultural role of the medieval city in nurturing independence and fostering trade, prosperity and technical and artistic skills. His faith in the emancipatory capacity of science and technology to promote material and cultural prosperity in a stateless world did not cancel out the attractions of autonomous urban as well as rural communities that could be linked together within mutually agreed federal structures. Like the Brighton-born gay socialist writer, Edward Carpenter, Kropotkin opposed capitalism not only because he was critical of the way goods were produced, distributed and consumed, but also because of the ontological assumption of superiority. These men 'wanted to change how human beings interrelated with nature and how they perceived their own beings'. By the second half of the nineteenth century this questioning of capitalist civilization did not appear 'cranky' – 'scientific paradigms were being overturned, the destructive aspects of technology were becoming evident, Eastern religion and Schopenhauer were in vogue, interest was growing in unconscious motivation, and artists and writers were asserting that positive values were to be found in societies dismissed as "primitive"'.[81] Both men were avid advocates of decentralization and looked to radically altered urban communities, not just rural villages, to effect radical social change. In a wide-ranging debate on the merits of 'harmonized labour' and an 'integral education', Kropotkin argued that 'man shows his best when he is in a position to apply his usually-varied capacities to several pursuits in the farm, the workshop, the factory, the study or the studio, instead of being riveted for life to one of these pursuits only'.[82] Prior to the mid nineteenth century, however, such a harmonious union between agricultural and industrial pursuits, as also between brainwork and manual work on the one hand, and town and country on the other, 'could only be a remote desideratum'. The conditions under which the factory system had asserted itself, including 'the obsolete forms of agriculture' which prevailed at the time, had prevented the development of a 'synthesis' between industry and agriculture, between manual and intellectual labour, and between town and country. However, technological change and the application of new scientific techniques had now resulted in the 'wonderful simplification' of production processes in both industry and agriculture. This opened up the possibility of 'a distinct tendency towards a synthesis of human activities', which in turn pointed towards a radically new direction in 'economical evolution'. Everywhere, Kropotkin argued, 'we see the same decentralization of industries going on, new nations continually entering the ranks of those which manufacture for the world market'. Each of these 'new-comers' endeavoured to develop on their own territory the principal industries, and to free themselves from being exploited by 'other nations more advanced in their technical evolutions'.[83]

Kropotkin also recognized that revolutions in the transmission of electricity had the potential to place local communities and small-scale economies on a par, in terms of socio-economic and cultural facilities, with the 'over-congested city'. By the same token, he argued, rural communities could have all the advantages of 'scientific intelligence, group organization, and animated activities' that were originally the monopoly of large cities. This had the potential not only to shatter the divisions between town and country, industrial work and rural work, but also to reduce the disparities between the metropolis and the periphery, thereby fostering the development of small units responsible for their own development, and responsive to local needs and cultural traditions. As noted above, Mumford considered *Fields, Factories and Workshops* a visionary work that 'laid the foundations for a more decentralized urban development in small units, responsive to direct human contact, and enjoying both urban and rural advantages'.[84] Not surprisingly, *Fields, Factories and Workshops*, together with *The Conquest of Bread*, had a profound influence on the social and economic teachings of such diverse thinkers as Mumford, Patrick Geddes, Mahatma Gandhi, Peter Hall, Julius Nyrere and Mao-Tse Tung. The former work in particular has also been popular with the pioneers in the smallholder movement in Britain since the 1950s. In both these works Kropotkin criticized those who believed that the scale and growing centralization of industrial and agricultural production were at once a rational and inevitable development because they were based on economies of scale and scientific laws of technical efficiency. Far from being a polemical work aimed at an exclusively anarchist readership, *Fields, Factories and Workshops* represented the accumulation of more than 20 years of observations on the history of mechanization, the centralization of production and the progressive dehumanization of labour from the sixteenth century to the late nineteenth.

   Kropotkin was also clearly ahead of his time in outlining the dangers of over-dependence upon imported foods. This, he argued, could threaten national security and lead to nations being starved into submission by their enemies in times of international conflict. Thus he called for the dispersal of food production and the decentralization of industry, arguing that a reconfiguration of the methods and scale of production could also satisfy the indigenous needs and cultural traditions of developed and underdeveloped countries alike. From an analysis of the history of social and economic change, he concluded that the trend for manufacturing industry to disperse throughout the world was already far advanced. He also demonstrated that the greater part of industrial production in many advanced economies in his day still occurred in small workshops rather than large factories. Well before the emergence of the 'green economy', and Green political parties, he realized the advantages of combining industry with agriculture, a practice adopted by several post-colonial African societies in the 1960s and 1970s. It is interesting to note that the persistence of mass unemployment in the core areas of global economy has revived interest in small-scale enterprises as alternatives to high-tech capital-intensive industry precisely because they generate employment at comparatively lower per-capita costs compared to large-scale industry where high levels of investment create jobs at an enormous cost.

Epilogue

Between 1872 and 1874, while he was a member of the revolutionary 'Circle of Chaikovsky' in St Petersburg, Kropotkin had been forced to dress as a peasant and adopt the assumed name 'Borodin' in order to evade detection by the police. He had just recently inherited his family's estate and at this stage of his life was dividing his time between setting up a peasant land league and presenting research findings on the physical geography and geomorphology of the glaciated landscape of southern Finland at meetings of the Imperial Geographic Society. To Lev Tikhominov, a fellow member of the circle, Kropotkin, who was already a self-confessed anarchist, was an intimidating figure. He was also an unlikely revolutionary. Unlike other members of the circle he was 'a European from head to foot'. Possessing the self-confidence of the 'pure aristocrat', he was nevertheless 'a revolutionary to the core' who appeared to be interested in many things. While he seemed to be 'completely flattered' to be associated with his plebeian fellow revolutionaries, other members of the circle were equally flattered to have this 'prince of Rurik blood' as a comrade in arms. Like all such coteries, the Chaikovsky Circle had its working-class pragmatists and revolutionary idealists. Kropotkin's could identify with both groups, but his Europeanism, still in its infancy at this stage, coupled with his advanced theoretical views on scientific anarchism, meant that he was not so much 'loved' as a 'comrade' 'valued as an educated and intelligent person'. He was also infinitely more experienced than other members of the circle. In November 1873, members of the Chaikovsky Circle were debating Kropotkin's proposals for a future society 'without government'. These included his demands for revolutionary discipline and a call for armed uprisings along the Volga, where legends about Pugachev and his followers were still in the air. It was at this stage that the police, with the aid of collaborators among the peasants and workers in the city, initiated a series of raids that effectively finished this revolutionary organization.

Throughout the opening weeks of 1874 Kropotkin was making plans to leave St Petersburg, but was detained because he wished to train a handful of new members in order to prolong the circle's existence. He also remained in the city in order to deliver a lecture to a meeting of the Imperial Geographic Society on 21 March, on the origins of Russia's ice age and its effects on the physical geography of Siberia and Finland. Before leaving for the meeting he had already burned all incriminating letters and papers, and packed all of his scientific works in preparation for a speedy departure to the rural south of the country. After the lecture, fearing that the police had discovered his true identity, he returned home late, and waited until dawn before leaving his apartment. He was nevertheless arrested by the police, who discovered the respected scientist, Prince Kropotkin, and the hunted revolutionary 'Borodin', were one and the same person.[1] He was 32 when he entered St Petersburg's notorious Peter and Paul Fortress. In a daring escape two years later, Kropotkin hid out in the countryside around the city, before leaving Russia with a false passport at one of the frontier posts along the Russian border with Finland. At a remote fishing port on the Gulf of Bothnia, he succeeded in boarding a steamer bound for Christiania in Sweden. From there he boarded a British steamer bound for England, and, one month after his escape from prison, landed at Hull. So began a period of some 42 years in exile from Russia. He had intended to remain in England only briefly, as he planned to return to Russia to proceed with the task of organizing a peasant land movement and preparing for peasant uprisings in the south of the country. In Russia he had been too well known to engage in 'open propaganda' to raise the social and political consciousness of workers and peasants and thereby deepen and widen the ideals and principles of the social revolution which he insisted should always precede any attempt at political revolution. In Western Europe he felt that he could 'be more useful' in helping the anarchist movement to 'find its proper expression', and he was 'soon taken up with the wave of the anarchist movement which was just then rising' in France and Switzerland in particular.[2] Initially at least, he found England deeply depressing. Unable to work under a sky without a sun, in a country that seemed to lack 'colour, atmosphere and air', he moved to Switzerland where he lived for five years, until he was 39.[3] He was expelled from the country following the assassination of Tsar Alexander II in the streets of St Petersburg in 1881 by a bomb thrown by a member of the revolutionary People's Will.

Finding refuge once more in England, he continued to function as an anarchist propagandist and may have contemplated settling there. The apathetic atmosphere prevailing in the country once again discouraged him. With his 'astute eye for grassroots consciousness', he concluded that working-class politics were characterized by 'periods of slumber and periods of sudden progress'.[4] In 1882 he decided to move to Thonon-les-Bains in the department of Haute-Savoie in eastern France. His arrival coincided with an outbreak of political violence in the region, and on 3 January 1883, together with 33 other anarchists, he appeared before the Lyon Police Correctional Court. Kropotkin took the opportunity of the court case to expound the views of his fellow anarchists and drafted a statement that outlined the principles to which they all subscribed. However, neither his eloquence as an anarchist philosopher, nor his aristocratic background, had any influence on the court. He and three other leading anarchist propagandists were condemned to 5 years imprisonment at the prison of Clairvaux in the old Abbey of St Bernard where they were accorded the privileged treatment of political prisoners. Despite the pleas for his release from a distinguished list of writers, academics and political leaders, he served out three years of his sentence and was finally released on 15 January 1886.[5] In March of that same year he once again landed in England, which was to become his home for the next 30-odd years. By the opening years of the 1890s, he was already turning increasingly further away from the political violence that continued to haunt the European anarchist movement. In a speech delivered as early as 1891 he suggested that the 'no-government' society should come about 'with the least possible disturbance', as a result of evolutionary change and 'the ripening of public opinion'.[6]

This turn towards peaceful methods and a reliance on social evolution was in keeping with his natural benevolence. However it was also motivated by the fact that in England he was in contact with leading socialists and able to renew his interests in scientific research. Hence he now began to react against the 'apocalyptic romanticism' of the Bakuninists, and was becoming increasingly less confident of the imminence of the anarchist revolution.[7] He made two trips to North America, the first in 1897 when he travelled to Toronto as a delegate of the British Association for the Advancement of Science. During this trip he helped the persecuted Russian Dukhobors find a suitable home in the Canadian countryside. During a second visit in 1901 he was enthusiastically received as an erstwhile member of the Russian aristocracy and a prominent representative of Russian culture. It was on this visit that he delivered a series of lectures that were published some four years later under the title *Ideals and Realities in Russian Literature*.[8] 'Sweet reasonableness' and a gentle amiability, rather than revolutionary fulminations and political propaganda, were to become his preferred tools for convincing leftist colleagues of the truths of his 'scientific anarchism'.

Casting a critical eye over economic and political developments in continental Europe, where German hegemony posed an increasingly real threat to the many varieties of political freedoms, he also began to revise his attitude towards the nation-state and nationalism. Thus he condemned the authoritarian character of the German state, and of German socialism, and was sure that Prussian militarism was paving the way towards continental domination. Convinced that there was a greater chance of an anarchist-inspired social revolution in England or France than in Germany, he insisted that the latter's defeat of France as far back as 1871 had been a major factor in the failure of revolution in Western Europe. After the suppression of his cherished Paris Commune in that year, he wrote that Germany had become 'the chief support of reaction' and a 'menace to European progress'.[9] Whereas many European anarchists regarded a popular war against the Prussian state as a prelude to a war that would obliterate all states, Kropotkin distanced himself from such views by adopting a state-centred position that called on all anarchists to support England and France in any forthcoming war against Germany. This caused his comrades in England, France and Switzerland to remind anarchists everywhere of their principled opposition to the state, and of their anti-militarist principles. Unlike Kropotkin, they continued to argue that support for allied governments in the war effort against Germany would turn anarchists into unlikely bed-fellows of all those who resorted to patriotism and nationalism in order to justify war.

At the height of the war, Errico Malatesta, his erstwhile colleague and a respected anarchist theorist, accused Kropotkin of being a 'Pro-government Anarchist' who championed the total defeat of Germany. Leon Trotsky, the cruellest of all his detractors, branded him a 'superannuated anarchist' who had a weakness ever since youth for populist causes, and accused him of using the war 'to disavow everything he had been teaching for nearly half a century'.[10] This break with his fellow anarchists and revolutionary socialists, many of whom were personal friends from the past, has been described as the 'most unhappy event of Kropotkin's life'. This, together with his penchant for scientific research and intellectual debate rather than polemics and political propaganda, meant that he was becoming an increasingly isolated, lonely and even melancholy figure as he entered his seventies.

When news arrived in March 1917 that the Russian people had finally overthrown the autocratic system that he had sacrificed so much to oppose, he was once again convinced that his final years could be spent in the service of his own people. In the summer of that year he left England. After more than 40 years in exile from his native land, he arrived at the Finland Station, in Petrograd, in June 1917. He was welcomed home by Alexander Kerensky, the leader of the provisional government. On the platform was a regiment of Russian Guards and a number of military bands that trumpeted out the Marseillaise as he stepped down from the train. Absent from these jubilant celebrations to mark the return of one who had done so much to champion the cause of the revolution-ary struggle against Russian autocracy were the Russian anarchists, the majority of whom had opposed the war with Germany.[11] Despite the fact that he refused Kerensky's offer of a cabinet position as Minister for Education, his association with liberal intellectuals and the provisional government, and especially his continued support for the war effort in a country that had grown weary of conflict, meant that he was cut off not only from his fellow anarchists, but also from revolutionary socialists and the Bolsheviks. Even though he was now 75 years old, he continued to take an active interest in the conduct of the war and in the revolutionary process in Russia, and joined a commission of intellectuals tasked with promoting social revolution as a prelude to political revolution. He also called for the establishment of a federal republic of Russia and continued to insist on revolutionary change without bloodshed. He criticized the Bolsheviks for adopting dictatorial methods and imitating the French Jacobins by calling for the socialization of land, industry and commerce. In April 1919 he wrote to the Danish critic and scholar, Georg Brandes, stating: 'Unfortunately, the method by which they seek to establish communism like Babeuf's in a strongly centralized state makes success absolutely impossible and paralyses the constructive work of the people.' Seven months later, by which time the Bolsheviks had seized power, he wrote: 'This buries the revolution.'[12]

At a meeting with Lenin early in 1919, he complained vehemently of the treatment of political prisoners at the hands of the Bolsheviks. He also criticized the suppression of workers cooperatives and the growing bureaucratization of the local authorities, which he believed should have been the foremost agents of social revolution in Russia. When Lenin defended the revolutionary authority of the Bolsheviks by arguing that it was impossible to 'make a revolution wearing white gloves', Kropotkin replied that it was entirely possible 'not to have authority' in the midst of revolution. Pointing to the successful establishment of a 'completely free' cooperative by English dockworkers and the recent successes of the syndicalist movement in France, he added: 'Everywhere you look around, a basis for non-authority flares up.' Praising him for his contribution to revolutionary theory, Lenin suggested that Kropotkin's magnum opus, *The Great French Revolution*, a work which he described as 'useful to everyone', should be available in libraries, villages reading rooms and regimental libraries throughout Russia. Kropotkin replied: 'Where can it be published? I will not permit a state-published edition.' With that, the meeting between Kropotkin, the anarchist philosopher and scientist, and Lenin, the leader of the Bolshevik Party, came to an end. Affection- ately bidding farewell to the aged theorist of scientific anarchism, Lenin assured him that he would always be glad to receive letters and advice from him, and that his views on the revolutionary process would always receive his considered attention.[13] Shortly after this historic meeting, Kropotkin penned a 'Letter to the Workers of the West' wherein he condemned foreign intervention to quell the Russian Revolution, arguing that this would only intensify the already existing 'dictatorial tendencies' of the country's Bolshevik leaders.

In 1920 he moved from Moscow to the small village of Dmitrov, 40 miles north of the city. He died here in a tiny house on 8 February 1921, at the age of 78. The Bolshevik government offered his family a state funeral, which they declined, and instead Moscow's anarchists arranged his memorial service in one of the city's trade union meeting houses. His funeral took place on 13 February, and he was buried at Novo-Devichiii Monastery.[14] It took the five-mile long procession of 20,000 mourners attending his funeral more than two hours to march to his grave. Among them were several anarchists who had been temporarily released from prison. This was the last occasion on which anarchists were permitted to parade in the Soviet Union. It was said that weather conditions were so cold that the musical instruments of the band accompanying the funeral actually froze, thus adding to the silent solemnity of the occasion. The black banners of the anarchists were inscribed with scarlet letters that bore the message 'Where there is authority there is no freedom'.[15] Among those who delivered graveside speeches were Emma Goldman, a handful of prominent Tolstoyan anarchists, a number of representatives of scientific and labour organizations, and delegates from the Communist Party. In the new revolutionary Russia that the Bolsheviks sought to construct Kropotkin's memory was to all intents and purposes obliterated. One of the few places where it was permitted to live on was in the name of a mountain range in Siberia that he first traversed in 1866 as a young officer in an unfashionable Cossack regiment.[16]

George Woodcock and Peter Marshall, two of anarchism's most sympathetic chroniclers over the *longue durée* who have also made very significant contributions to anarchist scholarship in their own right, have offered two quite different assessments of Kropotkin's place in the pantheon of anarchist thinkers. Woodcock held that Kropotkin himself would have claimed as his major contribution to anarchism 'the application of the scientific approach to its practical problems'.[17] For Woodcock, however, Kropotkin's 'irrepressible optimism, his exaggerated respect for the nineteenth-century cult of evolution, his irrational faith in the men of the people, deprived him of true scientific objectivity'. Kropotkin's approach to anarchism, he added, was 'as much intuitive as intellectual, and his compassionate emotion always overcame his cold reasoning'. Nevertheless, Woodcock conceded, his real contribution was 'the humanization of anarchism, the constant relating of theory to details of actual living, which gave the doctrine a concreteness and a relevance to everyday living that it rarely shows in the writings of Godwin, Proudhon or Bakunin'. Kropotkin's faith in anarchism's ability to solve some of the central dilemmas of modern life was also irradiated in his own personality. A man of 'unimpeachable honesty [who was] kind and conscious of the needs of others', he firmly believed in human solidarity 'because everything in his nature attracted him to the idea'. Yet in the end, Woodcock believed, Kropotkin's 'well-balanced goodness seems too bland and blameless in our modern times, when the assumption is easily made that genius must spring from frustration, and saintliness from some deep Dostoyevskian strain'.[18] Nevertheless, as I have been at pains to show in this study, that goodness was real and was based on a critical reading of evolutionary theory and the central role of mutual aid and cooperation in the progressive history of humankind. Belief in the essential goodness of humans also goes a long way towards accounting for Kropotkin's 'simple-hearted vision of an earthly and agnostic City of God with which he crowned the rambling edifice of anarchist thought'.

Writing some 30 years after Woodcock, Peter Marshall offered a far more critical appraisal of Kropotkin's contribution to the theory and practice of anarchism in his magisterial study, *Demanding the Impossible: A History of Anarchism* (1992). Marshall has written well-received biographies of William Godwin and William Blake, and also *Nature's Web*, an exploration of ecological thought, published in 1992. Describing Kropotkin as 'one of the most attractive of anarchist thinkers', Marshall acknowledges his influence on such diverse figures as Mahatma Ghandi in India, Lewis Mumford and Paul Goodman in the United States, and Patrick Geddes and garden-city pioneer Ebenezer Howard in England.[19] He remains for Marshall 'the greatest exponent of a decentralized society based on a harmonious balance between agriculture and industry'. His views on 'integrated education', the need to fuse the teaching of mental and manual skills, still deserve serious attention. In offering not so much a character assessment as a critical appraisal of Kropotkin's intellectual contribution to anarchism, Marshall went on to write:

Kropotkin's great value as a thinker lies in his endeavour to demonstrate that anarchism represents existing tendencies in society towards political liberty and economic equality. He further tried to adopt the methodology of the exact sciences in order to show that all the conclusions of anarchism could be scientifically verified. As a result, he attempted to prove that it is a philosophy which finds confirmation in evolutionary theory, sociology, anthropology and history.[20]

Nevertheless, Marshall argued, Kropotkin's scientific approach tended to be overly deductive rather than inductive, and he attempted to explain everything in terms of his interpretation of evolutionary theory. Quoting Malatesta, he accused Kropotkin of 'mechanistic fatalism' by adopting a materialist philosophy of human behaviour and history which suggested that social organization in a stateless society would be in keeping with natural law. For Marshall, Kropotkin's attempt to deduce a code of ethics from a philosophy of nature was also problematic. Here he was guilty of the 'naturalistic fallacy' of unjustifiably inferring an 'ought' from an 'is', and arriving at a statement of how things should be from how things actually are. In the end, Marshall pointed out, human values are human creations, 'and even if nature operates in a particular way it does not necessarily follow that we should follow suit'. Finally, however, he believed that 'Kropotkin's account of the origin of man-made laws from customs is excellent, and he brings out well the failure of prisons to reform wrongdoers and the immorality of punishment'. Marshall believed that Kropotkin's evolutionary perspective, with its emphasis on the close links between nature and society, made him a pioneer of modern social ecology. Thus he concluded:

> Even those who are generally hostile to anarchism single out Kropotkin as worth reading. He not only tried to base his anarchist philosophy on the findings of science, but to demonstrate its validity by appealing to existing trends in society. Although he countenanced violence and supported war in certain circumstances, he sought to create a society where they would no longer exist ... Indeed, perhaps his most important insight was that only a genuine community could allow the full development of the free individual.[21]

Following Kropotkin's death the rise of fascism and the emergence of authoritarian regimes saw 'organized anarchism' under attack and anarchists struggle to operate as a movement of rebellion rather than a revolutionary social force. Anarchist intellectuals persistently retaliated against all those who continued to equate anarchism with social chaos and political violence, or who branded them as utopian dreamers in an age of rising fascism. They continued to believe in the increasing possibility, and desirability, of a stateless society wherein social harmony would be predicated not on submission to law and authority, but on free agreements concluded between freely constituted territorial and social groups that could be constituted for the sake of production and consumption, and for the satisfaction of the infinite variety of needs and aspirations of civilized beings. They not only opposed the consolidation of military authority in Republican Spain and Vichy France, the classic heartlands of modern anarchism. They condemned global trends towards political and economic centralization, which progressively undermined personal and regional autonomy and subordinated the individual to the authority of states whose powers of surveillance had increased exponentially throughout the inter-war period.[22] In their desire to sustain local autonomy, resist capitalist modernization and protect the dignity of the individual, many anarchists chose to struggle alongside those who rebelled against the globalization of the state authority of the new superpowers in the post-war period. Those who remained outside state-centred revolutionary movements in order to offer their own anarchist critiques of state-centred socialism and national liberation struggles found themselves increasingly marginalized. In the event, they continued to be branded as utopian dreamers in a revolutionary world of 'realpolitik'. Nevertheless, many of these traditional anarchists kept the torch of classical anarchism alive by keeping faith with the human values of a dying past through their relentless opposition to the authoritarianism, consumerism, social conformity and the growing regimentation of modern state societies.

Throughout the revolutionary decades of the post-war period, when anti-colonial revolutions raged across India, Africa and South East Asia, these anarchists constituted a beleaguered minority who found it increasingly difficult to compete with the many varieties of revolutionary Marxism on the left, and with fascism, conservatism, populism and federalism on the right. Yet many of them still valiantly struggled to fulfil anarchism's historic mission not so much by reviving failed insurrectional strategies from the past, but by resorting, like Kropotkin, to the use of reason and sound scholarship in order to appeal to receptive minds in every generation since his death. In the late 1950s and 1960s the New Left in France, England and Germany emerged to champion a libertarian 'third way' between the one-dimensionality of Western capitalism and the bureaucratic centralism of Soviet Marxism. Thinkers such as C. Wright Mills, Herbert Marcuse, E.P. Thompson, Raymond Williams and Stuart Hall called on academics and intellectuals to challenge the prevailing orthodoxies of Marxism and Liberalism. Using arguments that would certainly have appealed to Kropotkin, modern anarchist theorists contended that such orthodoxies were largely irrelevant to the students and activists struggling to articulate an alternative to the post-scarcity society, an alternative that could be ushered in through participatory democracy, decentralized decision-making and consensual agreement, rather than at the behest of revolutionary vanguards purporting to represent the true interests of the working class. Suddenly now the traditional anarchist values of spontaneity, personal and regional autonomy, mutual aid, decentralized decision-making and participatory politics were being widely espoused by all those who challenged the pyramids of power in the university, the factory, the state and the family.[23] Similarly, rather than attempting to recreate forms of social organization that were already obsolete in Kropotkin's day, many of these anarchist theorists sought to persuade others on the left of the abiding truth of anarchism's foundational beliefs and of the viability of the stateless society and the urgent need for communitarian anarchist communities.

However, with the exception of a handful of truly original libertarian thinkers like Murray Bookchin, Noam Chomsky, Herbert Read and Paul Goodman, anarchists in the latter half of the twentieth century generally could not compete with the new mandarins of revolutionary thought and most traditional anarchist activists still struggled to keep alive the ideas of classical anarchists like Proudhon, Reclus, Kropotkin, Bakunin and Durutti. Nevertheless as Bookchin, Chomsky and others have testified, the heritage of classical anarchism was to be found not simply in the inspirational lives and self-sacrifices of these anarchists who dedicated themselves to the service of 'the wretched of the earth'. It was (and still is) to be found also in the stimulation that the writings of Proudhon, Kropotkin, Reclus and Godwin offered to those who continued to believe that moral self-realization must ultimately depend upon free choice, human dignity, sound ecological practice, social harmony and fair moral judgements. These, they insisted, must never be exchanged for material affluence, the false promises of political democracy, and the illusions of collective security. Thus the anarcho-communist intellectual tradition that Kropotkin did so much to sustain in the latter half of the nineteenth century continued to survive as a subaltern tradition, even if it sometimes seemed to lie dormant in the decades immediately after his death.

More recently that tradition has been experiencing a vibrant renaissance with the growth of 'academic anarchism' and the increasing popularity of anti-statist politics.[24] With the emergence of the anti-globalization movement, the rise of Occupy movements in New York, Cairo, Barcelona, London and Athens, the birth of the Democracy Project, and the political coming of age of new groupings like Podemos and People Before Profit, anarchism has emerged as one of the most vibrant and exciting political movements of our times. Despite the assertions of those critics who predicted that the emergence of affluent, industrial state-societies would sound the death knell of anarchism and usher in a new vibrantly democratic capitalist utopia, the passing of industrial society in the traditional core areas of global power has instead ushered in a new age of anarchism.[25] Prospects for the future growth and development of this new critical anarchism have rarely been better. The growing disillusionment with state-centred politics, the rise of the 'nanny state', and the increasingly intrusive 'regimes of domination' that have for so long structured modern life has meant that anarchism is once again attracting widespread support from political activists and social theorists alike. The rapid growth in trans-territorial modes of social and political organization, the bankruptcy of state-centred Marxism, the rejection of representative democracy and industrial capitalism, the denunciation of post-Keynesian austerity policies, the widespread appeal of 'low-footprint' lifestyles, the attractions of consensus decision-making, 'neighbourhood politics' and libertarian municipalism, and rising demands for socio-economic equality and social inclusion to be placed at the centre of debates about social and economic progress – all of these are pointing a growing proportion of well-educated and highly articulate young activists in the direction of vibrant new conceptualizations of the anarchist society.[26] Not only is 'advocacy anarchism' flourishing as a result of the growth of social media and the democratization of political discussion – debates within anarchism, and about anarchism, also continue to flourish, and have resulted in intellectually sustained and critical new studies of anarchist theory and practice. These have been fostered by a renewed quest for free communities of liberation and solidarity that must not only be socially and economically sustainable in the traditional sense, but must also be capable of self-determination, self-transformation and creative self-negation.

It is in this atmosphere that critical re-evaluations of the works of leading anarchist theorists such as Proudhon, Reclus, Kropotkin and Bakunin have been taking place. These founding fathers of anarchist theory lamented the unification of nation-states, the commercialization of social and environmental relations, the centralization and domination of society by states, the increased efficiency of state surveillance systems and the globalization of metropolitan authority on the imperial stage. Today's anarchists are operating in a very different global context as they witness the partial, albeit incomplete unravelling of many of these very processes.[27] This difference in context has already given rise to exciting new strategies that will inevitably shape the future of anarchist debate and anarchist society. This alone should give us hope that anarchists will be able to build on the intellectual foundations of classical anarchism to articulate an alternative to the failed state-centred strategies of both left and right. If, as a number of contemporary anarchist theorists insist, revolutionary Marxism and post-Marxist reformism have 'hit their historical limit', anarchists today face a new challenge, their response to which must live up to the intellectual standards of pioneers like Kropotkin and Reclus.[28] This will involve a robust re-evaluation of the logic of anarchist scholarship and a critical reappraisal of the classics of anarchist thought in the light of the vibrant critiques of Marxism, structuralism, authoritarianism, sexism, racism and post-colonialism that have added such intellectual vigour to antithetical theory and revolutionary praxis.

Notes

Chapter 1

1. I. McKay, *An Anarchist FAQ* (AK Press, 2007), p. 19.
2. R.E. Downes and J.A. Hughes, *Political Sociology* (Wiley, 1986), pp. 60–2.
3. P. Kropotkin, *Mutual Aid: A Factor of Evolution* (Pelican, 1939), pp. 157–61.
4. J. Mac Laughlin, 'European Gypsies and the Historical Geography of Loathing', *Journal of Fernand Braudel Center* 22:3 (1999), pp. 31–7.
5. M. Davis, *Planet of Slums* (Verso, 2007), pp. 53–5.
6. K. Bales, *Disposable People* (University of California Press, 1999); E. Wolf, *Europe and the People Without History* (University of Chicago Press, 1982).
7. S. Rowbotham, *Edward Carpenter* (Verso, 2008), p. 8.
8. J.P. Clark, *The Impossible Community: Realizing Communitarian Anarchism* (Bloomsbury, 2013), pp. 112–15.
9. R.J. Day, *Gramsci is Dead* (Orient Longman, 2008), pp. 140–2.
10. P. Kropotkin, 'Anarchism', in R.N. Baldwin (ed.), *Kropotkin's Revolutionary Pamphlets* (Dover, 1970), p. 288.
11. P. Kropotkin, *Fields, Factories and Workshops* (Greenwood Press, 1968), p. 17.
12. K. Sale, *Human Scale* (Coward, McCann and Geoghegan, 1980), pp. 12–19.
13. P. Kropotkin, *The State: Its Historic Role* (Freedom Press, 1987), p. 12.
14. Ibid., p. 10.
15. E. Hobsbawm, *Primitive Rebels* (Manchester University Press, 1958), p. 64.
16. C. Hill, *The World Turned Upside Down* (Pelican, 1972), pp. 72–6.
17. H. Butterfield, *Christianity and History* (Bell, 1949), p. 67.
18. G. Woodcock, *Anarchism* (Pelican, 1979), p. 42; P. Marshall, *Demanding the Impossible* (Fontana, 1993), pp. 96–101.
19. J. Mac Laughlin, *Travellers and Ireland* (Cork University Press, 1995), pp. 13–21.
20. E. Dell, 'Gerard Winstanley and the Diggers', *The Modern Quarterly* 4 (1996), pp. 138–9.
21. Woodcock, *Anarchism*, pp. 40–2.
22. Hill, *The World Turned Upside Down*, p. 76.
23. Ibid., pp. 27–30.
24. Quoted in ibid., p. 73.

25. G. Winstanley, *The Law of Freedom and Other Writings* (Cambridge University Press, 1983), pp. 92–3.

26. *The Works of Gerrard Winstanley*, ed. G.H. Sabine (Cornell University Press, 1941), p. 199.

27. Quoted in Hill, *The World Turned Upside Down*, p. 56.

28. Woodcock, *Anarchism*, pp. 41–2.

29. Quoted in Hill, *The World Turned Upside Down*, p. 59.

30. *The Works of Gerrard Winstanley*, p. 159.

31. P. Kropotkin, *Modern Science and Anarchism* (Freedom Press, 1912), p. 35.

32. Quoted in N. Cohn, *The Pursuit of the Millennium* (Paladin, 1984), p. 128.

33. Quoted in A.L. Morton, *The World of the Ranters* (Lawrence and Wishart, 1979), p. 70.

34. Winstanley, *The Law of Freedom and Other Writings*, p. 212.

35. Ibid., p. 108.

36. Hill, *The World Turned Upside Down*, pp. 98–100.

37. D. Purkiss, *The English Civil War* (Harper, 2007), p. 223.

38. Quoted in Woodcock, *Anarchism*, p. 46.

39. Hill, *The World Turned Upside Down*, p. 97.

40. *The Complete Works of Gerrard Winstanley*, ed. T.N. Corn, A. Hughes and D. Loewenstein (Oxford University Press, 2009), p. 69.

41. Marshall, *Demanding the Impossible*, p. 97.

42. J. Mac Laughlin, *Troubled Waters: A Social and Cultural History of Ireland's Sea Fisheries* (Four Courts, 2010), pp. 335–9.

43. S. Nissenbaum, *The Battle for Christmas* (Alfred N. Knopp, 1996), pp. 42–9.

44. E.P. Thompson, 'Patrician Society, Plebeian Culture', *Journal of Social History* 7 (1974), pp. 382–405.

45. Editors' Introduction, *The Complete Works of Gerrard Winstanley*, p. 76.

46. *The Complete Works of Gerrard Winstanley*, p. 175.

47. G. Orwell, *The Road to Wigan Pier* (Victor Gollancz, 1937); McCourt, F. Angela's Ashes (Doubleday, 2007).

48. *The Complete Works of Gerrard Winstanley*, p. 180.

49. Quoted in Woodcock, *Anarchism*, pp. 43–4.

50. Marshall, *Demanding the Impossible*, pp. 192–3.

51. W. Hazlitt, *The Spirit of the Age* (Oxford University Press, 1954), pp. 19–20.

52. Marshall, *Demanding the Impossible*, p. 196.

53. J. Joll, *The Anarchists* (Eyre and Spottiswode, 1964), p. 38.

54. W. Godwin, *An Enquiry Concerning Political Justice* (G.G. & J. Robinson, 1798), p. 331.

55. Kropotkin, 'Anarchism', *Revolutionary Pamphlets*, pp. 289–90.

56. Quoted in E. Hobsbawm, *The Age of Revolution* (Mentor, 1962), p. 286.

57. Marshall, *Demanding the Impossible*, pp. 79–80.

58. Ibid., pp. 192–3.
59. Godwin, *Political Justice*, p. 476.
60. Joll, *The Anarchists*, p. 39.
61. Ibid., p. 62.
62. Quoted in P. Marshall, ed. *The Anarchist Writings of William Godwin* (Freedom Press, 1986), p. 61.
63. Marshall, *The Anarchist Writings of William Godwin*, p. 140.
64. Quoted in Woodcock, *Anarchism*, pp. 69–70.
65. Quoted in Joll, *The Anarchists*, pp. 32–3.
66. Marshall, *Demanding the Impossible*, p. 194.
67. Ibid., p. 197.
68. Joll, *The Anarchists*, pp. 36–7.
69. Ibid., p. 93.
70. Marshall, *Demanding the Impossible*, p. 215.
71. J. Clark, *The Philosophical Anarchism of William Godwin* (Princeton University Press, 1977), p. 310.
72. Woodcock, *Anarchism*, p. 76.
73. Quoted in Marshall, *Demanding the Impossible*, p. 211.
74. Quoted in Woodcock, *Anarchism*, p. 81.
75. Marshall, *Anarchist Writings of William Godwin*, p. 171.
76. Woodcock, *Anarchism*, p. 71.
77. Ibid., p. 76.
78. Quoted in Joll, *The Anarchists*, p. 31.
79. Quoted in Woodcock, *Anarchism*, p. 75.
80. C. Ward, *Anarchism: A Very Short Introduction* (Oxford University Press, 2004), p. 13.
81. R.B. Rose, *Enragés: Socialists in the French Revolution* (Sydney University Press, 1965), pp. 73–9.
82. See Woodcock, *Anarchism*, pp. 53–4.
83. Marshall, *Demanding the Impossible*, p. 236; Pierre-Joseph Proudhon, *Selected Writings* (Macmillan, 1969), p. 261.
84. Proudhon, *Selected Writings*, p. 265.
85. Woodcock, *Anarchism*, p. 98.
86. Ibid., p. 99.
87. Ibid., p. 100.
88. Ibid., pp. 108–9.
89. Quoted in ibid., p. 103.
90. Ibid., p. 98.
91. Day, *Gramsci is Dead*, pp. 108–9.
92. Woodcock, *Anarchism*, p. 99.
93. Ibid., p. 100.

94. Pierre-Joseph Proudhon, *What Is Property?* (Dover, 1970), p. 5.

95. A. Ritter, *The Political Thought of Pierre-Joseph Proudhon* (John Murray, 1979), pp. 192–6.

96. Quoted in M. Williams (ed.), *Revolutions, 1775–1830* (Penguin Books, 1977), p. 216.

97. Kropotkin, 'Anarchism', *Revolutionary Pamphlets*, pp. 290–1.

98. K. Marx and F. Engels, *On Colonialism* (Lawrence and Wishart, 1976). For discussion on Marx's views on peasants and peasant society in history, see J. Mac Laughlin, *Reimagining the Nation-State* (Pluto, 2001), pp. 33–42.

99. Quoted in Woodcock, *Anarchism*, p. 107.

100. Quoted in Marshall, *Demanding the Impossible*, p. 241.

101. Quoted in ibid., pp. 242–3.

102. Quoted in Woodcock, *Anarchism*, p. 124.

103. Quoted in ibid., p. 109.

104. Quoted in Ritter, *Political Thought of Pierre-Joseph Proudhon*, p. 205.

105. Quoted in Woodcock, *Anarchism*, p. 110.

106. Quoted in ibid., p. 111.

107. Quoted in ibid., p. 112.

108. Quoted in ibid., p. 112.

Chapter 2

1. G. Woodcock and I. Avakumović, *The Anarchist Prince* (T.V. Boardman, 1950), p. 8.

2. R. Pipes, *Russia Under the Old Regime* (Weidenfeld and Nicolson, 1974), pp. 32–3.

3. C. Levi, *Christ Stopped at Eboli* (Penguin, 1982), p. 115.

4. Pipes, *Russia Under the Old Regime*, p. 98.

5. A. Herzen, *My Past and Thoughts* (Chatto and Windus, 1974), p. 23.

6. P. Kropotkin, *Memoirs of a Revolutionist* (Folio, 1978), p. 8.

7. A. Wexler, *Emma Goldman: An Intimate Life* (Virago, 1984), p. 67.

8. P. Avrich, *The Russian Anarchists* (Princeton, 1967), p. 75.

9. Quoted in Woodcock, *Anarchism*, p. 172.

10. V. Richards, *Errico Malatesta* (Freedom Press, 1965), p. 117.

11. See J. Mac Laughlin, 'State-centered Social Science and the Anarchist Critique', *Antipode* 18: 1 (1986), p. 33.

12. Woodcock, *Anarchism*, pp. 205–6.

13. R. Baldwin, Introduction to Kropotkin, *Revolutionary Pamphlets*, p. 13.

14. C. Ward, Introduction to Kropotkin, *Memoirs*, p. 9.

15. Ibid., p. 8.

16. Ibid., p. 14.

17. M. Miller, *Kropotkin* (University of Chicago Press, 1976), p. 115.
18. Quoted in Wexler, *Emma Goldman*, p. 167.
19. Kropotkin, *Memoirs*, p. 87.
20. Ibid., p. 26.
21. Ibid., p. 56.
22. Ibid., p. 61.
23. Ibid., pp. 73–4.
24. Ibid., p. 47.
25. M. Bánffy, *They Were Divided* (Vintage, 2011).
26. O. Figgis, *Natasha's Dance: A Cultural History of Russia* (Penguin, 2002), pp. 75–7.
27. Kropotkin, *Memoirs*, p. 17.
28. Ibid., p. 19.
29. Ibid., p. 20.
30. Ibid., p. 21.
31. Ibid., p. 30.
32. Ibid., p. 13.
33. Ibid., p. 23.
34. Ibid., pp. 26–7.
35. Ibid., p. 28.
36. Ibid., p. 31.
37. Ibid., p. 33.
38. Ibid., p. 91.
39. Ibid., p. 89.
40. Figgis, *Natasha's Dance*, pp. 72–7.
41. Mac Laughlin, *Reimagining the Nation-State*, pp. 112–5.
42. Nuala Johnson, 'Cast in Stone: Monuments, Geography and Nationalism', in J.A. Agnew (ed.), *Political Geography: A Reader* (Arnold, 1997), p. 353.
43. W. Sunderland, 'Imperial Space: Territorial Thought and Practice in the Eighteenth Century', in J. Burbank, M. von Hagen and A. Remnev (eds), *Russian Empire: Space, People and Power, 1700–1930* (Indiana University Press, 2007), p. 38.
44. Ibid., p. 67.
45. G.A. Hosking, *Russia: People and Empire, 1552–1917* (HarperCollins, 1979), pp. 127–8.
46. G.M. Hamburg, 'Russian Intelligentsias', in W. Leatherbarrow and D. Offord (eds), *A History of Russian Thought* (Cambridge University Press, 2001), p. 55.
47. Pipes, *Russia Under the Old Regime*, p. 116.
48. Kropotkin, *Memoirs*, p. 112.
49. Quoted in Miller, *Kropotkin*, p. 33.

50. Quoted in ibid., p. 42.

51. P. Kropotkin, 'Must We Occupy Ourselves with an Examination of the Ideal of a Future Society', *Selected Writings on Anarchism and Revolution*, ed. M. Miller (MIT Press, 1970), p. 89.

52. Kropotkin, *Memoirs*, p. 116.

53. Miller, *Kropotkin*, pp. 72–4.

54. Woodcock, *Anarchism*, p. 176.

55. Kropotkin, *Memoirs*, p. 214.

56. Leon Battista Alberti, *On Painting* (Penguin Classics, 1972), p. 98.

57. Sunderland, 'Imperial Space', pp. 45–9.

58. Kropotkin, *Memoirs*, p. 127.

59. Ibid., p. 141.

60. Hosking, *Russia*, p. 172.

61. Quoted in Figgis, *Natasha's Dance*, p. 386.

62. Ibid., p. 384.

63. Ibid., pp. 402–3.

64. Frederick Jackson Turner, *The Frontier in American History* (Henry Holt, 1921).

65. Kropotkin, *Memoirs*, p. 203.

66. Mac Laughlin, 'European Gypsies', pp. 43–4.

67. Kropotkin, *Memoirs*, p. 129.

68. Woodcock, *Anarchism*, p. 176.

69. Kropotkin, *Memoirs*, p. 141.

70. Figgis, *Natasha's Dance*, pp. 384–6.

71. Kropotkin, *Memoirs*, pp. 137–8.

72. Ibid., p. 139.

73. Ibid., pp. 142–3.

74. Ibid., pp. 142–3.

75. Quoted in Miller, *Kropotkin*, p. 72.

76. Woodcock, *Anarchism*, pp. 195–6.

77. Marshall, *Demanding the Impossible*, p. 313.

78. Richards, *Malatesta*, pp. 260–1.

79. Quoted in Woodcock and Akakumović, *Anarchist Prince*, p. 185.

80. Kropotkin, 'The Spirit of Revolt', *Revolutionary Pamphlets*, p. 39.

Chapter 3

1. Mac Laughlin, 'State-centered Social Science', pp. 14–17.

2. Mac Laughlin, *Reimagining the Nation-State*, pp. 65–72.

3. Kropotkin, *Modern Science and Anarchism*, p. 34.

4. Kropotkin, 'Anarchism', *Revolutionary Pamphlets*, p. 285.

5. Ibid., pp. 38–9.

6. Kropotkin, 'Anarchist Communism', *Revolutionary Pamphlets*, p. 47.

7. P. Kropotkin, *Ethics: Origin and Development* (McVeagh, 1924), p. 92.

8. Kropotkin, *Mutual Aid*, p. 18.

9. Kropotkin, *Ethics*, p. 23.

10. Ibid., p. 35.

11. Kropotkin, 'Anarchist Communism', *Revolutionary Pamphlets*, p. 47.

12. Miller, Introduction to Kropotkin, *Selected Writings on Anarchism and Revolution*, p. 20.

13. McKay, *Anarchist FAQ*, p. 18.

14. Ibid., p. 16.

15. Kropotkin, *Mutual Aid*, Chapters 3–4.

16. Kropotkin, Letter to Nettlau, 5 March 1902, *Selected Writings*, p. 298.

17. Ibid., p. 297.

18. Kropotkin, *Mutual Aid*, p. 121 (emphasis added).

19. Kropotkin, *Memoirs*, p. 217.

20. Kropotkin, *Memoirs*, p. 183 (emphasis added).

21. Hosking, *Russia*, pp. 86–9.

22. Figgis, *Natasha's Dance*, p. 134.

23. J. Mac Laughlin, *Donegal: The Making of a Northern County* (Cork University Press, 2007), pp. 6–8.

24. Figgis, *Natasha's Dance*, pp. 133–5.

25. Ibid., pp. 222–5.

26. Hosking, *Russia*, p. 263.

27. Leatherbarrow and Offord, Introduction to *History of Russian Thought*, p. 5.

28. Hamburg, 'Russian Intelligentsias', in Leatherbarrow and Offord, *History of Russian Thought*, pp. 44–8; R. Peace, 'Nihilism', in ibid., p. 119.

29. Quoted in Hosking, *Russia*, p. 268.

30. Kropotkin, *Memoirs*, p. 91.

31. Ibid., p. 96.

32. L. Spencer and A. Krauze, *The Enlightenment* (Icon, 1997), pp. 104–8.

33. Kropotkin, *Memoirs*, p. 23.

34. Woodcock, *Anarchism*, p. 175.

35. Joll, *The Anarchists*, pp. 34–6; Miller, *Kropotkin*, pp. 174–5.

36. Quoted in Joll, *The Anarchists*, p. 153.

37. Kropotkin, *Modern Science and Anarchism*, p. 23; 'The Spirit of Revolt', *Revolutionary Pamphlets*, pp. 42–3.

38. Kropotkin, 'Anarchist Morality', *Revolutionary Pamphlets*, p. 98; see also Kropotkin, 'Revolutionary Studies', *Commonweal*, 9 January 1892; Miller, Introduction to Kropotkin, *Selected Writings*, pp. 22–3.

39. Kropotkin, 'Revolutionary Government', *Revolutionary Pamphlets*, p. 243.

40. Quoted in Joll, *The Anarchists*, p. 154.

41. Miller, *Kropotkin*, p. 167.

42. Kropotkin, *Memoirs*, p. 231.

43. Baldwin, Introduction to Kropotkin, *Revolutionary Pamphlets*, pp. 31–2.

44. Ibid., p. 44.

45. Rowbotham, *Edward Carpenter*, p. 247.

46. Woodcock, *Anarchism*, pp. 195–8.

47. P. Kropotkin, *The Conquest of Bread* (Elephant Editions, 1985), p. 87.

48. Kropotkin, *Anarchism*, pp. 287–93.

49. J.R. Mintz, *The Anarchists of Casas Viejas* (University of Chicago Press, 1982), p. 120.

50. D. Graeber, *Debt: The First 5,000 Years* (Melville House, 2011).

51. Mac Laughlin, *Donegal*, pp. 10–15; Levi, *Christ Stopped at Eboli*, pp. 110–23.

52. Kropotkin, *Mutual Aid*, p. 12.

53. Ibid., p. 13.

54. Rowbotham, *Edward Carpenter*, p. 80.

55. E. Reclus, 'Anarchy: by an Anarchist', *Contemporary Review* 45 (1884), p. 641.

56. Kropotkin, *Modern Science and Anarchism*, p. 35.

57. Ibid., p. 34.

58. Ibid., p. 10.

59. Spencer and Krauze, *The Enlightenment*, p. 76.

60. J. Bronowski, *The Western Intellectual Tradition* (Penguin, 1969), pp. 155–63.

61. Kropotkin, *Modern Science and Anarchism*, p. 87.

62. Ibid., p. 92.

63. Mac Laughlin, 'State-centered Social Science', pp. 27–9.

64. Kropotkin, *Mutual Aid*, p. 16 (emphasis added).

65. Ibid., p. 32.

66. Kropotkin, *Conquest of Bread*, p. 108; 'Anarchist Communism', *Revolutionary Pamphlets*, p. 56.

67. Kropotkin, *Mutual Aid*, p. 18.

68. J. Mac Laughlin, 'The Political Geography of "Nation-building" and Nationalism in the Social Sciences', *Political Geography* 4 (1986), pp. 320–4.

69. Kropotkin, *Memoirs*, p. 92.

70. Ibid., p. 84.

71. Ibid., p. 129.

72. Ibid., pp. 88–90.

73. Ibid., p. 157.

74. Kropotkin, 'Anarchism: Its Philosophy and Ideal', *Revolutionary Pamphlets*, p. 135.

75. Kropotkin, *Memoirs*, p. 125.
76. Kropotkin, 'Anarchist Communism', *Revolutionary Pamphlets*, p. 47.
77. Ibid., p. 46.
78. Kropotkin, *Mutual Aid*, p. 102.
79. R.D. Putnam, *Bowling Alone: The Collapse and Revival of American Community* (Simon Schuster, 2000); R. Sennett, *Together: The Rituals, Pleasures and Politics of Cooperation* (Yale University Press, 2012).
80. Kropotkin, *Mutual Aid*, p. 74.
81. Kropotkin, 'Anarchist Communism', *Revolutionary Pamphlets*, pp. 289–90; *Mutual Aid*, p. 74.
82. Kropotkin, *Mutual Aid*, p. 154.
83. Ibid., pp. 138–40; Kropotkin, 'The State: Its Historic Role', *Selected Writings*, p. 227.
84. See L. Mumford, *The City in History* (Peregrine, 1961), pp. 312–15; Kropotkin, *Mutual Aid*, pp. 142–4.
85. Kropotkin, *Mutual Aid*, pp. 157–61.
86. Richard Sennett, *Flesh and Stone: The Body and City in Western Civilization* (Norton, 1996), pp. 200–2.
87. Kropotkin, *Mutual Aid*, p. 172.
88. P. Kropotkin, *The Great French Revolution* (Heinemann, 1909), p. 34; see also A. Carter, *The Political Theory of Anarchism* (Methuen, 1971), pp. 74–8.
89. Kropotkin, *Mutual Aid*, pp. 129–32.
90. Ibid., pp. 139–41; 'The State: Its Historic Role', *Selected Writings*, pp. 226–30.
91. Carter, *Political Theory of Anarchism*, pp. 27–9; Kropotkin, 'The State: Its Historic Role', *Selected Writings*, pp. 243–9.
92. Kropotkin, *Modern Science and Anarchism*, pp. 81–2.
93. Kropotkin, 'The State: Its Historic Role', *Selected Writings*, p. 245.
94. Ibid., p. 264.
95. Kropotkin, *Modern Science and Anarchism*, p. 93.
96. Marshall, *Demanding the Impossible*, pp. 323–6.
97. Kropotkin, *Modern Science and Anarchism*, p. 102.
98. Kropotkin, 'The State: Its Historic Role', *Selected Writings*, p. 257.
99. Kropotkin, 'Anarchist Communism', *Revolutionary Pamphlets*, p. 60; see also *Mutual Aid*, pp. 180–207.
100. Kropotkin, 'Anarchist Communism', *Revolutionary Pamphlets*, p. 58.

Chapter 4

1. S. Springer et al., 'Reanimating Anarchist Geographies: A New Burst of Colour', *Antipode* 44 (2012), pp. 591–604.

2. E. Hobsbawm, *The Age of Capital, 1845–1875* (Cardinal, 1975), pp. 192–4; *Revolutionaries* (Hachette, 2011), pp. 92–4.

3. Quoted in G. Woodcock, *The Anarchist Reader* (Fontana, 1977), p. 63.

4. Reclus, 'Anarchy: by an Anarchist', p. 627.

5. Mac Laughlin, 'State-centered Social Science', p. 11.

6. T.S. Kuhn, *The Structure of Scientific Revolutions* (University of Chicago Press, 1970).

7. J.A. Agnew, *Making Political Geography* (Arnold, 2002), pp. 9–10.

8. Mac Laughlin, *Reimagining the Nation-State*, pp. 62–6.

9. For an early critical analysis of ideological geography see D.R. Stoddart (ed.), *Geography, Ideology and Social Concern* (Barnes and Noble, 1979).

10. K. Marx, *The German Ideology* (Progress Press, 1968), p. 61; for a Leninist perspective on academics and scientists, see also L. Althusser, *Lenin and Philosophy* (New Left Books, 1977).

11. R. Williams, 'Base and Superstructure in Marxist Cultural Theory', *New Left Review* 82 (1973), p. 6.

12. On role of cultural capital, see P. Bourdieu, *Distinction: A Social Critique of the Judgment of Taste* (Routledge Kegan Paul, 1984).

13. Mac Laughlin, *Reimagining the Nation-State*, pp. 84–91.

14. J.D. Bernal, *Science in History: The Social Sciences* (Penguin, 1969), p. 1079.

15. Kropotkin, 'Anarchism: Its Philosophy and Ideal', *Revolutionary Pamphlets*, p. 114; *Fields, Factories and Workshops Tomorrow*, ed. C. Ward (Freedom Press, 1985), pp. 25–9.

16. For a detailed and critical discussion on the intricacies of ruling-class hegemony in colonial and ethnically divided authoritarian societies, see Mac Laughlin, *Reimagining the Nation-State*, pp. 29–42. See also J. Mac Laughlin and J.A. Agnew, 'Hegemony and the Regional Question', *Annals of the Association of American Geographers* 76:2 (1986), pp. 248–51. For the role of anarchists in anti-colonial struggles in the Philippines, Japan and China see B. Anderson, *The Age of Globalization* (Verso, 2013).

17. F. Fanon, *The Wretched of the Earth* (Penguin, 1967).

18. Kropotkin, *Anarchist Morality*, p. 85.

19. Kropotkin, 'Appeal to the Young', *Revolutionary Pamphlets*, p. 274.

20. See Marshall, *Demanding the Impossible*, pp. 262–5; Woodcock, *Anarchism*, pp. 134–9; Day, *Gramsci is Dead*, pp. 112–15.

21. Kropotkin, 'Must We Occupy Ourselves', *Selected Writings*, p. 58.

22. Kropotkin, *Conquest of Bread*, p. 115; H. Marcuse, *One Dimensional Man* (Sphere, 1968).

23. Kropotkin, *Fields, Factories and Workshops Tomorrow*, p. 25.

24. Kropotkin, *Modern Science and Anarchism*, p. 34.

25. Kropotkin, *Mutual Aid*, pp. 17–18.

26. P. Kropotkin, 'What Geography Ought to Be', *The Nineteenth Century* vol. 18 (1885), p. 942.
27. Ibid., p. 947.
28. A. Gramsci, *Selections from the Prison Notebooks* (Lawrence and Wishart, 1971), pp. 404–9.
29. Clark, *Impossible Community*, p. 89.
30. Kropotkin, 'Appeal to the Young', *Revolutionary Pamphlets*, p. 264.
31. Wexler, *Emma Goldman*, p. 69.
32. Quoted in Richards, *Malatesta*, p. 103.
33. Kropotkin, *Memoirs*, p. 224.
34. Ibid., p 118.
35. Ibid., p. 120.
36. Ibid., p. 115.
37. Ibid., p. 117.
38. Ibid., p. 157; see Woodcock, *Anarchism*, pp. 119–20.
39. T.H. Huxley, 'The Struggle for Existence and its Bearing on Human Society', *The Nineteenth Century* 23 (1888), pp. 195–236.
40. Kropotkin, *Mutual Aid*, pp. 24–5.
41. K. Kessler, 'On the Law of Mutual Aid', *Memoirs of the St. Petersburg Society of Naturalists* (1880), p. 297.
42. Kropotkin, 'Law and Authority', *Revolutionary Pamphlets*, p. 212; see also Woodcock, *Anarchist Reader*, pp. 115–6.
43. Kropotkin, *Fields, Factories and Workshops Tomorrow*, p. 18.
44. Ibid., p. 35.
45. Kropotkin, *Modern Science and Anarchism*, p. 45.
46. Kropotkin quoted in Woodcock, *Anarchism*, pp. 192–3; see also 'Must We Occupy Ourselves', *Selected Writings*, pp. 49–54.
47. Quoted in Woodcock, *Anarchism*, p. 196.
48. Kropotkin, *Modern Science and Anarchism*, p. 5.
49. Kropotkin, *Mutual Aid*, p. 208.
50. Kropotkin, *Anarchist Morality*, p. 88.
51. Ibid., p. 91.
52. Kropotkin, *Modern Science and Anarchism*, p. 92.
53. Kropotkin, *Anarchist Morality*, p. 95.
54. Kropotkin, 'Anarchist Communism', *Revolutionary Pamphlets*, p. 47.
55. Kropotkin, *Anarchist Morality*, p. 88.
56. Ibid., p. 95.
57. Kropotkin, 'The Spirit of Revolt', *Revolutionary Pamphlets*, p. 36.
58. Huxley, 'Struggle for Existence', p. 197.
59. Kropotkin, *Mutual Aid*, p. 6.
60. Ibid., pp. 32–3.

61. See my own discussion of the demographic implications of these arguments in J. Mac Laughlin, 'The Evolution of Modern Demography and the Debate on Sustainable Development', *Antipode* 31:3 (1999), pp. 324–33.

62. Ibid., p. 86.

63. Clark, *Impossible Community*, pp. 212–32; Day, *Gramsci is Dead*, pp. 117–24.

64. For a detailed discussion on the imminence of anarchism see Clark, *Impossible Community*, pp. 133–47.

65. See also G. Kearns, *Geopolitics and Empire: The Legacy of Halford Mackinder* (Oxford University Press, 2009), pp. 78–90.

66. Kropotkin, 'Anarchism: Its Philosophy and Ideal', *Revolutionary Pamphlets*, p. 137.

67. Ibid., p. 121.

Chapter 5

1. Kropotkin, *Memoirs*, p. 136; see also Miller, *Kropotkin*, pp. 72–6.

2. Ward, Introduction to Kropotkin, *Memoirs*, p. 8.

3. T.W. Freeman, *One Hundred Years of Geography* (Methuen, 1961), pp. 98–100.

4. See L. Hughes-Hallett, *The Pike. Gabrielle D'Annunzio: Poet, Seducer and Preacher of War* (Fourth Estate, 2013), pp. 290–2; E.J. Larson, *An Empire of Ice: Scott, Shackleton, and the Heroic Age of Antarctic Science* (Yale, 2011), pp. 145–6.

5. Kropotkin, Letter to Nettlau, *Selected Writings*, pp. 294–5.

6. Kropotkin, 'Must We Occupy Ourselves', *Selected Writings*, p. 89.

7. Kropotkin, *Memoirs*, p. 122.

8. See N. Tagirova, 'Mapping the Empire's Economic Regions from the Nineteenth to the Early Twentieth Century', in Burbank et al., *Russian Empire*, pp. 125–38.

9. Kropotkin, *Memoirs*, pp. 164–5.

10. Ibid., p. 161.

11. Ibid., p. 151.

12. Ibid., p. 126.

13. P. James and G. Martin, *All Possible Worlds: A History of Geographical Ideas* (Wiley, 1981), pp. 113–15.

14. Kropotkin, *Memoirs*, pp. 167–70.

15. Ibid., p. 355.

16. Kropotkin, *Memoirs*, p. 160.

17. See D.J.M. Hooson, 'The Development of Geography in Pre-Soviet Russia', *Annals of the Association of American Geographers* 58 (1977), pp. 250–72.

18. M.M. Breitbart, 'Peter Kropotkin, the Anarchist Geographer', in Stoddart (ed.), *Geography, Ideology and Social Concern*, p. 144.
19. Ibid., p. 142.
20. Woodcock, *Anarchism*, pp. 182–5; Miller, *Kropotkin*, pp. 160–4.
21. S. Keltie, 'Peter Kropotkin: Obituary', *The Geographical Journal* 57 (1921), pp. 317–18.
22. Woodcock and Avakumović, *Anarchist Prince*, p. 116.
23. Breitbart, 'Peter Kropotkin', p. 135.
24. Kearns, *Geopolitics and Empire*, p. 79.
25. Woodcock and Avakumović, *Anarchist Prince*, pp. 227–9.
26. R. Peet, *Modern Geographical Thought* (Blackwell, 1998).
27. See Kearns, *Geopolitics and Empire*, pp. 78–90; see also D. Livingstone, *The Geographical Tradition* (Wiley, 1994), pp. 254–6.
28. Hooson, 'The Development of Geography in Pre-Soviet Russia', pp. 258–60.
29. James and Martin, *All Possible Worlds*, pp. 116–19.
30. K. Sale, *After Eden: The Evolution of Human Domination* (Sphere, 2006), pp. 78–9.
31. Kropotkin, *Memoirs*, p. 205.
32. T. Veblen, *The Theory of the Leisure Class* (Dover, 1994), pp. 71–2.
33. Mac Laughlin, 'Political Geography of "Nation-building"', pp. 299–306.
34. B. Hudson, 'The New Geography and the New Imperialism, 1870–1919', *Antipode* 9:1 (1977), p. 252.
35. For these assessments of Humboldt see S.J. Gould, *I Have Landed: Splashes and Reflections in Natural History* (Jonathan Cape, 2002), p. 93; P. Watson, *The German Genius: Europe's Third Renaissance, the Second Scientific Revolution, and the Twentieth Century* (Harper, 2010), pp. 346–8.
36. F. Ratzel, *Politsche Geographie* (Oldenburg, 1903).
37. G. Ó'Tuathail, *Critical Geopolitics* (University of Minnesota Press, 1996).
38. V. Kiernan, *The Lords of Human Kind* (Penguin, 1972).
39. J.A. Agnew and J. Duncan, 'The Transfer of Ideas into Anglo-American Geography', *Progress in Human Geography* 5 (1981), pp. 42–57.
40. Hobsbawm, *The Age of Capital*, pp. 103–5.
41. E. Said, *Orientalism* (Penguin, 2003).
42. Hobsbawm, *Age of Capital*, p. 147.
43. W. Bagehot, *Physics and Politics* (Macmillan, 1873); G. Santayana, *The Life of Reason* (Constable, 1905), p. 67; see Mac Laughlin, *Reimagining the Nation-State*, pp. 92–5.
44. R. Hofstadter, *Social Darwinism in American Thought* (Beacon Press, 1955), p. 33.
45. Quoted in E. Churchill Semple, *Influences of Geographic Environment on the Basis of Ratzel's System of Anthropo-Geographie* (Henry Holt, 1911), p. 117.

46. Quoted in ibid., p. 121.

47. Ibid., pp. 5–6.

48. James and Martin, *All Possible Worlds*, pp. 203–7.

49. E. Huntington, 'Our Immigrant Problem', *Geographical Review* 2:6 (1916), p. 463 (emphasis added).

50. E. Huntington, *Civilization and Climate* (Yale, 1915), p. 18 (emphasis added).

51. Quoted in Ward, *Anarchism: A Very Short Introduction*, p. 86.

52. Kropotkin, 'Anarchist Communism', *Revolutionary Pamphlets*, pp. 68–9.

53. Kropotkin, *Memoirs*, pp. 170–1.

54. Ibid., pp. 156–8.

55. Kropotkin, 'What Geography Ought to Be', p. 945.

56. Ibid., p. 952.

57. Ibid., p. 954.

58. Quoted in Breitbart, 'Peter Kropotkin', p. 138.

59. Kropotkin, *Fields, Factories and Workshops Tomorrow*, p. 67.

60. Ibid., p. 25.

61. Ibid., pp. 141–2.

62. See Ward, Introduction to Kropotkin, *Fields, Factories and Workshops Tomorrow*, pp. iv–v.

63. Quoted in E. Capouya and K. Tompkins (eds), *Essential Kropotkin* (Macmillan, 1976), p. 11. See also H. Braverman, *Labour and Monopoly Capital* (Monthly Review, 1974), pp. 70–84.

64. Capouya and Tompkins, *Essential Kropotkin*, p. 11.

65. Ibid., p. 63.

66. Mac Laughlin and Agnew, 'Hegemony and the Regional Question', pp. 247–8.

67. Mumford, *The City in History*, p. 585.

68. Ibid., p. 385.

69. Kropotkin, 'The State: Its Historic Role', *Selected Writings*, p. 229.

70. H. Marcuse, *An Essay on Liberation* (Sphere, 1969); *Eros and Civilization* (Cardinal, 1955).

71. P. Hall, *Cities of Tomorrow: An Intellectual History of Urban Planning and Design in the Twentieth Century* (Blackwell, 2002), p. 156.

72. R. Bartlett, *Tolstoy: A Russian Life* (Houghton, Mifflin Harcourt, 2011), pp. 77–8.

73. Kropotkin, *Memoirs*, p. 147.

74. Rowbotham, *Edward Carpenter*, p. 129.

75. Kropotkin, 'The State: Its Historic Role', *Selected Writings*, p. 230.

76. Ibid., p. 233.

77. D. Harvey, *Rebel Cities: From the Right to the City to Urban Revolution* (Verso, 2012), pp. 8–9.
78. Kropotkin, 'The State: Its Historic Role', *Selected Writings*, pp. 229–31.
79. Kropotkin, *Mutual Aid*, p. 154.
80. Kropotkin, 'The Commune of Paris', *Selected Writings*, p. 127.
81. Rowbotham, *Edward Carpenter*, p. 252.
82. Kropotkin, *Fields, Factories and Workshops Tomorrow*, p. 18.
83. Ibid., p. 28.
84. Mumford, *The City in History*, p. 316.

Epilogue

1. Baldwin, 'The Story of Kropotkin's Life', in Kropotkin, *Revolutionary Pamphlets*, p. 18.
2. Ibid., p. 19.
3. Ibid., p. 20.
4. Rowbotham, *Edward Carpenter*, p. 69.
5. Woodcock, *Anarchism*, p. 194.
6. Ibid., p. 196.
7. Ibid., pp. 197–8.
8. Marshall, *Demanding the Impossible*, p. 332.
9. Woodcock, *Anarchism*, p. 202.
10. Marshall, *Demanding the Impossible*, pp. 332–3.
11. Woodcock, *Anarchism*, p. 203.
12. Marshall, *Demanding the Impossible*, p. 333.
13. Kropotkin, 'Conversation with Lenin', in *Selected Writings*, pp. 327–9.
14. Miller, *Kropotkin*, p. 247.
15. Woodcock, *Anarchism*, p. 205; Baldwin, 'The Story of Kropotkin's Life', p. 29.
16. Marshall, *Demanding the Impossible*, p. 335.
17. Woodcock, *Anarchism*, p. 205. Woodcock's other works include *Anarchy or Chaos* (1944), *Anarchism and Morality* (1945), *William Godwin* (1946), *The Crystal Spirit: A Study of George Orwell* (1966), *The Rejection of Politics* (1972) and *Herbert Read* (1972).
18. Ibid., pp. 205–6.
19. Marshall, *Demanding the Impossible*, p. 335.
20. Ibid., p. 336.
21. Ibid., p. 338.
22. Woodcock, *Anarchism*, pp. 444–6.
23. Marshall, *Demanding the Impossible*, pp. 540–2.

24. For excellent examples of erudite 'academic anarchism' see in particular Clark, *The Impossible Community*; J.P. Clark and Camille Martin, *Anarchy, Geography and Modernity* (Lexington Books, 2004); Day, *Gramsci is Dead*; Alex Prichard, *Justice, Order and Anarchy: The International Political Theory of Pierre-Joseph Proudhon* (Routledge, 2013); Todd May, *The Political Philosophy of Poststructuralist Anarchism* (Pennsylvania State University Press, 1994); and Laurence Davis and Ruth Kinna, *Anarchism and Utopianism* (Manchester University Press, 2009).

25. Prichard, *Justice, Order and Anarchy*, pp. 1–3.

26. On municipal anarchism see especially Clark, *The Impossible Community*, pp. 247–90.

27. Prichard, *Justice, Order and Anarchy*, pp. 163–4.

28. Day, *Gramsci is Dead*, p. 18.

Index

state-centralization, 4, 9, 11, 31, 136, 150–1, 159, 169, 192, 196, 220–33, 243–6
state functionaries, 103, 107, 128, 162–3
stateless society, 1, 3, 5, 25, 28–30
Stoics, 5
St. Peter and St. Paul Prison, 194, 236
subaltern groups, 104, 245
surveillance state, 66, 67, 118, 150, 152, 220, 243, 246
syndicalism, 41, 100, 177

terrorism, 110, 144
Tatars, 79–83, 86
The Times, 111, 13, 198
Thompson, E.P., 116, 148
Tolstoy, Leo, 25, 31, 36, 48, 51, 57, 67, 98, 102–5, 110, 115, 129, 145, 156, 193, 228, 241
trade unionism, 12, 41–2, 89, 100, 177, 240
True Levellers, 16, 21
tsarism, 71, 108, 194
Turgenev, Ivan, 52, 54

universal knowledge, 122
utopianism, 4, 36, 144, 178

Varlet, Jean, 34

Vichy France, 243
Vladivostok, 85, 189
vocabulary of desire, 4
vocational education, 71, 104
Volkonsky, Sergei, 68

Wallerstein, Immanuel, 144
Walton, Izaak, 10
War and Peace, 36, 67, 129
Ward, Colin, 34, 51, 183
wasteland cultivation, 14, 17, 19, 77, 84
What Geography Ought To Be, 37, 50, 114, 195, 241, 242
What Is Property, 38
White nation-states, 203
White supremacy, 214
Wilde, Oscar, 50
Williams, Raymond, 146, 149, 244
Winstanley, Gerrard, 7, 9–22, 33–5, 41, 112
Woodcock, George, 37, 50, 1105, 114, 195, 241, 242
World Power and Evolution, 211
World War I, 112, 212, 221
World War II, 24
Wretched of the Earth, 23, 154, 155, 245

Zeno of Citium, 5
Zola, Emil, 35